Freedom from the Free Will

SUNY series in Contemporary Continental Philosophy

Dennis J. Schmidt, editor

Freedom from the Free Will

On Kafka's Laughter

DIMITRIS VARDOULAKIS

SUNY
PRESS

Cover art by Lita Cabellut / "Franz Kafka" / 280 × 200 cm / mixed media on canvas
Portrait of Human Knowledge 2012 / Photography: Studio Tromp

Published by State University of New York Press, Albany

Printed in the United States of America

For information, contact State University of New York Press, Albany, NY
www.sunypress.edu

Production, Diane Ganeles
Marketing, Fran Keneston

Library of Congress Cataloging-in-Publication Data

Names: Vardoulakis, Dimitris, author.
Title: Freedom from the free will : on Kafka's laughter / Dimitris Vardoulakis.
Description: Albany : State University of New York Press, 2016. | Series: SUNY series in contemporary continental philosophy | Includes bibliographical references and index.
Identifiers: LCCN 2016005982 | ISBN 9781438462394 (hardcover : alk. paper) | ISBN 9781438462400 (pbk. alk. paper) | 9781438462417 (ebook)
Subjects: LCSH: Kafka, Franz, 1883–1924—Criticism and interpretation. | Kafka, Franz, 1883–1924—Humor. | Liberty in literature. | Free will and determinism in literature.
Classification: LCC PT2621.A26 Z957 2016 | DDC 833/.912—dc23
LC record available at https://lccn.loc.gov/2016005982

10 9 8 7 6 5 4 3 2 1

For Lukás

Contents

Acknowledgments

There are several people to thank for accompanying me in the writing of this book. There are, first, my students at the Western Sydney University, where I have taught the material contained in this book three times, in 2009, 2011, and 2014. I would particularly like to thank Norma Lam-Saw and Aleksandra Ilic for reading and commenting on chapter 4. I was especially lucky to have excellent teaching assistants while delivering these courses. I single out here Chris Conti and Hal Ginges, who produced their own articles in response to the material taught in the course. Thanks also to Mridula Chakraborty, Helen Koukoutsis, and Simon Fleming.

I am in the enviable position of being surrounded by intellectually stimulating colleagues whom I regard at the same time as friends. For discussions, intellectual stimulation, and for "being there," I'd like to thank Diego Bubbio and Charles Barbour, John Hadley and Jess Whyte, Anthony Uhlmann and Peter Hutchings, Alex Ling and Sabrina Achilles, and Mark Kelly and Lorrain Sim.

Over the years, I organized two Sydney Seminars for the Arts and Philosophy on Kafka. I am grateful to the Library of New South Wales for hosting the seminar, and to ABC RN for broadcasts related to the seminars. The first was seminar 14, titled "Kafka's Cages," which took place on July 3, 2009. The participants were Kiarina Kordela and Chris Fleming. The second was seminar 17, "Kafka and Philosophy," which took place on February 9, 2012. The participants were Henry Sussman, Paul Alberts, and Chris Conti.

In addition, I have learned a lot from all the colleagues who collaborated on the volume *Freedom and Confinement in Modernity: Kafka's Cages* (New York: Palgrave, 2011). I am particularly indebted to Kiarina Kordela, my coeditor for this volume and the fiercest interlocutor I have had the fortune to encounter.

I am also indebted to various colleagues around the world. I cannot possibly mention everybody, but I would like to single out the following: Gregg Lambert and Carry Wolfe invited me to participate in a gathering of the Society for the Study of Biopolitical Futures in Turing in June 2014, which was the first occasion that I presented the argument of the book as a whole in front of an engaged and demanding audience. Gerhard Richter organized a presentation of the general argument of the book at Brown University on November 7, 2014, where I was fortunate to receive excellent feedback from a number of participants. And Miguel Vatter, Vanessa Lemm, and Paul Patton invited me to present another part of the manuscript in another gathering of the Society for the Study of Biopolitical Futures in Sydney in February 2015.

Several other colleagues need to be mentioned. A number of discussions with Peter Szendy at a critical moment in the writing of the book left an indelible mark. Laura Odello showed me that the book is not just about Kafka, but it can also extend to other fields. Carlo Salzani and Brendan Moran were critical partners in conversation for developing chapter 4. Liesel Senn provided some much-needed and very competent research assistance at a late stage in the book's composition, and Amrita Tarr compiled the index and assisted with the galleys.

Over the years, Andrew Benjamin and Stathis Gourgouris have become—in different but equally significant ways—friends with whom I test my thoughts. I will always be in debt to their intellectual rigor and commitment.

I need to make special mention of my publishers, and in particular Andrew Kenyon, editor at SUNY, who welcomed the book project to the Press and handled the various stages with care and competence. Dennis Schmidt showed unbridled enthusiasm for the book ever since I mentioned it to him as something he could consider for his book series, for which I am profoundly grateful. This was not the first time that I have enjoyed Denny's generosity, and it will not be the last, I am sure, since chance has brought it about that we subsequently became colleagues.

The idea of the book was born in conversation with Amanda Third. Her generosity of spirit is such that it is impossible to ever repay my debt. Our son, Lukás, was born on September 23, 2011, on the ninety-ninth anniversary of the writing of Kafka's "The Judgment." This felicitous numerology compels me to dedicate the book to him.

A Note on Referencing Kafka's Works

All references to Franz Kafka's works in German are to the Fischer Kritische Ausgabe, edited by Jürgen Born, Gerhard Neumann, Malcolm Pasley, and Jost Schillemeit. I will specify in the notes only the particular editors of the volume that I am discussing.

I generally provide the page reference to the German only when there is an intrinsic reason, such as when I have altered the published translations or if I want to draw attention to an expression in the original. In these cases, the German page number follows the English one, and they are separated by a slash.

In general, I avoid entering into a number of well-rehearsed philological debates in Kafka scholarship when they do not relate directly to the substance of my argument, by appealing either to general usage or by following the solution of the translation that I reference. For instance, to give an obvious example, I retain the title *Amerika* for Kafka's earliest novel, even though we now know that Kafka's working title was *Der Verschollene*, which Brod changed to *Amerika*. I retain the title *Amerika* because it is the most commonly used title for this work, and because it is the one used in the translation that I reference—but without thereby suggesting that it is the "correct" title to use, whatever "correct" may mean in this context. Overall, my principle is to avoid philological disputes unless they are directly relevant to the argument.

Preamble

Kafka's Laughter

When I was invited to write a short piece for the catalog of a staging of *The Trial*, I argued that Franz Kafka's laughter enacts a critique of the prevalent concept of freedom as the free will of the individual, which has dominated both the political and the philosophical tradition in the Occident.[1] I had not anticipated the reaction this position would provoke. Several posts on blogs as well as personal communications informed me in no uncertain terms that the idea is preposterous: Not only is Kafka's world so overdetermined by tragedy that humor has no place in it, but Kafka's is a world of imprisonment where freedom is totally absent. This book is not so much a direct reply to these protestations against my short piece in the theater catalog, as a response to certain ingrained presuppositions about Kafka's work—and especially its "tragic" aspect, of which the replies to my short piece were symptomatic. I continue to maintain, and I develop here in some detail, that Kafka's humor is a response to the Western conception of freedom, which he tirelessly presents in this narratives, and that this response implies an alternative conception of freedom.

It is not unusual to talk about Kafka's humor. Those who knew him personally draw attention to the humor that characterized the person and that subsequently informed the work. There are, for instance, several references to Kafka's humor in Max Brod's biography. The most famous one is the following description of Kafka's reading of *The Trial* at a literary salon in Prague: "When Kafka read aloud himself, his humor became particularly clear. Thus, for example, we friends of his laughed quite immoderately when he first let us hear the first chapter of *The Trial*. And he himself laughed so much that there were moments he couldn't read any further. Astonishing enough, when you think of the fearful earnestness of this chapter. But that is how it was. Certainly it was not entirely good, comfortable laughter."[2] Brod is typical of Kafka scholarship in that he cites references that support a kind of laughter in Kafka, but he has no idea of how to integrate this laughter into the analysis of the texts themselves, other than by transforming its significance into a "higher" or "deeper" register. Thus, Brod subjugates this "not entirely comfortable laughter" to his own theological interpretation, which views Kafka as a kind of saint of modernity—as I will show in more detail in chapter 2.

A second, good example of this same maneuver is Felix Weltsch's *Religion und Humor im Leben und Werk Franz Kafkas*. Weltsch, who knew Kafka personally, introduces humor by saying that it is "totally impossible" to ignore it for anyone who knew Kafka. Soon, however, Weltsch qualifies this humor by saying that it is not lighthearted entertainment, but rather a "serious" humor that can thereby be linked to religion without any contradiction.[3] At the end, humor becomes a symptom of something else that is more profound. Kafka's laughter is presented as a reaction to something else that is more important, and never as producing ideas with literary as well as political import.

A significant advance over this uncomfortable transformation of laughter into theology is the argument that Kafka collapses the distinction between comedy and tragedy. Thus, for instance, Milan Kundera writes: "In the world of the *Kafkan,* the comic is not a counterpoint to the tragic (the tragi-comic) as in Shakespeare; it's not there to make the tragic more bearable by lightening the tone; it doesn't *accompany* the tragic, not at all, it *destroys it in the egg* and thus deprives the victims of the only consolation they could hope for: the consolation to be found in the (real or supposed) grandeur of tragedy."[4] And yet, despite its significance in relation to the earlier interpretations of Kafka's laughter, this insight does not say much more than that Kafka is a modernist author in the sense that modernism is concerned with the erasure of what is traditionally categorized as high art and fascinated with the mixing of genres. After all, as Mikhail Bakhtin shows in his study of Rabelais, laughter has always destabilized hierarchies, of both genre and power—notwithstanding the difficulty of drawing a demarcation line between the two.

More fruitful approaches to Kafka's laughter are concerned with the broader philosophical and political significance of laughter. I am thinking here, for instance, both of Walter Benjamin and of Gilles Deleuze and Felix Guattari, who place a significant emphasis on laughter—as I will show in chapters 1 and 2. To understand such broader philosophical significance, we can recall Umberto Eco's *The Name of the Rose* (1980), which dramatizes the repression of laughter in Western metaphysics. The reason this repression takes place can be easily gleaned by turning to Zarathustra's thunderous laughter. This laughter that Nietzsche describes had a determinative importance for his French interpreters precisely because of its metaphysical significance. To put it very simply, one can laugh at the idea that something transcendent determines our being. Simon Critchley puts it thus: "What makes us laugh . . . is the return of the physical into the metaphysical, where the pretended tragical sublimity of the human collapses into a comic ridiculousness which is perhaps even more tragic."[5] We can already glimpse the resonance of this conception of laughter within Kafka's stories. *The Metamorphosis* depicts the transformation of a human into a filthy insect. Such a transformation laughs at the idea that we—in our bodily existence—are made "in the image of God," while it remains tragic because of the transvaluation that the human has thereby undergone.

The problem with such an approach to Kafka's laughter is that it remains too broad. By contrast, my own approach narrows down the scope of laughter. This is to deny neither the generic implications of laughter noted by Kundera and others, nor the use of laughter in countering the Western metaphysical tradition. Rather, it is to show that laughter functions as a technical device with important discursive implications—in particular, implications that relate to how freedom is thought of in Kafka's writing.

In sum, my approach places humor at the center of Kafka's technique, which relies on plots in which the protagonists are seemingly totally deprived of their freedom. I argue that if there is political thinking in Kafka, this is only possible because of his laughter.[6] The reason is that Kafka's laughter is the tool he uses to deconstruct power. One of the most critical ways in which power is constructed depends on how we understand our freedom. As Foucault puts it, "power is exercised only over free subjects, and only insofar as they are free. . . . [F]reedom must exist for power to be exerted."[7] Freedom can be the means of our entrapment by power. The key to the exercise of power through freedom is the free will. We think that we have the freedom to exercise our will only by forgetting that power is exercised not simply by delimiting our freedom, but by confining our will to power's own operation and perpetuation. The more we exercise our free will, the more power proliferates. Hence, it is an illusion to think that we are free because we have a free will.

Kafka—I argue in this book—laughs at our illusion that we have a free will. And he also laughs at the correlate of the free will, namely, the separation between a world of ideal freedom and a fallen world of confinement. This separation corresponds to the metaphysical assumption that there is a spiritual realm that is separate from, and higher than, the material or corporeal realm. The question of the free will is always about how to connect these two worlds or these two realms—it is always about how our conceptions of "what we will" can come into being. The transcendence of an ideal world of freedom or of spirit is necessary for the free will to operate. As such, and pace interpreters such as Brod and Weltsch, Kafka's laughter performs also a critique of transcendence as the linchpin of both Western metaphysics and theology.[8] At the same time, this laughter is not only critical, but has a constructive aspect. Kafka's laughter suggests a different sense of freedom. This is a situated freedom—or *mediated freedom*, as I call it—that does not rely on ideals separated from the here and now. It is a *freedom from the free will.*

Let me describe the main idea in a different way. Mladen Dolar makes an astute observation about the presence of freedom and unfreedom in Kafka. After noting that "there is unfreedom everywhere in his [Kafka's] universe," Dolar insists that, nevertheless, "freedom is there at all times, everywhere, it is Kafka's *fin mot,* like the secret word one doesn't dare to utter although it is constantly on one's mind. The freedom that might not look like much, that might actually look wretched, but is there at all points, and once we spot it there is no way of going away from it, it is a possession to hold on to, it is the permanent line of flight, or rather the line of pursuit."[9] The present study can be understood as developing this observation by breaking down the question of freedom in Kafka into three distinct questions. First, what kind of unfreedom enchains Kafka's characters? The answer I will propose is that unfreedom is inextricable from the free will. Second, what kind of freedom is present in Kafka? The answer is a freedom from the free will—or as I also call it, mediated freedom. Third, how is the interaction between freedom and unfreedom presented? My contention is that laughter provides the means for this interaction and thus is central in how—technically—Kafka presents freedom and the free will.

My reading of this idea of the freedom from the will in Kafka rests on one important insight, namely, that the idea of the free will is tightly connected with the idea of the separation between an ideal world of freedom and a fallen world in which the human is imprisoned. This insight organizes the structure of the book:

I will show in chapter 1 how the conjunction between the idea of the free will and the separation of a paradisiacal world of freedom from a fallen world is developed by Augustine in his relating of the Fall. Kafka's own persistent return to narratives of confinement—narratives in which the protagonist is completely trapped and unable to exercise his free will—is counterbalanced by the idea of a space of complete freedom, best exemplified by the Nature Theater of Oklahoma in the last chapter of *Amerika*. Nevertheless, as I will show, Kafka actually laughs at the actors who are supposedly liberated. This will provide an *ontological* setting for the ideal of freedom from the free will.

Chapter 2 approaches Kafka's laughter from Maurice Blanchot's suggestion that Kafka resembles a comic presentation of Abraham, according to which Abraham is stranded in the desert because he is called by God to sacrifice his son, whereas in fact he is childless. I show how Kafka exploits the comical elements of the impossible task of pleasing a transcendent entity by reading closely "The Judgment" and *The Metamorphosis*. Chapter 2 will explore how the idea of the freedom from the free will also provides an *exegetical* matrix for reading Kafka.

The contrast between absolute imprisonment and absolute freedom is most clearly presented in the two short stories where the protagonists are literally encaged, "A Report to an Academy" and "A Hunger Artist," which I will discuss in chapter 3. I will show how they form a critique of the Western metaphysical tradition of the thinking of freedom by making Kafka's laughter resonate with the thought of Levinas and Spinoza and thus how it can be inscribed in an *ethical* register.

The function of the law in Kafka's writings, especially those from around 1914, the year of the broken engagement with Felice Bauer as well of the writing of *The Trial*, is often viewed as paradigmatic of the fallen, imprisoned world in Kafka. This does not preclude, however, the eruption of the Kafkaesque laughter in the moment of the greatest—seemingly—deprivation of freedom, as I will demonstrate in chapter 4. Laughter is also operative in the *legal* domain.

Ultimately, as I will argue in chapter 5, Kafka's reconceptualization of freedom as freedom from the free will has profound implications for how power is conceptualized. I will demonstrate this by contrasting Kafka's "In the Penal Colony" to Michel Foucault's description of the execution of

Damiens at the beginning of *Discipline and Punish*. The laughter at the illusion of the free will is, finally, situated in the *political* sphere.

This trajectory does not present Kafka as a political philosopher per se—since he did not develop a systematic theory, as would be expected from a philosopher. Rather, I show that Kafka offers invaluable insights to political philosophy about the function of freedom—insights that the disciplinary demands for systematic presentation may actually obstruct, occlude, and obscure.[10] And this makes it all the more valuable to recognize what Kafka laughs at: namely, the conjunction between the free will and the separation of a world of absolute liberation from a fallen world. And, further, it makes it more valuable to ponder the Kafkaesque insight that freedom may only be possible when we liberate ourselves from the free will.

I should note here that several attempts have been made to present Kafka's "politics." These have been aptly documented by Bill Dodd.[11] For the most part, they attempt to situate Kafka within the political debates of his time. The questions typically asked are what historical events and theoretical works may have influenced his political views and his thought—an exception here is Adorno's masterful "Notes on Kafka." Further, as Dodd observes, "much of this 'political' reading of Kafka has been engaged in the task of rescuing him from the aura of a *homo religiosus* with which Brod influentially announced him to the world."[12] I would like to point to two important articles that do not fit Dodd's observation in a straightforward way, but at the same time do not contradict it. First, as Peter Fenves has shown in a brilliant reading of the short fragment "Die besitzlose Arbeiterschaft"—a favorite with many political readings—the political interpretation of Kafka has the capacity to radically affect the way that the religious itself is thought of in his work. In this context, the religious is not simply opposed to the political.[13] This implies a premise of the present study, namely that the religious is not innocently separated from political commitments. Consequently, as I show, Brod's metaphysical reading has political repercussions, which include the construction of freedom, a central political concept par excellence. Second, as Judith Butler has demonstrated, the "political" in relation to Kafka cannot avoid tackling questions about the ownership of the proper name "Kafka," especially in the context of his manuscripts. Differently put, the political in Kafka is not confined to his political opinions or thoughts, but also relates to how the proper name "Kafka" has been mobilized in different political contexts.[14] I agree with this insight, even though the approach adopted in the present study is different, not only in that it concentrates in discovering the political in Kafka's texts themselves, but also in that I am concerned with one question—the issue of the presence of the free will in the midst of the most suffocating plots of confinement.

As the above suggests, I will present this idea of mediated freedom, or the freedom from the will, by reading selected Kafka texts in conjunction with the way that freedom has be theorized about in philosophy. Three caveats are necessary at this point: First, I do not intend to conduct here a holistic interpretation of Kafka. I am not offering a "key" that "unlocks" any "deeper" meanings of his entire oeuvre. Instead, I trace one idea—how Kafkaesque humor is tied up with political thinking, and in particular with thinking of freedom as free from the free will. And I do so by concentrating on a relatively small number of texts by Kafka. Second, I do not suggest that the entirety of Kafka's oeuvre needs to be read from the perspective of the interplay between laughter and freedom. There are innumerable other ways to approach his writings. I am contending, however, that a reading of Kafka's text that is concerned with their political significant cannot avoid dealing with Kafka's laughter. Third, I do not propose here a comprehensive theory of freedom. There are several philosophical issues that I have chosen to ignore. The reason is that I choose to concentrate on the constellation that laughter and freedom construct—a constellation that is illuminating about certain aspects of freedom but far from exhaustive of a philosophy of freedom.[15]

In addition, I want to allude to a further aspect, which I cannot take up here—not only because it would have made for an entirely different book but more crucially because I do not pretend to comprehend its implications. This has to do with the importance of the figure of confinement within the institution of literature. If we take a step back to contemplate some of the foundational texts of the literary canon, we cannot help but be struck by the crucial position of confinement plots. Thus, for instance, such a plot can be found in some of the first novels, such as Boccaccio's *Decameron*—where ten people narrate stories while they are confined to a villa for ten days to shelter themselves from the plague. Cervantes's *Don Quixote*, the narrative that inaugurates Hispanic literature, can also be read as a narrative of confinement, as Kafka's own reworking shows—a fragment that I discuss in chapter 1. And we can go much further back, all the way to the Homeric epics, first with the Greek army stranded at Troy and then with the desire for the *nostos*, which determines all of Ulysses's actions while his wife, Penelope, is trapped in the Ithacan palace waiting for his return. There is certainly something significant that connects plot development and confinement. And even if it is not the place here to investigate this relation, the crucial role of the plots of confinement historically suggests that the choice to concentrate on Kafka's plots of confinement is not a marginal issue in a modernist author from a provincial city in the Austro-Hungarian Empire, but a significant aspect of the institution of literature.

This brings me to the most significant, as well as the thorniest, methodological issue. It concerns the relation between literature and philosophy. I do not believe in the idea of "philosophical fiction" if what is meant by this is that there are certain fictional texts that can give us privileged access to certain ideas that in turn can enrich our lives or teach us how to live. There are various reasons why I reject this position. First, it reproduces the separation that characterizes the Western idea of freedom between a fallen world and an ideal world unalloyed with the vicissitudes of being. In this conception, the truth-seeking philosophy always occupies the position of the ideal, while fiction is harnessed to philosophy's truths like a servant—or a slave. Second, I hold that it reproduces a particular philosophical preoccupation, which seeks to unify the conceptual and the particular. In this conception, fiction can become the vehicle of this unification. Quentin Meillassoux recently described something like that under the concept of correlationism.[16] I describe it elsewhere under the concept of immediacy.[17] In any case, the figure of Kafka's cages questions and problematizes the assumption that thought and being can be separated. It is no wonder that the greatest critic of this metaphysical assumption, Baruch Spinoza, also arrives at a conception of freedom from the correlate of this metaphysical separation, namely, the separation of freedom and unfreedom. As Genevieve Lloyd and Moira Gatens put it, in Spinoza "freedom fundamentally is the emergence from the illusion of freedom—that is, from the illusion of free will."[18] It is for this reason that I will return to Spinoza on several occasions throughout this book.

One further implication ought to be noted, one that provides further reason for rejecting the possibility of "philosophical fiction": no concept is complete or autonomous. This suggests what Peter Szendy calls a "philosofiction"—which is to be strictly distinguished from a "philosophical fiction." According to Szendy, a philosofiction is the fictional element that "comes to haunt even the most formally rigorous philosophical works."[19] In other words, a philosofiction challenges the claim of concepts to occupy a space that is outside or beyond where they enjoy complete autonomy.

This point resonates with Kafka's cages. The fictional element dismantles the concept's autonomy in the sense that the concept remains anchored to particularity and dependent on singularity. In this sense, philosofiction is the freedom *from* the aspiration toward idealized values that are universal, or of an analysis that produces concepts thoroughly abstracted from experience, or the pursuit of truth at the expense of and by rejecting myth, or the insistence of a rational capacity that absolutely separates the human from the animal—and so on. Ultimately, a philosofiction is the liberation from the illusion that thought and being can be separated. No wonder that Deleuze insists on a Spinozan laughter that arises from the fact that "Spinoza is one of the most cheerful authors in the world."[20] This is a laughter in the face of all those sad emotions that arise from the separation of spirit and being.[21] The present book can be read as an invitation to join the chorus of this laughter.

1

Kafka's Cages

Laughter and the Free Will

Plots of Confinement and the Kafkaesque Laughter

One aspect of Kafka's work is readily noticeable: the plots for his stories regularly, almost without exception, consist of describing a situation of confinement.[1] The protagonist is invariably entrapped. This can be a physical entrapment. For instance, in *The Castle*, the land surveyor is presented as stuck in the village, unable either to gain access to the castle or to leave. In *The Metamorphosis* Gregor Samsa is confined—one could almost say, incarcerated—in his room. The same pattern is repeated in the stories. One of the most claustrophobic is "The Burrow," where the sole, concealed exit from the underground labyrinth does not lead to freedom but to torment and angst. The entrapment can also be nonphysical. *Amerika* and *The Trial* are good examples of this. While traversing the American continent in *Amerika*, Karl Rossmann is trapped by his powerlessness and the exploitation that haunts him everywhere. In *The Trial*, Josef K. is physically free to wander around the city, and yet his presumed guilt is unshakeable, following his every footstep. Or we can recall Josephine, trapped by her singing, which is what gives her identity, even though it is of a deficient standard. Kafka's appetite for plots depicting different configurations of confinement is insatiable.

These plots of confinement, however, always display an additional, crucial feature. Even though at first blush they may appear to construct tragic situations, in fact Kafka uses the presentations of the deprivation of freedom to animate his distinctive humor. Kafka seems to laugh out loud about the predicaments of his entrapped protagonists. Famously, Max Brod recounts how, while reading from *The Trial* at a literary salon, Kafka provoked such bouts of laughter in the audience that he constantly had to pause.[2] The moment one overcomes the impulse to read the plot development as inherently tragic, one notices Kafka's humor everywhere. One cannot help then but laugh out loud—just like the audience of *The Trial*. Recall, for instance, the land surveyor's hilarious attempts to gain access to the castle. His obsession is childishly stubborn. The means he employs are nothing but illusions—such as the notion that seducing the mistresses of the castle's officials will get him any closer to the castle; such illusions are so transparently futile as to be laughable. Josephine the singer is another good example of Kafka's humor. She is reminiscent of an old, exhausted, sad clown who provokes laughter by the sheer inability to live up to expectations.[3] This distinctive Kafkaesque humor is not sarcastic. Kafka does not laugh at his characters. His laughter does not have the judgmental ring of intellectual or moral superiority.[4] Rather, it is a gentle sympathetic laughter, which recognizes the difficult predicament that the characters find themselves in.

And yet, this is not to suggest that Kafka's laughter is uncritical. The aim of the present book is precisely to recover the critical import of Kafka's laughter. But if Kafka's humor is not directed against his characters, then what is its target? The thesis defended here is that Kafka's laughter is intimately related to his narratives of confinement—and in particular it is Kafka's way of critiquing the Occidental idea of freedom, according to which freedom is dialectically opposed to submission, unfreedom, and imprisonment. Kafka laughs at the idea that it is possible to conceive of an ideal freedom that is absolutely separated from confinement.[5] Differently put, Kafka's confinement plots are philosophical responses to how freedom and unfreedom have been conceptualized in the Western tradition. Such a critique is possible because of his laughter. Laughter is Kafka's tool for the critique of the Western tradition of freedom.[6]

At the same time, the critique enacted with Kafka's laughter is not merely a negative tool. There is also a constructive component. Laughter offers the possibility of an alternative conception of freedom. Such a freedom could be minimally defined at this point as distinct from the Western conception of freedom. This is a minimal definition only to the extent that I will offer more details about this different notion of freedom later. I do not use the word "minimal" here to make a qualitative judgment.

To the contrary, given that the Western tradition determining freedom in terms of the free will of the individual has so thoroughly and pervasively conditioned our way of thinking about freedom, even such a "minimal" description is hugely significant. A determination of freedom that is free from the free will is a tectonic shift in how freedom is conceived. Kafka's laughter performs such a shift.

I call "Kafka's cages" the constellation that consists of plots of confinement, the laughter that seems so naturally to arise within them, the critique of the Western conception of freedom performed by that laughter, and the chiseling out of a different conception of freedom through the use of laughter. Among the various scholars who have worked on Kafka's humor, Erica Weitzman is most explicitly concerned with the link between humor and freedom, although she concentrates only on Kant's conception of freedom.[7] I will emphasize instead the way that the plots of confinement respond to one particular, constitutive characteristic of the Western conceptualization of freedom, namely its dialectical opposition to the figure of confinement.

The Separation of Freedom and Unfreedom: Augustine's Invention of the Free Will

The designation of a "Western conception of freedom" may appear reductive and monolithic. After all, is it not easy to show that freedom is a political ideal that has had numerous actualizations over the centuries? Does not every geopolitical configuration produce its own idea of freedom? Is it not even a *fact* that every single individual understands freedom in a slightly different way, depending on the influence of various conceptual and contextual forces that determine that individual? I contend that even if all the above is the case—even if it is unwarranted to talk about Western freedom as if it is homogeneous, and even if Western freedom has received a wide array of determinations—it is still possible to identify its constitutive qualities. And there is one quality in particular that is distinctive and evident in the above objections about the multiplicity of the meanings of freedom. This is the idea that freedom is a property of the individual; differently put, this is the idea that the free will of the individual is constitutive of the idea of freedom.[8]

As I contended earlier, Kafka's cages present the idea of the free will as the unbridgeable separation between freedom and unfreedom. Kafka laughs in the face of this separation. In what sense are the freedom of the will and the separation of freedom and unfreedom interconnected? Are they the same? Does one imply the other? Or is there a causal relation between them? To answer these questions, we need a quick overview of the historical development of the idea of the free will. We will then discover that the free will is the obverse side of the separation of freedom and unfreedom. The free will and the separation of freedom and unfreedom are coimplicated in the production of the Western idea of freedom.

The free will is born as a solution to an intractable metaphysical problem faced by Christianity in the fourth century—that is, at the time when Christian dogma crystallizes its metaphysics. This is the problem of the existence of evil. If neo-Platonism provides Christianity with the means to construct a hierarchical ontology that installs the divine at the apex of the scale, it is Stoicism that provides the conceptual apparatus for the description of the divine. In particular, God's predicates "omniscient, omnipresent and omnipotent" have a Stoic provenance—they are the rearticulation of the Stoic idea of Providence.[9] This description is simple and powerful enough, and yet it contains one major problem, namely, how to account for the existence of evil. If indeed God knows everything, how could he be deceived by evil—for instance, why is the serpent allowed to manipulate the protoplasts in the Garden of Eden? If God is everywhere, does this mean that evil is a property of God? And, finally, if God is all powerful, why can he not eliminate evil? The stakes are high: the paradox of evil threatens the entire metaphysical edifice, having the power to undermine not only the description of the divine, but as a consequence, also its hierarchical metaphysics. And this is not only a metaphysical problem. It is also—maybe even *primarily*—a political one, since the translation of the neo-Platonic hierarchical structure into the political realm provides the legitimation for the sovereign, the "mortal God," as Hobbes accurately captures this idea.[10]

Augustine invents the idea of the free will to circumvent the paradox of evil. Evil, contends the Church Father, is not a property of the divine, but rather reflects the choices between good and sinful actions perpetrated by agents. The paradigmatic description of the genesis of the free will is the Fall, which in Augustine's writings attains a pivotal metaphysical significance. Augustine emphasizes two aspects, which are not present in the Biblical story from Genesis. First, the Garden of Eden is no longer a bucolic setting. Rather, Augustine refers to it as Paradise, thereby signifying a space of absolute harmony and freedom. Second, the expulsion from

Paradise is a result of the free choice of Adam and Eve. It has nothing to do with the divine will.[11] The repercussions of this account—the so-called Augustinian theodicy—are profound, since they ground Christian morality.[12] This consists in the existence of an ideal space and time of absolute harmony and freedom, such as the paradisiacal Garden of Eden, and its irrevocable separation from the Fallen world where humanity subsists. This is a genuinely neo-Platonic solution because it relies on a hierarchical determination: It shifts the existence of evil to the lower level of existence, which is in turn absolutely separated from the higher level. The effect of this is the radical separation of the Fallen world and Paradise, as well as an entire series of terms associated with each world, such as unfreedom and freedom. The doctrinal articulation of this separation is the theory of the original sin—the fact that the first expression of the free will by the protoplasts was a sin—which condemns humanity to the Fallen world. Differently put, the exercise of the free will is not only the starting point of morality but also the confinement of the human within a mortal body and a world of suffering. For Augustine, then, and for the Christian tradition in general, there is free will because we are fundamentally unfree right here and now, but we retain the promise that the right free choices will return us sometime in the future—even at the end of time, on the last day (*der letzte Tag*, the day of Judgment)—to that ideal space of freedom from which we are expunged.

Kafka's response to this future promise of freedom is typical of the way in which laughter operates. The Augustinian structure is presented so matter-of-factly, so blatantly, as to be distorted and inverted. One of the famous instances of this is a conversation reported by Max Brod, which Walter Benjamin emphasizes—and I will shortly return to Benjamin since he is also fascinated by the contrast between freedom and unfreedom in Kafka's work. Brod contends that "there is hope outside this manifestation of the world that we know." In other words, hope exists beyond the spatio-temporal dimension of the Fallen world we live in. Brod notes that Kafka smiled at this assertion, and then responded: "Oh, plenty of hope, an infinite amount of hope—but not for us."[13] Benjamin takes this statement as a "bridge" to a series of figures who are liberated from the oppressive world of the family constructed in so many of Kafka's narratives. Benjamin is correct to point out that hopelessness is a sign of freedom—but this is not a freedom of the Augustinian type, according to which freedom is the ideal that will be realized in a future time beyond the world of the here and now. Rather, these figures that fascinate Benjamin express a different sense of freedom. It is a freedom that rejects the supposition of a separation between the "Fallen" world and an ideal world of freedom. Consequently, theirs is a freedom that requires no ideal, whereas Brod posited such an ideal by referring to a world "outside" or beyond "the world we know." Kafka's response—such a hope is "not for us"—does not discard hope or freedom as a possibility, but rather rejects the separation between the world of the here and now and a future, inaccessible world. And this entails a positive assertion too: If there is a hope, and if there is freedom, they are of the here and now. The critique enacts a constructive movement. Kafka presents an alternative conception of freedom. Specifically, this freedom of the hopeless is characterized by the freedom *from* the conception of an ideal freedom that is separated from the here and now.

Let me provide one more example of the Kafkaesque idea of freedom *from* the Western conceptualization of freedom, since it indicates the transition from a laughter that performs a critical function to the construction of an alternative idea of freedom. "The Fall is the proof of our freedom," says Kafka to the young Gustav Janouch, in a statement that performs the same reversal of the Augustinian paradigm that fascinated Benjamin—a reversal, which, as I show later, is also characteristic of Spinoza's conception of freedom.[14] In this reversal, the Fall—instead of being the mark of an imprisonment in the present whose only possibility of redemption relies on an inaccessible future—turns into the "proof of our freedom." Instead of the now being the prison within which humans are condemned to suffer their mortal lives, the now is transfigured into the condition of the possibility of freedom. This condition is realized because there is no future to enact or guarantee the redemption. Freedom as imbued in the Fall means that freedom has no future and hence lacks an ideal that is separated from the now. This reversal is performed through a gentle laughter at the expense of the puzzled and bemused young Janouch. Thus, laughter becomes the technical expedient to breach—and bridge—the radical separation of freedom and unfreedom, characteristic of the conception of the free will in the Western tradition.[15]

I call the freedom that is distinct from the Western conception of freedom "freedom from the free will." This is to highlight the essential feature of freedom in the Western tradition, namely, the attempt to locate freedom within the actions of the individual. However, we should not forget that Augustine manages to define the free will only by drawing a distinction between an ideal freedom characteristic of Paradise and the Fallen world of imprisonment. This separation is part and parcel of the free will. This remains constant in the Western tradition, despite the fact that both the free will and the separation have received a variety of articulations in philosophy, as I will also discuss in the following section.

I should note that I regularly use two further terms to designate the freedom from the free will to draw attention to different aspects of this concept. One of them is "mediated freedom." I use this term to emphasize the situated aspect of freedom from the free will. Mediated freedom is a freedom that determines itself through responding to one's environment—that is, without recourse to an abstract ideal freedom beyond being. I also use the term "ethical freedom." As I explain in more detail in chapter 3, I use this term to highlight the interpersonal aspect of freedom. Freedom is not the prerogative of the individual, but rather arises through one's interactions with others. One is never free alone. All these three ways to designate the freedom that I see arising through the Kafkaesque laughter—freedom from, mediated freedom, and ethical freedom—rely on relation. They tell us that freedom is a relational concept. I will take up this idea in the final section of the present chapter.

Freedom From: Negative and Positive Freedom

It is important to forestall here a possible confusion about the use of the term "freedom from" to describe the conception of freedom that arises through Kafka's laughter. The confusion can arise from the fact that Isaiah Berlin uses the same expression—"freedom from"—to designate what he calls "negative freedom." And there are additional reasons for turning to Berlin's celebrated essay "Two Concepts of Liberty" at this point. The distinction that he adumbrates between the two fundamental senses of freedom in the Western tradition—namely, the distinction between negative and positive freedom—is useful for further elaborating some of the key features of Kafka's laughter and for further developing the historical sketch of the conception of freedom in the Western tradition.[16]

The first point about Berlin's essay is the often-overlooked assumption that grounds his entire approach. Berlin states it en passant, without emphasizing it or elaborating on it, without even arguing for it, assuming that it is a self-evident fact. In Berlin's words: "Political theory is a branch of moral philosophy, which starts from the discovery, or application, of moral notions in the sphere of political relations."[17] There are in fact two fundamental assumptions in this formulation. The first one accords with the Augustinian separation between two realms—one that corresponds to some ideal sphere, and the other to the here and now. Berlin articulates this as the separation between moral notions and the tumult of politics. Berlin's immediate concern is to show how this separation operates. He rejects the idealist notion that there is a necessary connection between the conceptual content of the moral notions and "historical movements," favoring instead to bridge this separation as the necessary effort to understand such "movements."[18] In other words, Berlin assumes an ontology that posits the separation between the moral notions and the particularity of the historical unfolding. And he is concerned to show that this separation is not an epistemological question that seeks to connect the mind with the external world, but rather the motor for a hermeneutics of history. Simply put, ideas help us make sense of the material world. This "common sense" position presupposes the Augustinian separation between this world of particularity and another, higher world, which Berlin identifies with morality.

The Christian Father and the Jewish intellectual hold in unison that without the separation between a higher realm toward which action is directed and the historical or Fallen world, there is no free will. But they significantly part ways in how they conceive of the function of morality in relation to this separation. According to the second assumption contained in Berlin's statement above, the ideal is commensurate with morality. This is the reason why political theory is "a branch of moral philosophy." This is a Kantian position—even though Berlin seems to assume it while Kant was acutely aware of the difficulty in bridging the divide between morality and politics.[19] This is not the place to address in any detail Kant's position. Suffice it to point out that Berlin's installation of morality as the ideal of politics is a Kantian move, and more importantly, that this move revises in a fundamental sense the Augustinian separation of freedom. Whereas for Augustine the free will is required so that moral choices can be made and hence morality can function, the existence of freedom for Kant relies on the moral realm. It is a matter of priority. For Augustine, the free will precedes morality, since it is only by the first decision of the protoplasts leading to the Fall that moral law comes into being. Conversely, for Kant the universality of the moral realm precedes freedom in the sense that it comes to supervene politics and the expression of freedom. Or, as Berlin puts it, to understand the vicissitudes of history, we need to presuppose the precedence of moral theory over politics. Put in yet another way: the Augustinian conception requires the free will so that the Fall takes place and so that the separation with Paradise is enacted, whereas the Kantian position requires the separation of the moral kingdom from particularity as the condition of the possibility of freedom. This reconfiguration is important, since it signals a different conception of power in Christianity from modernity and biopolitics. I cannot address these conceptions of power in detail now, but I return to this issue elsewhere in the book, especially in chapter 5. I will only briefly sketch here how Kafka's response to negative freedom laughs at the conception of freedom in the modern articulations of power, while his engagement with positive freedom laughs at biopower.

Negative freedom designates the absence of coercion. An individual or a community experiences negative freedom to the extent that they are unobstructed to pursue what they will. Berlin summarizes the sense of negative freedom as "liberty *from*."[20] Such a negative freedom presupposes that coercion, unfreedom, even slavery, are its opposites; it also presupposes an individual who possesses a free will to do something, and that that individual enjoys negative freedom so long as his or her will is not obstructed. The idea of negative freedom can also be placed within a historical perspective. If we think of the exercise of the will as what the individual has the right to do, then negative freedom can be linked to the social contract tradition, which occupies a pivotal position in the development of the modern conception of power. From this perspective, negative freedom is a natural right.

The subversion of negative freedom in Kafka's narratives of confinement is stark. There are several reasons of this. First, the shorter narratives especially tend to describe a situation where there is a physical sense of confinement from which there is no way out. The idea that there will be liberation from this state of affairs is absent as a possibility. The prospect of physical liberation is not even entertained by the mole in his burrow or by Gregor Samsa in his room. Second, and more significantly, it seems as if these oppressed individuals have no free will of their own. Thus, Gregor is described as being trapped by his father's debt, forcing him to do a job that he did not like. But when, after his transformation into an insect, he overhears his father saying that he actually has some hidden funds, he is elated—instead of feeling betrayed and angry that these funds were not used to improve his professional predicament. Gregor has no free will in the sense that he has no sense of an obstacle from which he wants to be freed—Gregor lacks negative freedom. Third, and most importantly, there is a series of characters in Kafka's works who seem totally incompatible with the idea of free will. One good example that I will deal with in detail later are the secondary characters in "In the Penal Colony." Another is the women characters, especially in *The Castle* and *The Trial*. In both these novels, the women seem to have no free will at all, since all they "will" is to fall in love with the male protagonist. It would surely be possible to conduct a gender analysis of this lack of free will. But the important point is not to see this lack as a deficiency but rather as a liberation from the conception of the free will in the Western tradition. Notice also—and this is the confusion that I want to eliminate—how different Berlin's conception of "freedom from" is from the Kafkaesque one. Whereas Berlin's "freedom from" highlights the freedom from coercion as an exercise of the free will, the Kafkaesque "freedom from" presupposes neither the sharp separation of freedom and unfreedom, nor the free will, and as such it is a freedom from negative freedom.

Berlin designates the sense of positive freedom with the expression "freedom to." This indicates the institutional, political, and legal apparatuses put in place to enable the individual to enjoy freedom. Negative freedom remains unconcerned with regimes of power—Berlin aptly suggests that a benevolent dictator can conceivably provide his subjects with more negative freedom than a liberal democratic regime. Conversely, positive freedom is concerned with the external conditions that give the individual the liberty *to* exercise free will. Berlin argues that the danger of positive liberty is that it can become difficult to distinguish where a regime of power starts eroding rights in the name of affording the subjects instituted liberties. This description is perceptive, but does not go far enough, since it still has no premonition of what Foucault described as "biopolitics." According to Foucault, biopolitics is an expansion of power through controlling every aspect of life.[21] If the tyrannical regimes evoked by Berlin are bad enough but still an identifiable enemy—freedom is, after all, the battle cry of any revolution—the biopolitical spread of power invades every aspect of life to the extent that a revolution is now unimaginable, not only because there is no target, but, more importantly, because within this state of biopolitical unfreedom the subject actually enjoys certain freedoms and may submit itself through its own free will to unfreedom. Biopower subverts positive freedom to the extent that it appears as a mirage—not just the shadow of freedom, but rather the dissimulation of unfreedom as freedom.

The Kafkaesque strategy for undercutting the sense of positive freedom is two-pronged. On the one hand, Kafka refrains from situating his plots in an identifiable historical moment or place. Even the only seeming exception, *Amerika*, describes a place that Kafka never visited and that he does not even make a great effort to represent realistically. Instead, America is the figure of a sense of freedom—even though, as Karl Rossmann discovers, that sense is illusory. In general, however, the reader is in the dark about the actual location of the story. We do not know the geographical coordinates of *The Castle*, and its political regime does not have a "direct" correlative in the "real," historical world. And yet it is for this reason, Theodor Adorno contends, that Kafka's stories are all the more political. Specifically, Adorno notes that "[a]ll of his stories take place in the same spaceless space." This allows Kafka an invaluable insight about power: "Consummate untruth is the contradiction of itself; it need not, therefore, be explicitly contradicted."[22] There is no need to criticize specific regimes of power—there is a more urgent critique, namely the critique of the logic of power. As such, Kafka is not concerned with particular manifestations of positive freedom, but rather with the illusion of positive freedom tout court. This consists in the recognition that what worried Berlin—namely, that it is easy for the institutions supposedly safeguarding freedom to erode civil liberties—has actually become the norm.

At the same time, Kafka seems to trump even Foucault's bleak description of a widely dispersed biopower that sees fit to intervene in every subject's life. In *The Trial*, Josef K. is free to wander around the city. He does not encounter any physical constraints. And yet, he is also hounded by an invisible guilt, whose source is an invisible law and judiciary. This is not just a subversion of natural justice, nor simply an indication that power has extended its control to the entire field of living; this simultaneous subversion and expansion of power reintroduces the mystical element of invisibility. Foucault suggests that racism is a biopolitical exercise of power, which however has the capacity to reanimate older forms of sovereign power that rely on the right of life and death.[23] Kafka amplifies this insight by showing the codependence of the various modalities of sovereignty, as I discuss with reference to "In the Penal Colony" in chapter 5. This amplification of power to make it appear omnipresent is also often attributed to the father in Kafka's narratives, such as the father in "The Judgment." But Kafka does not present this expansion of power to lament the tragic loss of freedom. On the contrary, the expansion of power allows him to laugh freely at the futile attempts to achieve freedom on the part of those characters who still believe in a notion of positive freedom—characters such as Josef K., who stubbornly persists in searching for a complete acquittal, or the land surveyor who harbors the hope that all will be explained as soon as he gains access to the castle officials. The reason these attempts are futile and laughable is that the illusion of positive freedom and the expansion of power control only further amplify the chasm between freedom and unfreedom.

There is one text by Kafka that exemplifies the rejection of the opposition between negative and positive freedom—or at least, it is possible to read it that way if we take Jacques Derrida's essay on it as an essay on freedom. I am referring to "Before the Law," the short parable in the chapter "At the Cathedral" of *The Trial*, which was also published independently under the title "Before the Law"—and Derrida's text, which bears exactly the same title.[24]

In fact, Derrida foregrounds the issue of the title in his opening sentence: "A title occasionally resonates like the citation of another title. But as soon as it names something else, it no longer simply cites, it diverts the other title under cover of a homonym. All this could never occur without some degree of prejudice or usurpation."[25] A title is something singular, something unique, which is meant to identify the individual and singular creation of a particular author. When the title is repeated, it is no longer a synonym—signifying the same thing—but rather a homonym, which denotes something different. For this play of identity and repetition to unfold, certain "prejudices" are required—certain framing devices that may go hardly noticed but that nevertheless determine the interplay between the singularity and the repeatability of the title and its homonym. Derrida proceeds to list several conditions that make this interplay possible, such as that an "original version" of the text is assumed to exist; the presence of a "signatory" who is the "real" author of the text; the assumption that a literary text relates fictional events; and, the assumption that the title guarantees the "identity" of the work.[26] Derrida asks a question at this point—"who decides, who judges, and with what entitlement, what belongs to literature?"—which actually entails that these are political issues since they pertain to who has the authority to make decisions and draw judgments. There is, then, on the one hand, the author's personal experience, which is transmitted to the page as a unique piece of writing, and there is, on the other hand, the wide legal, institutional, and conventional framework that both enables and regulates this transmission. Or, more simply, there is, on the one hand, singularity, and, on the other, the law. The details of this interplay cannot be definitively determined; it is impossible to settle where singularity ends and where the law begins. According to Derrida, this interplay is enacted in Kafka's parable, too.

I hardly need to summarize Kafka's "Before the Law," since it so well known. A man from the country arrives before the gate to the law. The gatekeeper tells him that he can go through, but that there are also other, more fierce gatekeepers down the road. The man from the country decides to wait—and wait he does, for a long time, in fact till the end of his time. When he is about to expire, the gatekeeper whispers in his ear that this gate was only for him and no one else could possibly have been admitted through it. I will return to an analysis of this parable in chapter 4, but for the moment I will read from the perspective offered by Derrida.

It is certainly permissible to assume the metaphor of the gate as *the* metaphor for freedom. After all, Augustine's invention of the free will is dramatized as the narrative of the Fall, that is, the narrative that "showed the door" out of Paradise to Adam and Eve, because they freely chose evil. The whole discourse of the free will and of choice can be depicted in terms of what doors are open to us. Thus, the opposite of freedom is the state in which "they throw away the key." So the parable is inter alia about freedom. Furthermore, and even though Derrida is not explicit about his, the interplay he stages between singularity and the law bears strong, unmistakable traces of the free will, too. Derrida says, for instance, that the man from the country "has the natural, physical freedom to penetrate spaces" and that therefore we are "compelled to admit that he must forbid himself from entering" the door.[27] More broadly, it is possible to relate Derrida's account to Berlin's distinction between negative and positive freedom. The force of singularity would, then, correspond to Berlin's negative freedom—the freedom from coercion that each individual can aspire to. And the legal framework would be the correlate of positive freedom that sets the conditions in which an individual can exercise its freedom.

There is only one moment in Derrida's essay in which freedom reverberates explicitly with the interplay between singularity and the law. Shortly after having asserted that the man from the country does not exercise his natural freedom to enter the gate to the law, Derrida writes: "The law is prohibited. But this contradictory self-prohibition allows man the freedom of self-determination, even though this freedom cancels itself through the self-prohibition of the law." The man does not face a physical obstacle from actually entering the gate to the law. This allows the determination of his negative freedom. He can exercise his free will—as the gatekeeper admits. The man retains his singularity. But even if he enters the gate, the law remains distant, elusive—prohibited. The man is singular because he is subject to the law, even though, paradoxically, his subjection to the law—the fact that he is also subject to positive freedom—entails that his singularity is no longer unalloyed. Derrida expresses this point thus: "Before the law, the man is a subject of the law in appearing before it. This is obvious, but since he is *before* it because he cannot enter it, he is also *outside the law* (an outlaw)." And then he concludes: "He is neither under the law nor in the law. He is both a subject of the law and an outlaw."[28] It is instructive to dwell on this logic of a "neither/nor" that is not exclusive but rather equivalent to a "both/and." We can reformulate this logic in terms of the separation between an ideal freedom and an absolute unfreedom, which is the logic of the Western conception of freedom. Is the ideal freedom something singular—the individual's unique experience of eradicating obstacles? Or is it, conversely, the freedom to embed oneself in the law so as to participate in the prohibitions that are necessary for a polity to function and for authority to exist? Is ideal freedom a negative or a positive freedom? To say it is both entails that no such thing as an ideal freedom exists, since the two opposing meanings cancel each other out in an infinite spiral of uncertainty. To say that it is neither entails that the double bind between an ideal freedom that is both negative and positive enacts a disentanglement from the premise of the double bind—it enacts the freedom *from* the separation between an ideal freedom and an absolute unfreedom.

The freedom from the free will is incommensurate with the negative and the positive freedoms that Berlin describes. Rather, Kafka's "freedom from" is closer to the sense of freedom we find in Derrida's reading of "Before the Law." This is a freedom that shakes off the shackles of the free will. I have also called this freedom from the free will "mediated freedom." We see here another reason for using this term: Freedom is not something that persists independently in an autonomous individual. Rather, it exists in relation to the free will. This relation can be understood as the inclusive logic of the "neither/nor" Derrida describes. We will find several other ways in which its operative presence is mediated. And it is always mediated—enacting relations with practices and conceptualizations that seem to contradict it. Kafka's particular way of presenting such a mediated freedom—the means at his disposal or his technique—is laughter.

Laughter and Freedom: On Kafka's Political Technique

This historical and discursive detour through Augustine and the two senses of freedom—negative and positive freedom—has furnished us with at least three important components of Kafka's cages. First, the laughter is directed at the chasm posited between the Fallen world and a world of ideal freedom. But this is not only critical—it also proposes that freedom can be achieved by freeing ourselves from the illusions of pursuing an ideal freedom. Second, Kafka laughs at the idea that one enjoys freedom through the exercise of the free will. He even goes so far as to construct characters who lack free will and who mechanistically act according to their desires and the dictates of their whims or their environment. Third, Kafka laughs at the illusion that power can facilitate the individual's free will. Instead, the accentuation of power shows an ever-widening gap between freedom and unfreedom.

Gilles Deleuze and Félix Guattari are acutely aware of Kafka's reformulation of the concept of freedom. Their privileged example in this regard is Rotpeter from "A Report to an Academy." They underscore that for the encaged ape, "it isn't a question of liberty as against submission, but only a question of a line of escape."[29] A line of escape, or a line of flight, as they also call it, is a sense of freedom that is free from the separation "of liberty as against submission." In this sense, a line of escape is the same as what I call "freedom from." Further, Deleuze and Guattari point to Kafka's laughter and its political significance: "Only two principles are necessary to accord with Kafka. He is an author who laughs with a profound joy. . . . And from one end to the other, he is a political author."[30] Deleuze and Guattari are acutely aware of the political import of Kafka's laughter. Despite these significant insights, Deleuze and Guattari do not explicitly synthesize Kafka's laughter with the conception of a line of escape. It is this synthesis that I call "Kafka's cages" and that I want to pursue in this book.

The reader most attuned to Kafka's cages is Walter Benjamin. Both his essay on Kafka, which he prepared for the tenth anniversary of his death, as well as the extensive notes that he collected as part of a book project that he never completed, testify to a profound and sustained engagement with the interweaving of freedom and laughter in Kafka. The reason Benjamin is so sensitive to Kafka's cages is his acute awareness of the importance of the separation between the Fallen world and an ideal world of absolute freedom. In a fragment from his notes, we read the following crucial observation: "'I imitated because I was looking for an exit, and for no other reason,' said the ape in his 'Report to an Academy.' This sentence also holds the key for the place of the actors of the Nature Theater. 'Right here' they must be congratulated, since they are allowed to play *themselves*, they are freed from imitation. If there is in Kafka something like a contrast between damnation and salvation, it has to be searched for entirely on the contrast between the world theater and the Nature Theater."[31] Benjamin is concerned here with the notion of freedom in Kafka, as the reference to Rotpeter's assertion that he was looking for a way out shows. This desire for freedom is consummated by the participants in the Nature Theater of Oklahoma, as described in the final chapter of *Amerika*. The actors are totally free from constraints; they do not even need a script since they play themselves. But to understand exactly what kind of freedom the actors of the Nature Theater of Oklahoma enjoy, Benjamin suggests that it is fundamental to keep in mind the contrast with the world of unfreedom, the Fallen world in which live the "holders of power," as Benjamin describes them in his essay. For instance, the consummation of freedom in the Nature Theater of Oklahoma is not a straightforwardly positive achievement. Let us not forget that on the train ride back to Oklahoma, the actors gradually become terribly bored. Their absolute freedom, their "transparent character," as Benjamin puts it, makes them thoroughly uninteresting. At the same time, the landscape outside becomes interesting. In fact, the mountain rocks are animated in Kafka's description to such an extent that they appear as more human than the liberated human actors.[32] Here is an instance of Kafka's laughter in the face of the separation between the Fallen world and the world of ideal freedom.

As his essay demonstrates, Benjamin was fascinated by Kafka's laughter—precisely because it intervenes in the contrast between unfreedom and ideal freedom. The laughter is not explicitly thematized by Benjamin. Jokes, however, litter his essay.[33] In fact the entire essay is framed by two humorous narratives, which are at the same time related to the question that Benjamin foregrounds in his notes, the "contrast between the world theater and the Nature Theater." The first is the anecdote about Potemkin, whose prolonged bout of melancholia would paralyze the bureaucratic apparatus. A particularly prolonged outbreak had the civil servants in despair, as the documents that required the Chancellor's urgent signature were accumulating. Brazenly, a minor clerk called Shuvalkin grabbed the documents and took them to the bedroom that Potemkin was refusing to leave, put them under his nose, and asked him to sign them. The Chancellor obliged, but when the clerk triumphantly showed the documents to his colleagues, they saw that Potemkin actually had signed them in Shuvalkin's name. Benjamin comments: "This story is like a herald of Kafka's work. . . . The world of offices and registries, of musty, shabby, dark rooms, is Kafka's world. The obliging Shuvalkin, who takes everything so lightly and is finally left empty-handed, is Kafka's K."[34] This anecdote is "like a herald" because it depicts with irreverent humor the absolute unfreedom effected by the holders of power. Kafka responds to unfreedom with laughter—a laughter that is not mocking of the characters but that rather softens the blows that result from the separation of freedom and unfreedom, that is, the blows of the free will.

How different is the story with which Benjamin essay concludes! There is here also the figure of imprisonment that traverses Kafka's works. And we can also find the unmistakable humor. But here the laughter points to an outright possibility of freedom. Benjamin is discussing a short fragment by Kafka that reimagines the relation between Sancho Panza and Don Quixote. Benjamin raises the stakes by introducing it as the narrative that is "at least one occasion" in which Kafka can present justice, and also as Kafka's "most complete [*vollendetste*] narrative."[35] Why is this short piece Kafka's "most complete" story? I contend it is because it presents in condensed form all the elements of what I call "Kafka's cages," including a positive articulation of freedom, which was lacking in the opening anecdote. I cite Kafka's entire story titled "The Truth about Sancho Panza":

> Without ever boasting about it, Sancho Panza succeeds in the course of the years, by supplying a lot of romances of chivalry and adventure for the evening and night hours, in so *diverting from him* his demon, whom he later called Don Quixote, that his demon thereupon *freely* performed the maddest exploits, which, however, lacking a preordained object, which Sancho Panza himself was supposed to have been, did no one any harm. A *free man*, Sancho Panza serenely followed Don Quixote on his crusades, perhaps out of a sense of responsibility, and thus enjoyed a great and profitable entertainment to the end of his days.[36]

This is a story about liberation.[37] Benjamin acknowledges as much, even if only elliptically, by writing that "the burden is taken off the back."[38] The story is the most complete, then, because Sancho Panza has succeeded where Shuvalkin had failed: in liberating himself. But this is a sense of freedom that is incommensurate with the idea of freedom as the exercise of the free will. Sancho Panza diverts the demon who has been controlling him, so that the demon now performs the maddest exploits. It is as if the demon, Don Quixote, enjoys the free will to do what he wants. He is unencumbered by constraints, he enjoys negative freedom—and yet, the "free man" is Sancho Panza, even though he still has to follow his demon around. But what a great joy it is to follow such a demon, what a profound sense of entertainment one gets from watching Don Quixote's mad exploits caused by his freedom of the will! It is as if the free will is, according to Kafka's "most complete" story, the greatest joke that mankind has concocted for itself. It is a joke, however, only so long as one can free oneself *from* such madness. And this is only possible by following Don Quixote—which means, by being tied to the here and now, renouncing the ideal of an absolute freedom in another world beyond the Fallen one by developing a sense of mediated freedom. And, further, this is only possible because Sancho Panza assumes his responsibility to look after Don Quixote and his demonic free will. Sancho Panza's freedom is then an ethical one in the sense that it is not confined to his desires and wants, but rather arises through the mediation of alterity. Benjamin's essay concludes with this positive image of a sense of freedom that is free from the free will and thus liberates the subject to actualize itself in the now and in relation to others.

Kafka's cages, then, are a figure, a constellation. They are the laughter that arises as a result of the representation of the separation of an ideal freedom from a thorough, devastating unfreedom. That laughter provides the means to construct a different sense of mediated freedom, one that no longer requires an ideal but is rather embedded in the practices of the here and now. It is an ethical freedom that renounces the egoism of the free will so as to assume its responsibility toward the other. Such a freedom resembles a theatrical scene in the sense that its performance is singular and unrepeated, even though there is a "script" that can be accessed "universally" by everyone—a script that describes the freedom *from* the free will.

The Cage and Its Relations: Laughter, Freedom, Ontology

There are two easy ways to misconstrue the idea of Kafka's cages that I am putting forward here. I will take them in term, not only as a strategy to forestall misunderstandings, but also because they bring to the fore one crucial aspect of the freedom from the free will, namely, its relational aspect.

The first way to misconstrue Kafka's cages is to place an inordinate value on encagement. It is not uncommon to "glamorize" the element of confinement since it is so compulsively present in Kafka's writings. His private writings—the diaries and the letters—can also be mobilized toward such a reading of the cage. The most famous example of this is a letter he wrote to Felice Bauer. I quote extensively:

> I have often thought that the best mode of life for me would be to sit in the innermost room of a spacious locked cellar with my writing things and a lamp. Food would be brought and always put down far away from my room, outside the cellar's outermost door. The walk to my food, in my dressing gown, through the vaulted cellars, would be my only exercise. I would then return to my table, eat slowly and with deliberation, then start writing again at once. And how I would write! From what depths I would drag it up! Without effort! For extreme concentration knows no effort. The trouble is that I might not be able to keep it up for long, and at the first failure—which perhaps even in these circumstances could not be avoided—would be bound to end in a grandiose fit of madness. What do you think, dearest? Don't be reticent with your cellar-dweller.[39]

This letter from January 1913 comes from the end of the first phase of Kafka's relation to the woman to whom he is going to be engaged twice, only for the engagement to be dissolved almost immediately on both occasions. Kafka meets Felice in the Brod house at the end of the summer of 1912. He writes his first letter to her in late September, just before he composes his breakthrough story, "The Judgment." The initial correspondence is quite exuberant. Kafka is clearly fascinated by Felice. It may also have helped that for the first time in his life he feels he is a writer—this is a hugely creative period for Kafka, as I explain in chapter 2. In any case, by January of the following year, just as the writing is running out of steam and just as Kafka realizes that he has committed himself to Felice through their correspondence, he starts making references to a possible union between them. But this is not a usual courtship. Instead, he tries to woo her by describing how singularly unsuitable he is to married life because of his devotion to writing. He outlines his dream to be a "cellar-dweller," a voluntary prisoner to the vocation of writing. It is easy to make the inference that his life, his being, is imprisoned by or within writing. He is a prisoner of literature. He is a martyr for writing.

The concept of "Kafka's cages" that I have outlined in this chapter has nothing to do with such a glorification of the writer's "imprisonment" in literature. Instead, what is crucial in Kafka's cages is the way that relation infuses with and determines being. Thus, we can read the above letter in a way that does not resolve it in a transfiguration of the author to a martyr for literature, but rather indicates the relations it opens up. The first point to note is that in writing to Felice, in relating to Felice, Kafka talks about a kind of existing or being. This is the being of the "cellar-dweller." Regardless of the details of this kind of being, it is important that relation is a description of existence. There is an ontological import to relation. Second, this ontology engages the other. The description of the cellar-dweller is Kafka's way—his means—of communicating to Felice his need to write. He is telling her that to be with him, she would have to accept—nay, accommodate—his innate need to write. The figure of the cellar-dweller forges a kind of relation with Felice. There is also a third kind of relation, one that relates the cellar-dweller to the institution of literature itself. Kafka's self-description as a writer locked up in an underground basement evokes Dostoyevsky's man from the underground. The suggestion that at the end he may suffer a "grandiose madness" strengthens this reference. But here this relation to Dostoyevsky's figure is within a context that gives it a decidedly humorous register. Kafka is supposedly communicating, to the woman he is about to be engaged to, his vision of his preferred existence, and who in his right mind would tell someone he is wooing that he wants to lock himself up in a cellar—unless, that is, there is a playful tone in the message? In addition, in typical Kafkaesque fashion, the image of this triumphant writing in the cellar is shattered by the recognition that he will turn mad.[40] This is not simply a confession of despair, but also an engagement with Dostoyevsky's figure of the man from the underground, as if Kafka is winking to Felice, telling her, "You know of course whom I personify here, you get my reference to Dostoyevsky, you get my joke?" Felice, alas, always practical, always pragmatic, always with both feet on the ground, probably does not notice Kafka's wink. But this does not mean that we have to revert to the description of Kafka's cages as the imprisonment of the tortured author. Instead, I suggest, we should avoid this perspective—

which is ultimately Felice's perspective—and notice instead the relations that Kafka's figure of confinement mobilizes.[41]

The second way to misconstrue Kafka's cages is the obverse of the first one. According to this move, the cage becomes the springboard to greatness. Differently put, the cage is the condition of the possibility of redemption or transcendence. The origins of this interpretation can be traced to Max Brod, Kafka's friend and literary executor. After Kafka's death in 1924, Brod devised a program to publish his friend's works. He started with the novels, which he did not publish in order of composition. The first to appear was *The Trial* in 1925, followed by *The Castle* in 1926 and then *Amerika* in 1927. This initial publication frenzy almost instantaneously established Kafka as a major author. Four years later, in 1931, Brod edited the first collection of Kafka's short stories to appear after his death, *The Great Wall of China*. In the same volume, Brod included a series of aphorisms for which he chose the title *Reflections on Sin, Hope, Suffering, and the True Way*.[42] The title was indicative of the interpretation that Brod was already working on and that was going to be contained in his biography of Kafka, published in 1937. According to this interpretation, Kafka was on a spiritual journey, which gave his writings a distinctly spiritual dimension. The aphorisms contained in *Reflections on Sin, Hope, Suffering, and the True Way* are presented as exemplary of this spiritual journey. This journey goes through a lot of hardship, of course, but it culminates in a transcendence by affirming the divine. In Brod's extrapolation: "He believed in a world of Rightness, he believed in 'The Indestructible' of which so many of his aphorisms speak.[43] We are too weak always to recognize this real world. But it is there. Truth is visible everywhere. It glints through the mesh of what we call 'reality.' "[44] The "Indestructible," according to this interpretation, is indicative of Kafka looking past the cages within which humanity is trapped and into a divine presence as the guarantee of "truth." The cage is the condition of the possibility of redemption.

Nowadays, the usual way of referring to these thoughts is as *The Zürau Aphorisms*.[45] This name derives from the place where they were composed, but also serves to blunt Brod's interpretation of these aphorisms within a squarely theological register. Roberto Calasso provides a useful context of the manner of composition of these aphorisms.[46] In September 1917, a month after he coughed blood for the first time, Kafka and his sister Ottla went to Zürau, a Bohemian village, where they stayed for eight months. Kafka did not write literature during that time, but he was writing in his diary, as was his usual practice. The aphorisms comprising *The Zürau Aphorisms* were thoughts extracted from his diary by Kafka himself, and arranged in numerical sequence in a separate notebook. The care with which Kafka undertook this task may suggest that he was contemplating their publication, although he would have had ample opportunity to pursue this should he have wanted to, before he died seven years later. In any case, there is a metaphysical tenor in these thoughts that could have certainly justified Brod's reading them as theological reflections. But a totally different reading is also possible.

One of the overarching themes of the aphorisms is the concept of freedom. Moreover, Kafka repeatedly returns to the story of the Fall. Thus, the aphorisms written in Zürau have a unique status in examining the question of the free will in Kafka. They appear as a "meta-text" that accompanies the laughter that the idea of the free will generates in his stories. At the same time, it is not so easy to separate them from the "literary writings," since they persistently exhibit precisely the same kind of humor in order to refer to freedom. What I suggest is this: The idea of freedom put forward by Kafka has nothing to do with transcendence. Freedom is not an overcoming of a stage of encagement. Freedom is not redemptive. Rather, it is the transformation of the separation between a world of paradisiacal freedom and a Fallen world of confinement. Let us turn to aphorism 64/65: "The Expulsion from Paradise is eternal in its principal aspect: this makes it irrevocable, and our living in this world inevitable, but the eternal nature of the process has the effect that not only could we remain forever in Paradise, but that we are currently there, whether we know it or not." Kafka starts by describing the Fall as an imprisonment in the human world. But then he immediately subverts this description. Now, suddenly, the eternal expulsion to the Fallen world makes this world itself eternal, just like the Garden of Eden. From this, Kafka concludes that such an eternal process means that we have always been in Paradise. We actually never left it, whether we recognize it or not. The freedom implicated in this thought is a freedom from the free will, in the sense that the genesis of the free will is precisely the point of the separation between Paradise and the Fallen world, which aphorism 64/65 subverts. In addition, we can understand this new freedom in terms of mediation. There is no transcendent freedom outside our experience. We are currently in this state of freedom, we are experiencing it now, avers Kafka. This is a freedom mediated through our existence. This is an important point. We are not dealing here with a metaphysics whose ontology requires the determination of that which exists in relation to something ideal, something that is of a temporality other than the now. Instead, the freedom from the free will mobilizes a conception of ontology as relation.

This idea of a relational ontology can be discerned in the aphorism that immediately follows, aphorism 66. I quote it here in its entirety:

> He is a free and secure citizen of the world because he is on a chain that is long enough to allow him access to all parts of the earth, and yet not so long that he could be swept over the edge of it. At the same time he is also a free and secure citizen of heaven because he is also attached to a similar heavenly chain. If he wants to go to earth, the heavenly manacles will throttle him, if he wants to go to heaven, the earthly manacles will. But for all that, all possibilities are open to him, as he is well aware, yes, he even refuses to believe the whole thing is predicated on a mistake going back to the time of his first enchainment.

The imagery of both freedom and imprisonment is present here. One is free because one is in chains. Moreover, these chains are of two kinds. They are both earthly and heavenly—that is, both material and spiritual. They pull him in two opposing directions. This is the structure of the free will, which, as we have seen, is predicated on the separation between the idealized freedom of Paradise and the confinement in the Fallen world of the earth. A single word obscures this separation: "But." But, says Kafka, who cares about these chains, which were a mistake from a long time ago anyway? One can ponder whether Kafka means the mistake made by the protoplasts leading to the "first enchainment," that is, what Augustine designates as the first instance of the human exercise of the free will. Or whether this structure as a whole is the mistake: whether it is a mistake to see freedom as chained between heaven and earth, that is, to reduce freedom to the free will and the "first enchainment." He "refuses to believe" that the free will is a mistake, even though he has freedom right there, in front of him, in the guise of "all possibilities [that] are open to him." Besides the point that I made earlier about freedom as the relations established in one's existence—freedom as the way that one is in the world—this passage gives an additional insight. Mediated freedom also establishes a relation with the free will. One can realize the possibilities at one's disposal only in relation to the terrestrial and heavenly chains that bind him.

At this point arises the most delicate problem, which has led to some of the most disastrous solutions to the conception of the relational ontology that expresses the freedom from the free will. It is also a problem that can receive a surprisingly simple and straightforward resolution. Let me describe the problem first: If freedom from is related to the free will, then this threatens the reintroduction of transcendence and the reconstruction of the separation between idealized freedom and absolute imprisonment in different, but related, metaphysical registers. The reason is that as soon as one speaks of overcoming, what is mobilized is precisely the kind of vocabulary and imagery used by Brod to describe Kafka's discovery of the "Indestructible" as the vector of "Truth." Thus, Brod—or this line of thinking—could very well concede that the correct conception of freedom is indeed freedom from the free will, but still point out that what is called in this context "freedom from" is not all that different from his "Indestructible," in the sense that it does point to some "truth" that transcends a mistaken or deficient state—in this case, the free will and the "first enchainment." More broadly, this can be articulated as the problem of negation: a direct negation of something—what Hegel calls a "determinate negation"—is nothing but its reaffirmation. Does not the negation of the free will establish two realms, one of the free will and the other of "true" freedom—two realms that are strictly analogous to the separation between the Fallen world and paradise?

The ontology of mediated freedom that I put forward here is not such a negation. Instead of an overcoming, what I am proposing here—and what I hold that Kafka proposes—is the idea that the freedom from the free will is more primary than the free will. Differently put, the free will is an aftereffect of mediated freedom. Or, in yet another way, freedom from the free will precedes the free will and is its cause.[47] Let us turn to aphorism 84: "We were created to live in Paradise, and Paradise was designed to serve us. Our designation has been changed; we are not told whether this has happened to Paradise as well." "We," says Kafka, "we" as an idea of the human being, is created in Paradise. "We" were meant to be in Paradise as a space of freedom. Then, "we" were told that "we" were expelled. "We" find ourselves in a world of imprisonment. But if "we" are not imprisoned, does this mean that paradise remains the transcendent ideal that negates the imprisonment of the Fallen world and toward which "we" should, or ought to, strive? Maybe—and here is the

Kafkaesque humor again—maybe Paradise is not such a transcendent end, because Paradise has changed too. Maybe, as aphorism 64/65 suggests, "we" are already in paradise. The pronoun "we" now is infused with a significant ontological force. Being persists in relation not to that which is transcendent, but to that which is more primary than the transcendent. The transcendent has mutated into something earthly, something immanent, which pertains to "our" existence. Kafka's compulsive return to the Fall in *The Zürau Aphorisms* invariably makes the same point: Being is not determined by the Fall. It is the other way round: Being determines the Fall. The Fall is the construct, a "mistake" in the language of aphorism 66, which we do not need to overcome, but rather to rectify.

Kafka's means of presenting this mistake—so simple, so naïve, and yet so pervasive—is humor. Laughter is his reflex reaction to every manifestation of the idea that we can simply transcend the free will—through our sheer willpower! This is the impossible task that the land surveyor sets for himself in *The Castle*, and Kafka laughs with him. And as the testimonies about his public readings inform us, Kafka also invites his audience to laugh along. This laughter is only possible by noting the ontological priority of mediated freedom over the free will. I will present this idea of the ontological primacy of mediated freedom in various registers in the following chapters. The Kafkaesque laughter will reverberate only so long as we avoid the two mistakes that are so tempting to make—like the mistake of eating from the tree of knowledge—in relation to Kafka's cages: They are neither symbols of disaster that turn Kafka into a martyr for literature (as in Felice's horror), nor proofs of a metaphysical triumph, as if Kafka were a modern prophet (as in Brod's misguided optimism). They are, rather, injunctions to take existence, in all its relationality, seriously—and this also means armed with laughter. It means that living is what is more primary than transcendence. I leave the last word of this first chapter to Kafka himself. "We are sinful, not only because we have eaten of the Tree of Knowledge, but also because we have not yet eaten of the Tree of Life. The condition in which we find ourselves is sinful, guilt or no guilt" (Aphorism 83).

2

The Abrahamic Laughter

The Topography of Freedom in "The Judgment" and *The Metamorphosis*

Abrahamic Laughter: Between the Theological and the Political

Maurice Blanchot pays close attention to Kafka's futile desire to reconcile the calling of literature with his daily activities, such as his job and the prospect of married life. As Blanchot puts it in "Kafka and the Work's Demand," Kafka's torment consists in the increasing recognition "that he cannot live alone and that he cannot live with others."[1]

In the midst of the description of this despair, Blanchot acknowledges the possibility of laughter. He first observes that Kafka is comparable to Abraham because Kafka thought that one had to sacrifice the calling of writing—which resembles Abraham's sacrifice of Isaac.[2] And then Blanchot further elaborates by drawing a distinction between the modernist writer and the biblical figure: "For Kafka the ordeal is all the graver because of everything that makes it weigh lightly upon him. (What would the testing of Abraham be if, having no son, he were nevertheless required to sacrifice this son? He couldn't be taken seriously; he could only be laughed at. That laughter is the form of Kafka's pain.)"[3] Why is Kafka's weight light in comparison to Abraham's? In Genesis, the source of this weight is God himself. As an authority whose command is Law and who personifies the ideal, rebellion against the injunction to sacrifice Isaac is meaningless. To put it in the terms introduced in the previous chapter: Abraham persists in the Fallen world of suffering and unfreedom, whereas real freedom—the freedom to command, the freedom to demand the son's sacrifice—resides in the position occupied by the ideal. But, notes Blanchot, this is not Kafka's predicament. There is no incontestable authority commanding him to write. Thus, Kafka's position is not indicative of the impossibility to rebel, since not only is there no one to rebel against, there is not even a command to be explicitly resisted. The Abrahamic laughter is generated by Kafka's pain at the ordeal, which he is *not* forced—through a deprivation of his freedom—to undergo. Differently put, Kafka suffers from the implications of the absence of an ideal, even though that ideal no longer condemns him to the suffering of an absolute unfreedom—which is laughable.[4]

The Abrahamic logic, then, presents the idea of the free will and the separation of the two realms—an ideal one and the Fallen world of imprisonment. At the same time, a laughter enables the transition to a different realm, one that is not riven in two. If the world that relies on separation to make the free will possible can be described as a political theology, then the second world, which enacts a freedom from the free will, can be distinguished by referring to it as theologico-political.[5] In other words, the logic of the Abrahamic laughter sets the basis of what was called in the previous chapter "Kafka's cages." Before we proceed, let me sketch some salient features of the theologico-political topography. There are at least three fundamental issues at stake:

First, there is the theological recognition of what we can call, after Nietzsche, the death of God. The divine command to sacrifice a nonexistent son puts into question the omniscience and hence the very existence of the divine authority itself. If ideals are dead, then the only response to their representations is to laugh in their face—even though they keep on returning to haunt us. The ideal is the attempt to represent nothing, a void—which is laughable. From this perspective, the land surveyor's prerogative in *The Castle* is indeed laughable. His actions are premised on the "mystical" valence of the castle and its officials. They define his mission, they determine his raison d'être. The castle and the officials—unlike their equivalents in *The Trial*—are not invisible and remote.[6] Instead, their mystical purchase should have been debunked by their actual appearance—there is, for instance, nothing remotely mystical about Klamm. And yet, K. is ensnared by this all-too-visibly-debunked ideal, by this illusion that holds him prisoner in the village. There is something distinctly laughable about this predicament. In discussing *The Castle*, Jane

Bennett expresses this point with precision: "Noting the presence in the foreground of . . . the unreality of ideals that nevertheless provide preconditions to action . . . you *laugh*. The ideal sets a goal and a standard, the laughter reminds that it too will have its limits and its hidden or forgotten moral ambiguities. You laugh at the intensity of your quest to access the inaccessible ideal, but your laughter includes the knowledge that you'll do it again, and that doing it now and doing it again may in fact make a *critical* difference."[7] We see here why Blanchot calls Abrahamic laughter painful. Laughing at the absent ideal may make a critical difference, but the ideals keep on returning—eternally. *There is no outside from this theological submission to the dead ideal.* The reason is that as soon as an outside is posited, this very positing creates a new ideal, a new idol, which pushes us back to suffering yet again. To return to the figure of the Kafkaesque Abraham, even though there is no son to sacrifice to obey a higher order, the divine injunction for such a sacrifice returns to haunt Abraham—which is why "he could only be laughed at."

Second, this is also a political issue, as James Martel clearly recognizes. The question is how to resist an ideal that is dead. As is well recognized, resistance can produce counter-resistance.[8] This happens, in this instance, by countering the dead ideal head-on, which only leads to its substitution by another ideal.[9] All too aware of this problem, Martel proposes instead a politics of resistance as "recognizing misrecognition," and he discovers in Kafka a paradigmatic exponent. Such a politics unfolds in a double move. The first one consists of a failure of Kafka's characters "to conform to the various powers that they see as organizing their life." But, notes Martel, "such a failure can . . . be turned into an asset; it becomes a failure to read a faux mythology 'correctly,' a failure to make sense of a symbolic universe that they seem to have no choice but to submit to." Thus failure becomes the means to resist the ideals that ensnare Kafka's characters. This has a further implication. The ideal thereby finds itself in a position of self-implosion. Or, in Martel's words, this resembles "a messiah that voids or destroys its own symbols of power, its own mythologies." Not only is God dead, as in the theological moment that we noted above, but any political idea is also dead, voided by its own innermost vacuity. The political praxis that arises here consists in recognizing this failure and this voiding. It consists, in other words, in "a politics of 'recognizing misrecognition' wherein signs are neither worshipped as true nor abandoned altogether."[10] The price to pay for a resistance that resists in such a way as to avoid reinstating the ideal is that there is no end to the resistance. *There is no outside resistance.* This does not provide any certainty or comfort. Blanchot cites from Kafka's *Diary* an entry dated January 28, 1922: "I have been forty years wandering from Canaan."[11] Such a self-conception of the Abrahamic ordeal justifies Blanchot's insistence on Kafka's torment. At the same time, an Abraham wondering aimlessly without a son to sacrifice also provides the opportunity for comic relief. Characters such as K., the land surveyor, keep on trying to reach the ideal, and their attempts become increasingly frustrated—and laughable—the more they (mis)recognize that the ideal is already dead.

Third, we can synthesize the theological and the political moments in what I call the "theologico-political" by noting that they both have a certain indefinite temporality: the dead ideal returns, the resistance is perpetual. But this temporality also corresponds to a topography. (Is this the reason that K. is a land surveyor, a topographer?)[12] This can be read as the topography of the free will. As explained in the previous chapter, there is no free will unless there is a separation between an ideal freedom and an absolute unfreedom. This separation produces the free will in its various guises. Differently put, there is unfreedom in the outside—in the land of banishment and endless pilgrimage toward the city of God, as Augustine puts it; and there is freedom inside that city, inside the ideal of a paradise where harmony and peace persist. This is the topography of freedom that corresponds to the metaphor of the door, which we also saw in the previous chapter. The door creates an inside and an outside, one corresponding to freedom and the other to unfreedom. Conversely, Abrahamic laughter creates a different topography, in which the outside/inside distinction is effaced. If the ideal is generated by this topography's separation of the outside and the inside, now that the ideal is dead there is no longer any other space where one is condemned to suffer in unfreedom. And if, despite its death, we still encounter the ideal in various representations of the topography of outside/inside, then we can outflank this represented separation by laughing at it. Laughter is the Kafkaesque mechanics of introducing a sense of freedom that does not rely on the free will, and hence it does not rely on the topography that separates an ideal freedom from an absolute unfreedom.

The Abrahamic laughter erupts in response to the topography of separation that characterizes the free will. It introduces a theologico-political conception that nevertheless lacks an outside, thereby eschewing the topography that requires a separation between an inside and an outside. Such a topography without an outside testifies to the death of the ideal, since there is no longer an inaccessible topos where the ideal can be placed. And yet, representations of the ideal return. Abraham still feels compelled to sacrifice Isaac, even though he in fact has no son. The Abrahamic laughter is a response to the futile attempts to deal with the representations of the ideal, while also resisting that political theology that requires the return of the representation of ideals.

In this chapter I further describe this Abrahamic laughter. I will do so by concentrating on Kafka's early, breakthrough story, "The Judgment," while also considering *The Metamorphosis*. This analysis will also turn to Maurice Blanchot, who more than anyone else has paid close attention to what he calls "the outside." Blanchot's outside describes a topography that is not reliant on a separation of an inside and an outside—it is "outside" such a separation. Not surprisingly, given the importance of such a separation for the free will, Blanchot associates his notion of the outside with "the origin of a new freedom."[13]

Who Is Gustav Blenkelt? The Two Interpretations

September 23, 1912 is a—perhaps, *the*—fateful day in the Kafka calendar. That morning, the aspiring writer from Prague sees the dawn rise without having gone to bed. The reason is that he has spent the night writing the piece—"The Judgment"—that confirms in his mind that he has what it takes to be a writer. "The Judgment"—the story as well as the process of its creation—remain till his death a constant point of reference, the standard against which everything else he writes is measured.

"The Judgment" is written in the midst of an exceptional set of circumstances. A week before the fateful night in which the short story is written, Kafka sends off his first book, *Meditations*, to his publisher, and two days earlier he writes his first letter to Felice Bauer. It is a very productive period for Kafka. Max Brod notes that immediately afterward, Kafka writes the first chapter of *Amerika*, titled "The Stoker," followed by *The Metamorphosis* in November and December. Essentially, then, Kafka composes, in the space of around three months, the three stories—"The Judgment," "The Stoker," and *The Metamorphosis*—that he wants to collect as a volume under the title *Sons*. During the same period he writes most of the rest of his first novel, *Amerika*. Kafka had not seen such a productive period in his life before—and he will have to wait for another two years to have a similarly productive period, as we will see in chapter 4.

The night of September 22 to 23 is the pivotal date for this first significant burst of productivity.

Kafka knows as he is composing "The Judgment" that it is a great story. The evidence is the entry of September 23 in his diary—that is, the same journal in which the story itself was written. This long and often-quoted entry is a joyous one. "Only in this way can writing be done, only with such coherence, with such a complete opening out of the body and the soul. . . . Many emotions carried along in the writing, joy, for example."[14] The mirth continues the following day. After reading the story, Ottla, his sister, remarks on the similarity between their house and the one in the story. Kafka records the exchange as follows: "24 September. My sister said: The house (in the story) is very like ours. I said: How? In that case, then, Father would have to be living in the toilet."[15] Kafka is not trying to avoid the comparison. Instead, he takes it so matter-of-factly as to make it absurd and to generate humor.[16] The levity of these pages of his journal is palpable.

In the same joyous day of September 23, even though he had spent the entire night writing, Kafka returns to his journal to compose one of the entries whose status is ambiguous, appearing both as sketches for a longer piece of writing and as self-contained, autonomous parables. I will turn to this entry before examining "The Judgment," because examining this diary entry adds further nuances to the Abrahamic logic, and it does so by presenting it in a succinct, condensed form. Thus the analysis of the Blenkelt story paves the way to the analysis of "The Judgment."

The entry consists of two paragraphs about "a simple man with regular habits" called Gustav Blenkelt. The first paragraph provides a strictly matter-of-fact description of Blenkelt, concentrating on external characteristics: "He didn't like any unnecessary display and had a definite opinion about people who went in for such display." Further, Kafka writes that Blenkelt "felt he had an absolute right" to comment on "the marital affairs of his acquaintances," and he "used to speak his mind freely." This meant that some admired him, others honored him, some tolerated him and, finally, there were "those who wanted to have nothing to do with him." This description makes Gustav Blenkelt "an exceptionally social person," says Kafka. One can rightfully wonder whether this sociality is a description of Blenkelt's standing in the community—a large part of which clearly could not stand him—or whether, instead, it is a description of what constitutes sociality in Blenkelt's community. If the inference of his being "exceptionally social" does not follow from the matter-of-fact description, then the last sentence of the first paragraph can only be a statement about the sociality tout court of the community of which Blenkelt is a member.

The second paragraph makes logical sense only if we take the latter view—that is, that we have here a description of sociality, and more precisely a sociality presented as a Fallen world. The second paragraph reads:

> In his thirty-fifth year, the last year of his life, he spent an unusual amount of time with a young couple named Strong. It is certain that for Mr. Strong, who had opened a furniture store with his wife's money, the acquaintance with Blenkelt had numerous advantages, since the largest part of the latter's acquaintances consisted of young, marriageable people who sooner or later had to think of providing new furniture for themselves and who, out of old habit, were usually accustomed not to neglect Blenkelt's advice in this matter, either. "I keep them on a tight rein [*Ich halte sie an festen Zügeln*]," Blenkelt used to say.[17]

The society described here is premised on a principle of imprisonment or ensnarement. Blenkelt's conception of his right to the freedom of speech and his acquaintance with a number of members of his community means that he can use that freedom to ensnare the Strongs, who need him for their young business to flourish. Thus, Kafka starts with the description of an individual, but it becomes a description of the society in which that individual resides, and then it reveals its principle of sociality as one of imprisonment. How are we to understand this movement? There are two ways, depending on how we understand the topography of the story as well as the operative presence or absence of laughter in it.

The first one can be traced back to Max Brod, who is in fact one of the few commentators pointing out this entry from the *Diaries* in connection to the writing of "The Judgment," even though he offers no direct explanation for their relation.[18] Such a link, however, can be readily discovered in Brod's theological interpretation of Kafka's writings. Such a theological interpretation is premised on the separation between the world of earthly reality and a higher, truer world. I am quoting here a passage from Brod's biography of Kafka that I also quoted in the previous chapter: "He believed in a world of Rightness, he believed in 'The Indestructible' of which so many of his aphorisms speak. We are too weak always to recognize this real world. But it is there. Truth is visible everywhere. It glints through the mesh of what we call 'reality.' This explains Kafka's deep interest in every detail, every wrinkle of reality."[19] "The Indestructible" is that higher reality which is more profound than the here and now and toward which Kafka's own writings aspire, contends Brod. Blanchot points out that Kafka's notes on the "The Indestructible" in the journals seem to be references to an idea that Brod develops in *Paganism, Christianity, Judaism*, thereby making Brod's emphasis on these journal entries self-referential.[20] Leaving this aside, Brod's reading conforms to a theological interpretation of Kafka because of the separation between two realities—one of freedom and the other of imprisonment and suffering. In this interpretation, the theological ideal is not a void that returns as a specter to haunt us—as is the case in Bennett's interpretation we saw earlier. Rather, the ideal is given substance, named as the "The Indestructible," and indexed as reality. There is nothing to laugh at about such an ideal, since it condemns us to live in an inferior world of unfreedom.[21]

We can find several versions of this theological interpretation. A recent and influential attempt derives from Walter Sokel, who interprets this separation as a form of Gnosticism. The main characteristic of Gnosticism is a radical duality between a deficient world of imprisonment in which we live, and a higher, ideal world in which the true God resides. This can be expressed also as the idea that our own world is dominated by an evil deity holding us captive. Sokel recognizes Gnosticism in Kafka's obsessive return to such images of imprisonment. For instance, he writes that "[v]ery much in the Gnostic vein, Kafka perceived life as imprisonment" and that Kafka's movement toward Gnosticism "tends to strengthen Kafka's natural disposition to experience the world as a prison, a place of intolerable confinement."[22] At the same time, there is a higher, true God who retains the promise of freedom, even though that God is of another world separated from ours.[23] Such a higher God can be read as "The Indestructible." The piece about Blenkelt can be understood in gnostic terms. The way that society is described results in keeping others "on a tight rein." Blenkelt is the representative of the evil deity—an avatar of the power of that political theology that condemns us to ensnarement and to a lower reality.

Regardless of the particular details of Brod's "Indestructible" or the deities of Gnosticism, their common denominator is the separation between a higher reality that stands for the ideal, and a lower reality of suffering. It is not accidental that both such interpretations—their differences notwithstanding—posit being as an expression of unfreedom. The reason is that, as we saw in the previous chapter, the separation between the ideal and its demoted state of unfreedom is the precondition of the creation of the free will, which in this sense is a theological idea. As Kafka notes, Blenkelt spoke "his mind freely" and it is this free will that justifies his meddling in married couples' affairs and gives him the means to keep the Strongs "on a tight rein." Blenkelt, as a representative of an ensnared sociality, which at the same time posits a higher reality of freedom, posits a radical separation between two worlds, which is a precondition of the free will. This interpretation, then, mobilizes the logic of political theology's topography.

And yet, Kafka's matter-of-fact description makes no allusion whatsoever to such a higher reality of freedom and ideality that the gnostic schema and the topography of the free will require. To take Kafka's text literally, Blenkelt is not an evil deity, but a self-righteous meddler, a confidence man who poses like a god to keep his friends "on a tight rein." Adorno contends that one has to read Kafka literally. His insight functions as a riposte to those interpretations that assert an ideal in Kafka's writings—and Adorno names several such interpretations.[24] If we read the Blenkelt story literally, the ideal is missing. The ideal is dead, just like Blenkelt, whose death is prefigured in the opening sentence of the second paragraph of the story. Thus, the representations of the ideal—through the representation of the opposite of the ideal, such as the evil figure holding the world "on a tight rein"—are nothing but representations of a void, a nothing. They are representations of Blenkelt's fantasy of his own omnipotence, which he seeks to fulfil on his friends.

Such a move can be summarized by saying that Kafka posits the lack of an outside or the lack of a higher authority, supposedly separated from our reality while it nevertheless supervenes over our world. The "moral" of the Blenkelt story is that there is no outside. But this is not all. In addition, it is fundamental to recognize how Kafka makes this move. This lack of an outside is not asserted explicitly. Rather, the lack of an outside is presented in its being misconceived as a generalized description of being, which presents the entire society as a prison. The particular sociality described through Blenkelt is one of perceived imprisonment. This manner of presentation provides Kafka with the means to laugh at such a conception. This laughter introduces the topography of the theologico-political.

According to Bennett, the dead ideal returns to haunt K. in *The Castle* because there is no outside of the representations of the dead ideals. We will always be haunted by misconceptions that will hold us "on a tight rein." In this case, the dead ideal is personified by Blenkelt himself who, by Kafka's own account, is far from a particularly charismatic figure, let alone an evil deity who can hold us captive through his omnipotence. Thus the reaction to Blenkelt occupying the position of the representation of the ideal can only be one of mirthful disbelief: "Who, Blenkelt? How can such a miserable, intervening sod be even close to an evil deity holding us captive?" The theological moment is this laughter *at* the debunked ideal.

According to Martel, there is no outside of the political ideals, because such an outside would only reinstate a new political ideal. Kafka's laughter at Blenkelt is also the means to resist a sense of political ensnarement. Kafka laughs as a means to counter the illusion that freedom is the exercise of one's free will. Blenkelt freely expresses his opinions about married couples, and he exercises his free will to keep them under his power, but there is something comical in this pitiable character who deludes himself that overpowering others through his will is a sign of omnipotence and a token of freedom. Laughter *resists* such a power.

Who is Blenkelt? By one account he is a representation of the divine itself, in the sense that he performs the split between this Fallen world of suffering and a higher, free world associated with the divine. By another account, Blenkelt is nothing but the delusion of omnipotence, in both a theological and a political register. The Blenkelt story shows in its bare essentials this fundamental dichotomy. The topography of the story's landscape can be read in two radically opposed ways. This insight is fundamental for the logic of Abrahamic laughter. We do not recognize the dead ideals unless they are represented. The topography of the theologico-political without an outside also requires the opposite topography of political theology, which requires the separation of a higher realm and a lower realm, no less than the separation of an inside and an outside. The Abrahamic logic requires this dichotomy so that it can ask: "Who is Abraham? Who is that figure aimlessly wandering the desert without a son to sacrifice?" Differently put, this dichotomy puts into question the identity of the individual, just as we have seen in Blenkelt's case: Does he retain his autonomy and hence his free will, only for the world to be condemned to an inescapable interment? Or is he a delusional vehicle for the representations of that ideal which is dead? The confusion generates laughter through the introduction of typical devices of comedies of error, where the identities of the characters are misrecognized.

The Transformation of the Ideal in "The Judgment": The Primacy of the Theologico-Political

"The Judgment" stages the dichotomy between the two topographies that we discovered in the Blenkelt story—the topography of the theologico-political without an outside and the topography a political theology in need of the separation.[25] This dichotomy generates an even greater confusion of identity in "The Judgment." This confusion is necessary for the Abrahamic logic to introduce the topography of the theologico-political, as we saw in the Blenkelt story. At the same time, "The Judgment" adds a further element. Namely, the topography without an outside is presented as *more primary* than the one that enforces the separation between two realms and that underwrites the concept of the free will. Laughter here is nuanced as the theologico-political (mis)recognition of this primacy. Differently put, the comedy of misrecognition generated by the confusion of identity is now extended from the characters to the identity of the two topographies themselves.[26] But whereas the topography of political theology requires the secured identity of the borders that separate a higher from a lower realm, the theologico-political requires no such secure borders or identity. Thus the confusion of identity is amenable only to the theologico-political topography—it only follows if we assume the theologico-political topography.

We need look no further than the two opening sentences to discover the distinction between the two contrasting realms. (I am using the term "distinction" instead of "separation" to suggest that it may in fact be no separation at all but rather, as we will see, the misrecognition of separation.) The story begins by identifying the time. "It was a Sunday morning in the most beautiful time of spring [*im schönsten Frühjahr*]" (77/43). This is not the calendar time. The story is set in the apogee of the time of rebirth and procreation. The expression *im schönsten Frühjahr* brings to mind something like Botticelli's "Primavera"—a luscious and joyous scene. The second sentence immediately contrasts this image: "Georg Bendemann, a young merchant, was sitting in his own room on the first floor of one of a long row of small, ramshackle houses stretching beside the river which were scarcely distinguishable from each other in height and coloring" (77). Georg is a young man who we will soon learn has been doing exceedingly well in business. Yet he is still trapped in his paternal home and in his old room. In addition, that home itself appears like a cell, standing beside other, almost identical cells. One is left to ponder the misery that such cell-like houses accommodate. If a painterly analogue were to be sought, one could conjure here something like a Goya etching. This contrast between the height of spring and the cell-houses looks like the contrast between the world of paradise and the Fallen world of suffering. As such a separation, this contrast indicates that freedom is a fundamental concern of "The Judgment." But is this the freedom of the free will, according to which this separation can never be bridged? Or is this setting the stage for laughing at the illusion of such a separation? With these two possibilities the Abrahamic logic is operative.

The third sentence, the final sentence of the first paragraph, reads: "He had just finished a letter to an old friend of his who was now living abroad had put it into its envelope in a slow and dreamy fashion, and with his elbows propped on the writing table was gazing out of the window at the river, the bridge, and the hills on the farther bank with their tender green" (77). This sentence contains three elements that correspond to what we can identify as three sections of the short story. The determination of the three elements will define—just as in Blenkelt—two radically different interpretations of "The Judgment." Let us take the two readings in turn to see how they lead to a confusion of identity. Only then will we be in a position to discover the additional element to the Abrahamic logic introduced by "The Judgment," namely, the primacy of the topography without an outside. I will start with the interpretation that identifies the operation of a free will.

The first element pertains to his friend, who lives in Petersburg. The first few pages of "The Judgment" describe Georg's thoughts about his friend, whose voluntary exile in a foreign land without friends appears to destine him for the life of a bachelor. In these first few pages, it appears as if Georg's predicament corresponds to the first sentence of the story, since he is happy with his engagement to a young woman "from a well-to-do family" (79), whereas his friend is presented as corresponding to the second sentence, trapped and lacking friends in a distant land deprived of opportunities and success. Georg initially did not want to inform his friend about his engagement, fearing that the news of his joyful predicament would make his friend resentful. But on that beautiful spring

Sunday morning, he writes the letter that informs his friend about the happy news.[27]

The second element pertains to his dreamy state. Georg appears relaxed. In the beautiful spring morning, he lowers his guard. He has no inkling of his actual predicament when he goes into his father's room to tell him about writing to his friend in Petersburg. His father's room is dark, the old man looks feeble, and his memory seems to have started to fail him as he does not recall Georg's friend from Petersburg. Georg lovingly lifts his father from the chair to take him to bed. The father clutches on Georg's watch chain, as if he has regressed to a young child fascinated with such glittering objects. But then, all of a sudden, his father revives. He starts accusing Georg of being infatuated with his fiancée "because she lifted her skirts like this, the nasty creature" (85), and he informs Georg that he has been in touch with the friend from Petersburg to keep him abreast with the news. He jumps up and stands threateningly on the bed, shouting to Georg: " 'So now you know what else there was in the world besides yourself, till now you've known only about yourself! An innocent child, yes, that you were, truly, but still more truly have you been a devilish human being!—And therefore take note: I sentence you now to death by drowning' " (87). The appearance in the first part of the story that Georg occupied the position of bliss signified by the blooming spring and that his friend corresponded to the second position of generalized imprisonment is now reversed. Having dropped his guard, Georg had not realized that in fact he is the prisoner of this father who, as an evil spirit, thoroughly monitors his every move. Even more than Blenkelt, whose power extended only to keeping others "on a tight rein," the father has the power to induce Georg's actions. Thus, Georg appears as thoroughly deprived of any vestige of freedom to act, since the sole free will dominating the scene is his father's.

The third element of the third sentence of "The Judgment" pertains to the scene Georg observes outside his window just after sealing the letter to his friend. Instead of a picturesque view of the bridge framed by the pastoral background of the green hills, Georg is actually looking at the setting of his death. Just after the death sentence is delivered by his father, Georg feels "himself driven out of the room [*fühlte sich aus dem Zimmer gejagt*]" (87/60). The verb *jagen* means hunting, and the reflexive *sich gejagt fühlen* signifies something like being haunted by a power so fierce as to be thoroughly deprived of any sense of freedom. This force drives him toward the river, to the same bridge that he was contemplating from his open window. He jumps over the rail to drown himself. The story concludes with the following sentence: "At this moment an unending stream of traffic was just going over the bridge [*ging über die Brücke ein geradezu unendlicher Verkehr*]" (88/61). Not only is Georg deprived of any experience of the joyous image represented in the opening sentence as the most beautiful moment of spring, this paradise is foreclosed to all of humanity. The unending traffic signifies the generalization of the second sentence, that is, the generalization of imprisonment. Instead of the joys of spring, everyone is condemned to cross the bridge where death awaits.

In the first reading, which evidences the free will as the will of the father, the ideal of spring remains inaccessible to all characters as well as to the society they live in. The bright sun only throws a spotlight from afar onto the suffering, imprisonment, and death unfolding below. There is an absolute separation between the two realms signified by the first two sentences of the story. The shift to the second reading consists in discovering a topography that is incompatible with the separation of the first interpretation. In fact, we will see that the father's sudden transformation evidences the apotheosis of the joyous ideal of the spring in a remarkable reversal between the first two sentences. As I will argue, this is ultimately a radical transformation of the ideal itself. But let us start from the beginning. The theologico-political reading of "The Judgment"—very much like the Blenkelt story—is intimately linked to the disestablishment of identities. Identities are both established and, almost simultaneously, undercut. This culminates in a veritable paroxysm of misidentifications. We will follow the traces of this transformation of identities, which is part of the same process that transforms the ideal.

The first section of the story concerns, as we saw, Georg's ruminations about this friend from Petersburg. It appears to establish a contrast between the two. And yet gradually their identities become unstable. Here are a couple of indicative passages. First, the second sentence describes the house in which Georg and his father live as being like a cell—a box of a house in a row of almost identical houses. At the same time, the contrast between Georg and the friend from Petersburg is built on the former's success and the latter's failure in professional life. Kafka places a lot of emphasis on this. For instance, Georg feels he could not advise his friend to return because everybody would have been looking at him as a failure, whereas his own business is thriving. One is left to ponder why Georg is living in such a cell of a house, when business is thriving: the income has increased significantly, while the overheads are under tight control—"the staff had to be doubled and the turnover was five times as great" (79)—thereby generating a significant increase in the profit margins. Such details in the narrative from the beginning undermine the contrast between Georg and his friend. Second, Georg talks twice about how fortunate he is to be with his fiancée. On both occasions he repeats twice that he is happy. For instance, he writes to his friend: " 'For today let me just say that I am very happy [*glücklich*] and as between you and me the only difference in the relationship is that instead of a quite ordinary kind of friend you will now have in me a happy [*glücklichen*] friend' " (80/48–49).[28] This insistent repetition of the same word is one of the typical symptoms of lying. This may not be intentional lying, but rather the mark of lying to oneself, or of disavowal as a symptom of repression. Regardless, by the time Georg walks into his father's dark room, one who takes the text literally could not help but feel that there are details that do not "stack up" and that ultimately undermine the certainty of who Georg Bendemann is.

The gradual doubts as to the characters' identities rapidly increase during the encounter in the father's room. The ostensible reason for this is the father's transformation. He initially questions whether the friend from Petersburg actually exists, only to divulge subsequently that the father has been his "representative [*Vertreter*]" (86/57), as if there is a formal, legal connection between them. Moreover, there are various allusions that the friend is actually a son to the father. For instance, the father announces that the friend "would have been a son after my own heart" (85). Further, the friend is referred to as *verloren* (lost) in Russia. Given that there is no indication why he is lost there, the word may be used as an allusion to *verlorene Son* or the prodigal son.[29]

Besides the erosion of the identities of Georg and the friend, the father's own transformation from a feeble, hopeless old man playing like a child with Georg's watch chain one moment, to a powerful man who jumps with "strength [*Kraft*]" (84/56) on his bed the next, not only calls into question the identity of the father in relation to Georg, but even problematizes the distinction with which the story opened—that is, the contrast between the procreational image of spring and the world of generalized imprisonment. The reason is that the father asserts his power to ensnare Georg with recourse to the sexuality symbolized by the spring. The allusions to the father's sexuality start from the moment Georg enters his dark room: " 'Ah, Georg,' said his father, rising at once to meet him. His heavy dressing gown swung open as he walked and the skirts of it fluttered around him.—'My father is still a giant [*ein Riese*],' said Georg to himself" (81/50). Georg could not be referring to his father's actual body size when he calls him a "giant," since only moments later he lifts him with ease in his arms. One is left to assume that the word "giant" springs into Georg's mind by what he observes under the parted gown. The lifting of garments persists as an image. While deriding the fiancée, the father says: " 'because she lifted her skirt like this, the nasty creature,' and he lifted his shirt so high that one could see the scar on his thigh from his war wound" (85). The scar is a metonym for the father's manhood, not only because of his war exploits but, one has to assume, for his contiguous, exposed member. These exposures indicate a sexual delirium that even includes the threat that the father will copulate with Georg's fiancée: " 'Just take your bride on your arm and try getting in my way! I'll sweep her from your very side, you don't know how!' " (86). Is this actually a reenactment of the primal combat for supremacy between father and son, or is it a comical presentation of such a scene? Georg has every reason to shout at his father: "You comedian!" (86). But the comedy is not so much due to the recreation of primal myths as to the uncertainty about who has copulated with whom, so that the relation between Georg and his friend is unclear—are they brothers?—and as to who is going to copulate with whom—Georg or the father with Fräulein Frieda Brandenfeld? This comedy of errors is possible because the father appears—or, rather, is *meant to* appear—as an evil deity condemning Georg to death, because he assumes the properties not of the generalized imprisonment but of the sexual crescendo indicated by the most beautiful spring day. Thus the disestablishment of identities also creates a confusion—even reversal—of the separation between the ideal signified by spring and the suffering signified by the cell-like abodes. Or, more accurately, there is confusion generating laughter *because* the separation has collapsed.

From this perspective, the father's condemnation of Georg to death by drowning is the opposite of the expression of his free will. Instead, this death sentence is caused by the collapse of the separation that guarantees the free will. There is no free will when there are no longer any stable identities—for at this point, whose will is it? Here is how Kafka describes the reaction of the only "independent witness" of the story. The father has just condemned Georg to death: "On the staircase, which he rushed down as if its steps were an inclined plane, he ran into his charwoman on her way to do the morning cleaning of the room. 'Jesus!' she cried, and covered her face with her apron, but he was already gone"

(87). Her exclamation cannot be an allusion to Georg being a martyr like Christ (that is, the figure who mediates the separation between the ideal world of the divine and the earthly world of suffering). If that were the case, her reaction would not have been to cover her face to obscure an obscene view. The exclamation "Jesus!" suggests a reaction to such an indecent sight. Georg is exposed, just like his father who flaunted the "scar" from his wound alongside his exposed member. Thus the father and the son assume a similar appearance—naked, powerful, virile. Their identities merge at this point, making the idea untenable that the father is an independent entity from Georg so that he has the power to exercise his free will to condemn him.

Even Georg's death is, upon closer inspection, rather joyous. Let us note again that the father's transformation has asserted the primacy of the sexual delirium of the spring. Georg holds onto the railing of the bridge as a "gymnast" (88)—a gesture of corporeal strength. And when he lets go of the railing to fall into the water, the expression used by Kafka—"ließ sich hinfallen"—can mean not only that he let himself fall from the railing, but also that he let himself go, penetrating the wetness of the river. Is this the description of a death or of *la petite morte*? Did the father condemn Georg to death, or did he command him to "go forth and multiply"? The short story concludes with a sentence that may appear nonsensical: "At this moment [i.e. just as Georg "let himself go"] an unending stream of traffic was just going over the bridge [*In diesem Augeblick ging über die Brücke ein geradezu unendlicher Verkehr*]" (88/61). Brod records the following conversation: "He told me, in fact, and to the best of my recollection, more or less in so many words, 'Do you know what the last sentence means? When I wrote it, I had in mind a violent ejaculation.' "[30] Brod's discomfort, evidenced by his scrupulous exactness—"to the best of my recollection . . . in so many words"—is an exegetical discomfort. The sexual crescendo of the last sentence challenges Brod's own vision of the separation between our world and a higher reality of "The Indestructible." Instead of a generalized imprisonment, we are presented with the vision of generalized copulation. From this perspective, there is no more joyous story in Kafka's oeuvre than "The Judgment."

This joyous conclusion is possible because of the collapse of the separation between the ideal world, signified in the first sentence as the joyful spring, and the Fallen world of suffering in which the human is interned. The sexual crescendo of "The Judgment" invites us to take the ideal presented in the first sentence literally. It is an "ideal" of the here and now, an immanent ideal, which does not require a higher topos for it to be realized. Rather, it is realized in the materiality of *ein geradezu unendlicher Verkehr*—the incessant joy of sexuality.

The ideals as instituting an otherworldly topos separated from the here and now of generalized imprisonment are dead. But they also keep on returning. They return like the father, who seeks to overpower Georg. At the same time, the political task—as Martel astutely indicates—is to "recognize misrecognition." In "The Judgment," this consists in recognizing the disestablishment of identities, whereby all three main characters, Georg, the friend, and the father, merge in various ways, and to such an extent that none of them can lay a claim to individual autonomy. Consequently, none of them can claim that he freely wills. The dead ideal is exposed through laughter. The misidentifications present a vision of a generalized copulation, which laughs in the face of transcendent ideals. This laughter resists the imposition of an authority as the representative of the ideal on earth. It resists the political implication of the free will.

This means that the second interpretation includes within it the first one—just as the suffering of the here and now of the second sentence is folded within the joyous materiality of the sexuality of spring in the first sentence. The transformation of the father consists in a transformation of the world of suffering to a world of joy. And this is also a transformation of the topography that separates another realm and the here and now to a topography without an outside. The dichotomy between the two topographies is crucial for the Abrahamic logic to function, as we already saw in the Blenkelt story. But the transformation that we now see in "The Judgment" entails that the two interpretations cannot be opposed—as if one could freely will to choose one over the other. The confusion of identity through the comedy of errors generated by the misattribution of signs of identity is registered in the transformation of the father from a feeble old man to a fierce judge who condemns Georg to death. At the same time, this confusion is also inscribed in the very distinction between the identities of Georg and his father. These transformations are only possible because the world of imprisonment in the second sentence of the story is confused with the ideal of spring registered in the first sentence. Imprisonment is thereby transformed into joyous sexuality. And also transformed in this same process is the ideal, which is transformed from something transcendent to an "ideal" of material joy. Thus, as soon as identities start transforming, the stable identification of the two separate realms required by the topography of political theology collapses.

Or, rather, it is folded into the topography of the theologico-political as a representation that is to be laughed at.

"The world of freedom" and Its Essential Fault: Blanchot's Kafka

Can this theologico-political topography without the separation between a transcendent realm and a Fallen world of suffering, without a division between an inside and an outside—that is, this topography that works around the ground of the free will—point to a new experience of freedom? Blanchot wrote several essays on Kafka, and some of the most powerful pages of this entire corpus are precisely on this question.[31] They are contained in "Kafka and the Work's Demand" under the rubric of a description of what Blanchot calls the "outside."

The "outside"—or, the outside, without qualifying quotation marks from now on—is intimately linked to the Abrahamic logic.[32] Blanchot describes Kafka as torn between the world of the everyday life—the world of his family, his job, and his prospective marriage—and the world of literature. Literature in this context does not mean simply the writing down of stories or one's thoughts, as Michel Foucault clearly recognizes in his essay on Blanchot, to which I will turn shortly. Rather, literature in this context is the abandonment of the world of everyday life. This abandonment is simultaneously the institution of another world, one that Blanchot links with freedom: "deprivation of the world is reversed, becoming a positive experience, that of another world where Kafka is already a citizen, where . . . he knows staggering heights and enjoys a freedom whose value other men sense, whose prestige they acknowledge." Kafka is "deprived" of the world of the everyday only to gain another world, a world of freedom. Blanchot immediately qualifies this new world: "it is necessary to read them, not from the common Christian perspective (according to which there is this world, then the world beyond, the only one which has value, reality, and majesty)." The new world is not a world of a higher reality. Instead, such a world must be seen "always from the 'Abraham' perspective." The Abrahamic logic, as we saw earlier, eschews the separation between the higher world and a lower world of suffering. What does this world consist of, then, according to Blanchot? This is an experience of infinite exclusion and migration: "to be excluded from the world means to be excluded from Canaan, to wander in the desert, and it is this situation which makes his struggle pathetic, his hope hopeless. It is as if, cast out of the world, into the error of infinite migration, he [i.e., Kafka] had to struggle ceaselessly to make of this outside another world and of this error the principle, the origin of a new freedom."[33] There is no stable topography in this other world. Commanded to sacrifice a non-existent son, Abraham can only wander in the desert without a specific goal, without a specific purpose, deprived of a secured meaning guiding his peregrinations. This may be an infinite task, and hence a hopeless struggle, but it introduces also a new hope, since what has been gained is this outside, which is the "origin of a new freedom."

Blanchot is quick to acknowledge the Jewish affinities of this infinite wandering, and at the same time acknowledges Kafka's fascination with the Zionist project. But ultimately, to remain faithful to the Abrahamic logic consists in giving up all political projects, especially if they are underwritten by a theology: "He already belongs to the other shore, and his wandering does not consist in nearing Canaan, but in nearing the desert, the truth of the desert—in going always further in that direction even when, finding no favor in that other world either, and tempted again by the joys of the real world . . . he tries to persuade himself that perhaps he still keeps in Canaan." Blanchot is sensitive to the temptation that the world of the everyday can play, and it does play for Kafka: "if the force of the human world's attraction remains great enough to draw him back to the border and keep him there as though crushed, no less great is the pull of his own world, the one where he is free, where he has the liberty he speaks of with a tremor, a tone of prophetic authority which contrasts with his habitual modesty."[34] It is, at the end of the day, this sense of freedom that is determinative—the freedom of the outside is more important than the temptations of the everyday world.

Literature is pivotal at this point. Literature is the experience of the outside: "Here literature is proclaimed as the power which frees, the force that allays the oppressions of the world 'where everything feels throttled'; it is the liberating passage from the first to the third person, from observation of oneself, which was Kafka's torment, to a higher observation, rising above mortal reality toward the other world, the world of freedom."[35] Kafka resides in the desert—like a wandering Abraham without a son to sacrifice—through the practice of literature. But here literature is understood in a much broader way than usual. Literature is the passage away from the Fallen world of suffering where we are oppressed. It is also the erasure of the first-person perspective—of the power to say "I" and hence of the power to exercise one's free will.[36] Through the liberation from the structure of the free will, one can experience "the other world, the world of freedom." Blanchot's description at this point approximates the idea of the positive description of freedom that I outlined in the previous chapter. One is free by freeing oneself from the shackles of the free will. Blanchot describes this as the experience of literature.

In one of the most perceptive and sensitive essays on Blanchot, Michel Foucault emphasizes the importance of literature, which he associates with the thought of the outside. Foucault demonstrates how the outside undoes all structures of representation, which includes all structures that determine the subject as a form of interiority—as a form of consciousness that can reason in order to exercise its free will. Foucault's description of Blanchot is in fact reminiscent of Blanchot's own description of the Abrahamic logic in Kafka: "To negate one's discourse, as Blanchot does, is to cast it ceaselessly outside of itself, to deprive it at every moment not only of what it has just said, but of the very ability to speak. It is to leave it where it lies, far beyond one, in order to be free for a new beginning."[37] If "speaking" in this context corresponds to the world of the everyday in Kafka, then the experience outside speech is what Kafka discovers in literature. Foucault affirms the theological no less than the political implications of Blanchot's—and, by extension, Kafka's—outside.

An important problem arises at this juncture—one that Foucault is acutely aware of. If this outside were to negate the world of the everyday, would that not simply reinstitute a topography of separation, whereby the Abrahamic logic will efface itself? Differently put, the moment the outside excludes itself from the separation between an inside and an outside, by that very exclusion the separation reinstates itself as the separation between the outside and the topography of the inside/outside—or the separation between the Abrahamic and the Christian logics. This also applies to the operation of power. Foucault puts it as follows: "Anyone who attempts to oppose the law in order to found a new order . . . will encounter the silent and infinitely accommodating welcome of the law. The law does not change: it subsided into the grave once and for all, and each of its forms is only a metamorphosis of that never-ending death."[38] As we also said earlier, the death of God is articulated as the eternal return of the representation of this dead ideal. Blanchot places this problem at the heart of Kafka's search for the outside: "Kafka's entire work is in search of an affirmation that it wants to gain by negation." This is the affirmation of the outside, which Kafka seeks to establish through overcoming the Christian logic relying on a topography of separation. But such an affirmation through negation is in danger of reaffirming that which is negated: "It is for this reason that it seems so strange to say of such a world that it is unaware of transcendence. Transcendence is exactly this affirmation that can assert itself only by negation. It exists as a result of being denied; it is present because it is not there. The dead God has found a kind of impressive revenge in this work. For his death does not deprive him of his power, his infinite authority, or his infallibility: dead, he is even more terrible, more invulnerable, in a combat in which there is no longer any possibility of defeating him."[39] Kafka's characters are battling with this dead transcendence.

This creates a tension central in Kafka's writings. The tension exists because the death of transcendence can instate itself as a new transcendence, as a new ideal. In other words, Blanchot's outside signifies a topography that is outside the separation between inside and outside—and yet that very separation reinstates an inside/outside separation. This is the pivot of Kafka's entire work, to which Blanchot repeatedly returns. For instance, in "Kafka and the Work's Demand," he expresses it as follows: "And yet, in this region where the conditions of a real dwelling are lacking . . . in this region which is the region of error because in it one does nothing but stray without end, there subsists a tension: the very possibility of erring, of going all the way to the end of error, of nearing its limit, of transforming wayfaring without any goal into the certitude of the goal without any way there."[40] It is as if Abraham, banished to aimlessly wander in the desert because he has no Isaac to sacrifice, elevates that wandering and that lack into a principle that justifies his actions no less than the world he finds himself in. Canaan is substituted by the desert. Blanchot further elaborates this tension as the "essential fault" that characterizes the land-surveyor in *The Castle*, who impatiently strives to gain access to the castle and its officials: "The impatience at the heart of error is the essential fault, because it misconstrues the very trueness of error which, like a law, requires that one never believe the goal is close or that one is coming nearer to it."[41] Ultimately, for Blanchot, one who finds the world of the outside but suffers from impatience is a "condemned" man. Here, the imagery of imprisonment returns, all the more terrible, all the more tormenting, since a different kind of freedom had been glimpsed in the outside.

The Essential Transformation: Laughter in *The Metamorphosis*

Despite the positive aspects of the outside, regardless of the fundamental significance of Abraham, Blanchot's picture of Kafka is a bleak one. The essential fault condemns his characters. I contend that the reason Blanchot's picture is ultimately so bleak is that he fails to recognize the significance of Abrahamic laughter that his own logic accounted for. Is not the endless wandering in the desert without a son to sacrifice similar to the endless fretting about how to gain access to the castle and its officials? Is not the laughter Abraham invites also the same laughter that K. should invite?

The reason Blanchot fails to realize the potential of the Abrahamic laughter is that he never asks the question about the relation between the two worlds that he describes—the world of the everyday and the world of the outside, or the Christian and the Abrahamic worlds. For Blanchot, it is as if a choice has to be made at every point—Kafka and his characters have to choose the world they belong to. Surely, the choice is not clear-cut. They may choose the outside, but their attributes or actions—for instance, their impatience—may return them to the opposite world. For this reason, Blanchot can never notice the transformative aspect of laughter. Failing to explore how the confusion of identity and the comedy it generates also confuses the separation between a higher and a Fallen world prevents Blanchot from ever considering the possibility that the world of separation is dependent on the outside. And, failing to pursue the Abrahamic logic to its logical conclusion, Blanchot persists with the logic of two separate worlds. But this is the logic of the topography of political theology. Instead, the theologico-political topography requires a logic that is transformative. As we saw in "The Judgment," the transformation of the topography of separation and imprisonment into a topography of joyous laughter also enacts a liberation from the free will.

In other words, Blanchot glimpses the liberating potential of the outside to the extent that it is distinct from the world of the free will, but nevertheless this insight remains curtailed, stunted in its development. The most glaring example of this is Blanchot's reading of the ending of *Metamorphosis*.[42] Gregor Samsa wakes up one morning to find himself transformed into a giant vermin. He is trapped in this new body, and also in his room, which he is no longer able to leave—or at least, he can no longer leave without being chased back into it by his father. His sister shows him some kindness, but this also quickly wears away. Blanchot describes Gregor's state as one of "exclusion," "imprisonment," and "exile." Gregor, then, embodies the Abrahamic wandering in the desert. In fact, Gregor embodies the ontological principle of Abraham: "This existence is an exile in the fullest sense: we are not there, we are elsewhere, and we will never stop being there." Gregor's being is exile. Blanchot continues: "Gregor's state is the state of the being who cannot depart from existence; for him, to exist is to be condemned to falling continually back into existence." Gregor is a condemned man. Gradually his condition deteriorates. He is almost forgotten to starve to death in his room, and "he dies: an unbearable death, abandoned and alone—and yet almost a happy death by the feeling of deliverance it represents, by the new hope of an end that is final for now."[43] Death puts an end to the continuous dying that Gregor's existence was.

After the vermin is dead and unceremoniously disposed of, the remaining Samsas go out on an excursion. Here is Kafka's description:

> While they were thus conversing, it struck both Mr. and Mrs. Samsa, almost at the same moment, as they became aware of their daughter's increasing vivacity, that in spite of all the sorrow of recent times, which has made her cheeks pale, she has bloomed into a pretty girl with a good figure. They grew quieter and half unconsciously exchanged glances of complete agreement, having come to the conclusion that it would soon be time to find a good husband for her. And it was like a confirmation of their new dreams and excellent intentions that at the end of their journey their daughter sprang to her feet first and stretched her young body. (139)

Blanchot sees this as a bleak conclusion. The last remaining hope, namely that Gregor's death is a deliverance, "is also stripped away; it is not true, there is no end, life goes on, and the young sister's gesture, her movement of awakening to life, the call to the sensual on which the story ends, is the height of horror; there is nothing more frightening in the entire story." The ideals return as soon as they are proclaimed dead. The dead transcendence is more than a life-long sentence: it is the sentence of existence as such. Hence the inference: "Kafka's narratives are among the darkest in literature, the most rooted in absolute disaster."[44]

Unlike Blanchot, Max Brod discovers a positive ending here: "the whole of the free world is revealed [because it is based on a principle that is] healthy, positive, inclined to everything that desires to live, everything gentle and good, the blooming girlish body that shines over the hero."[45] Presumably the restoration of the nuclear family acts as an affirmation of "The Indestructible." Blanchot's reading is the exact opposite, in the sense that the outside where Gregor languishes is not amenable to the topography of the higher place represented by "The Indestructible" and the Fallen world of everyday life. In this sense, Blanchot is attuned to the insight we found in the Blenkelt story, namely, of the possibility of two readings that affirm the two different topographies. And yet Blanchot, by not asking the question of the relation between the two different topographies—a transformative relation mediated by laughter—fails to fully grasp the transformation that we found in "The Judgment" and that shows that the topography of separation is incorporated in the topography of the outside. Let us see how this works in *The Metamorphosis*.

There are two obvious differences between the transformation in *The Metamorphosis* and the one in "The Judgment." First, the one transformed now is the son—not the father—and the transformation is explicitly corporeal. I contend that these are less important than the similarities. For instance, the maid's averted gaze from the indecent sight of Gregor descending the stairs is reproduced on the cover of the first edition *The Metamorphosis*. The drawing by Ottomar Starke shows the father, in his dressing gown—just like the attire of the father from "The Judgment"—standing in front of Gregor's ajar door and covering his eyes at the sight behind the door. Kafka had a strong input in this cover, since Kurt Wolff, the publisher, initially wanted to depict the transformed Gregor. In a letter dated October 25, 1915, Kafka vehemently protested: "Not that, please not that! . . . The insect itself cannot be depicted. It cannot even be shown from a distance."[46] Even more importantly, this aversion to vision is intimately linked to the sexual element, which, just as in "The Judgment," is introduced from the very beginning and determines the transformative process in *The Metamorphosis* to its end.

The sexual element in *The Metamorphosis* is introduced at the very beginning, through the first thing observed after the description of Gregor's transformation into a vermin. The narrative gaze turns to the bedroom. It is too small for a human being, says Kafka, but is nevertheless peaceful and familiar. And the first thing noted in this room is a picture: "Above the table . . . hung the picture which he had recently cut out from an illustrated magazine and put into a pretty gilt frame. It showed a lady with a fur cap on and fur stole, sitting upright and holding out to the spectator a huge fur muff, into which the whole of her forearm had vanished!" (89). As many commentators note, this is a reference to Leopold von Sacher-Masoch's *Venus in Furs*.[47] This reference would have been unmistakable to Kafka's contemporaries, who would have thereby perceived the sexual connotations. Has Gregor been looking at "dirty" magazines? Or is his sexuality so repressed that he does not even realize that the photographs he looks at are sexually charged? The correct answer to these questions is of little importance. What is more important is that—just as in "The Judgment"—the introduction of sexuality through the lady in furs mobilizes theological and political concerns. *Venus in Furs* starts with an explicit reference to Hegel's dialectic of master and slave from the *Phenomenology*, which establishes the setting for the entire recollection of the love affair. In addition, as Gilles Deleuze shows, *Venus in Furs* is important in how we construe human relations, and thus it can be read as a political text par excellence.[48] The structure then unmistakably parallels "The Judgment." There is an imprisonment, even encagement—in a cell-like house or in a room that is too small for humans. But this encagement is folded into the sexual element.

The folding of the principle of imprisonment within the sexual, just as in "the Judgment," provides Kafka with ample—one could claim, relentless—opportunity for amusement. Let me provide a few indicative examples, confining myself to the picture of the lady in furs. When the chief clerk comes to inquire why Gregor has not turned up for work, the mother is quick to jump to his defense: "The only amusement he gets is doing fret work. For instance, he spent two or three evenings cutting out a little picture frame . . . it is hanging in this room" (96). There is something slightly perverse in this statement—something that mobilizes sexual taboos. How can the mother praise Gregor for doing fret work, something that kids do at school? This infantilization of Gregor is immediately followed by the reference to the sexually charged picture of the lady in furs. One is left to ponder exactly what the relation between the mother and the son is—but, more importantly, this sexual innuendo is produced by the comedic device of destabilizing identities: What is Gregor's real age? What kind of magazines does he read? Who is Gregor Samsa?

The comedy that confuses identity in relation to the lady in furs culminates later in the novella, when the sister and the mother are clearing Gregor's room of its furniture. This creates mixed feelings in Gregor: "Did he really want his warm room, so comfortably fitted with old family furniture, to be turned into a naked den in which he would certainly be able to crawl unhampered in all directions but at the price of shedding simultaneously all recollection of his human background?" (116). The clearing of the room becomes an issue about freedom. Is Gregor going to enjoy being "unhampered" to crawl around the room, like an animal, or will the cleared room entrap him in a nonhuman nature, thereby depriving him of his free will? In other words, what is Gregor, a human or an animal? When the sister and the mother are catching their breath after moving the heavy desk—the furniture used by Georg to write the letter to the friend in Petersburg and by Kafka himself to write "The Judgment" and *The Metamorphosis*—Gregor rushes out from his hiding place under the couch—for the "deal" is that his mother is not to see him, his sight is indecent—

> and four times changes direction, since he really did not know what to rescue first, then on the wall opposite, which was already otherwise cleared, he was struck by the picture of the lady muffled in so much fur and quickly crawled up to it and pressed himself to the glass, which was a good surface to hold on to and comfort his hot belly. This picture at least, which was entirely hidden beneath him, was going to be removed by nobody. He turned his head toward the door of the living room so as to observe the women when he came back (118).

Unlike his near namesake, Gregor cannot plunge into a river to cool his "hot belly." Instead, emulating copulation, he puts it on the lady, and turns his gaze to see the women's reaction. He desires to see their reaction to a broken taboo. But again here, confusion reigns: Is this the taboo of bestiality, whereby an animal is having or simulating sex with a human? Or is it a kind of reversed primal scene whereby the mother is seeing the son—a human—during intercourse? The comedy is here blatant, and it is generated by the confusion of Gregor's identity, caught between being transformed into an animal and remaining the—human—son and brother of the women clearing his room. Further, sexuality is directly related to the issue of freedom. A character finds imprisonment folded into this sexuality through a transformation, which also contains the seeds of liberation through sexual release.

From this perspective, which emphasizes the sexual element of the transformation as a parallel feature of "The Judgment" and *The Metamorphosis*, the conclusion of the novella attains a radically different perspective than simply the bleak, utter disaster Blanchot notices. The excursion of the Samsa family sees the *transformation* of the sister from a girl to a woman. Recalling that transformation is the symptom of sexuality, both in "The Judgment" and in *The Metamorphosis*, the signs are ominous for the sister. The sexual innuendo and double entendre again is the stuff of comedy.[49] The father and the mother exchange knowing glances, and the idea crosses their minds to find a good husband for the sister. It is "a confirmation of their new dreams and excellent intentions that at the end of their journey their daughter sprang to her feet first and stretched her young body" (139). Is such a thought a possibility within a universe in which imprisonment has been incorporated into sexuality?

The answer to the above question cannot be a simple "no," for such a negation would simply reintroduce that which is negated, in the self-referential return of the power of separation, of which both Blanchot and Foucault are acutely aware, as we saw earlier. Instead, the answer should be the burst of laughter at the illusion that the patriarchal structure the Samsa parents assert will be liberating. The liberation resides in the resistance to such structures provided by the laughter generated by the sexual innuendo. Laughter—not outright negation—provides Kafka with the means to free himself from that which is the most invisible, and hence the most pervasive, cage: the free will. If the essential fault of Kafka's characters is their impatience to transfigure their aimless wandering in the outside into a (goalless) goal, then the great asset of their futile endeavors is the laughter they generate. It is this laughter in the midst of the ideals that persistently return—the laughter in the midst of hopelessness—that makes resistance possible as an enactment of a different freedom.

This laughter is possible because of the confusion of identities. Sexuality generates transformation. The sister is transformed—Kafka shows that this transforming is taking place. But he does not show us what she is transformed into. Given the confusions of identity that the transformations within the Abrahamic logic generate, we could safely guess that the sister's transformation will have nothing to do with finding happiness in a secure married life. Instead of such a happy image, we are left to ponder how the transformation of sexuality propagates an escalating paroxysm of misidentifications. And we are thus left with an indefinite comedy of errors resulting from this transformation. Transformation is not a disaster—it is an affirmation of the joyous represented by the most beautiful spring day in the first sentence of "The Judgment" and the conclusion of *The Metamorphosis*.

There is no higher topos posited here. Kafka's projected book *Sons*—had it ever been published—would have been enclosed within these two affirmations of the spring. The characters would have been interned in their sexuality. But this is an interment not in a world of suffering, which presupposes a higher reality of freedom. This is not the political theological interment of the free will. Instead, it is the transformation of the topology of political theology to the topography of the theologico-political. In this new topography, the ideal may return, but only to contribute to a confusion of identity and hence to merriment and laughter. The ideal returns in order to be laughed at. And this also means that the free will is transformed into the freedom *from* the free will.

3

The Return of the Body

The Ethics of Laughter

Ethical Freedom: Levinas's Critique of the Free Will

We saw in the previous chapter that the confrontation between the two exegetical paradigms of Kafka's work is not simply a matter of interpretation. In addition, the determination of theology and politics is at stake depending on whether we read Kafka's writings as asserting a topography relying on a separation between the inside and the outside, or as undercutting such a separation. As we saw, an effect of the former is to secure a subjective autonomy leading to a notion of the free will, whereas an effect of the latter is to destabilize subjective identity, thereby putting into jeopardy the idea of the free will. Further, the separation of the inside and the outside is effectively the reformulation of the separation between an ideal space of peace and absolute freedom—the space Augustine calls "Paradise"—and a Fallen world of suffering and unfreedom. Kafka laughs at this separation. This laughter performs a critique of the theological topography, whereby it also affects the political by suggesting that freedom is only possible by liberating ourselves from political theology—that is, by freeing ourselves from the free will. Thus, the exegetical stakes exceed the limits of a philological interpretation of a modernist Austro-Hungarian author, and have significant philosophical repercussions.

In particular, the most important philosophical inference to be drawn from the juxtaposition of the two opposing interpretative paradigms in the previous chapter pertains to the primacy of laughter and the destabilization of the topography of political theology. This suggests that we can discover in Kafka's texts a sense of freedom that is more primary than the free will. Having arrived at this important notion, it is now necessary to view it from a different perspective so as to broaden the inquiry. We need to move from the register of political theology and to ask about the ethical implications of freedom from the free will. I am not suggesting that the theological and the ethical are two discursive spheres that can be thoroughly segregated—I will be shortly turning to Emmanuel Levinas, who is acutely aware of the impossibility of such a segregation. On the contrary, I am suggesting that the reformulation of the political theology that we encountered in the previous chapter is intimately connected to ethical concerns, even though these concerns articulate a series of different—or differently inflected—questions. In particular, the ethical concerns come to the fore when we ask about the subject's responsibility to others as well as to oneself. How does one exist in relation with others? Further, this raises the issue of whether it is possible to overlay the exegetical conclusion from the previous chapter onto the ethico-political register. This would entail showing that the ethical concerns formulated by the above questions are more primary and are presupposed by Western metaphysics, which reduces freedom to the free will.

In *Totality and Infinity*, Levinas takes up this problematic.[1] *Totality and Infinity* shows that the stakes of the ethical question are not merely—or not at all—to determine the normative dimension of one's actions. Rather, they call for a rethinking of the entire Western metaphysical tradition, that is, the tradition that establishes the free will as a political ideal. As part of this ambitious and broad project, Levinas proffers a radical critique of philosophy from the ancient Greeks to Martin Heidegger. This consists of questioning the assumption that philosophy starts with the question, "*ti esti*" or "what is." The question of existence inevitably leads to totality, that is, to a structure that eliminates difference, because it seeks to subsume alterity to sameness. According to the tradition that asks "what is?," the ideal of human fulfillment is freedom. Conversely, Levinas proposes a sense of ontology that relies on the presence of the other. Differently put, ontology is simultaneously ethical and political—a position that inevitably requires Levinas to reformulate the notion of freedom as free will.[2]

I am not concerned here with the particular articulation of the Other in Levinas. Rather, I am stressing the ineliminable presence of alterity in constituting an ontology and subjectivity. It is in this minimal sense that I want for the moment to indicate what I call elsewhere the imbrication of ontology, the ethical and the political.[3] Or, as I also put it, being is being with. In any case, and returning to Levinas, such an emphasis on alterity leads him to challenge the free will as an expression of the subjectivity of the individual. The question of freedom arises early in *Totality and Infinity*, in the first section titled "The Same and the Other." Freedom is used to provide a critique of the political presuppositions of Western metaphysics. Howard Caygill puts it thus: "By separating justice from its subordination to discourses of the true, of being, and of freedom, Levinas is able to translate his ethical critique of morality into a political theory."[4] Freedom plays this central function in Levinas's argumentation—alongside the more traditional discourses of being and truth—because it allows Levinas to develop a critique of the free will that debunks the idea of subjective autonomy that presupposes a topography of the inside and the outside.[5]

This positioning of freedom in *Totality and Infinity* resonates with Kafka's critique of the traditional conceptualization of freedom as the free will, which is in turn supported by the separation between an ideal freedom and a Fallen world of imprisonment. What Levinas's philosophy can offer the analysis of Kafka's laughter is the argument for the primacy of the ethico-political considerations at the expense of the dominance of being in the Western philosophical tradition.[6] (Thus, Levinas allows us to expand the move we saw in the previous chapter, whereby the theologico-political exegetical schema was shown to be presupposed by the schema that relies on the free will. Levinas shows us that we can apply the same idea from the exegetical to the ethico-ontologico-political apparatus.) Differently put, the free will cannot stand on its own, but rather presupposes something that is more primary as well as incommensurable. Crucially, Levinas arrives at this position by showing that embodiment—that is, one's being—presupposes a freedom as relation to others. Freedom from the free will is ethical freedom. We have a body when we are not alone. Or, loneliness leads to disembodiment. We will see how this idea is operative in Kafka's "A Report to an Academy" and "A Hunger Artist." But first we need to see how Levinas fleshes out this idea in *Totality and Infinity*.

Levinas introduces the idea of the need to overcome the free will with reference to Gyges. According to Plato, who seems in this context to be Levinas's source, Gyges was a shepherd who discovered a ring that made him invisible.[7] He used this power to kill the king, marry the queen, and install himself in the throne.[8] In Levinas's reading, the myth of Gyges is a fable about the free will. The subject acquires a magical accessory that helps him to assert his absolute will and hence to usurp absolute authority. No sooner has Levinas presented this position than he moves to criticize it on the grounds that it leads the subject to a profound ontological isolation: "Gyges' position involve[s] the impunity of being alone" (90). The free will presents the subject as suffering from the sovereign illusion of a subject that it is free from being judged, as if it were limitless, as if it were the personification of justice. Such a freedom is "an-archic," that is, without a law, groundless and unable to lead to discourse—it is silent (90). The description of this profound isolation and silence of the subject performs a critique of a conception of free will that holds a hegemonic position in the Western philosophical tradition. Or, as Caygill puts it: "Levinas proposes a radical separation of the concept of freedom from that of autonomy, a link almost taken for granted in the modern tradition of ethical and political thought and shared by thinkers as diverse as Rousseau, Kant, Hegel, Marx and Nietzsche."[9] The radical isolation of the subject does not lead to its autonomy—to its giving itself its own law—but rather to an an-archy, which is the absence of law but at the expense of relations to others and hence at the expense of the subject's own being in the world. This anarchy implied by the free will is the destruction of one's embodiment.

As soon as he presents the story of Gyges as the epitome of the free will, Levinas advances various reasons why this notion of the free will does not hold up to scrutiny. But this is not a simple opposition, as if there are two notions of freedom, one that asserts the free will and another that rejects it, and as if the latter prevails. No, instead of such a dialectic of mastery, Levinas argues that the free will presupposes alterity and hence undermines its own autonomy: "The silent world is a world that comes to us from the Other" (91). The real absence of freedom is the illusion of the free will. This illusion leads to isolation as a form of imprisonment. Conversely, a freedom *from* the silence and loneliness of the free will is only possible by recognizing that it comes from what Levinas calls "the Other." In other words, alterity is inscribed even in the most radical, in the most decisive moments, when isolation and silence seem to have prevailed. Levinas continues: "This silence is not a simple absence of speech; speech lies in the depths of silence like a laughter perfidiously held back" (91). This laughter in the midst of the most silent and most isolated free will aligns Levinas's and Kafka's projects—even though Levinas mentions this laughter in passing, whereas, as I have been arguing, this laughter is the most important technique in Kafka's attempt to communicate a political message within his writings. But, before turning to this perfidious laughter in Kafka, one more element in Levinas's critique of the free will is needed.

Levinas is not content with a critique of the traditional conception of the free will. He also forges a reconceptualization of freedom in ethico-political terms. According to Levinas, it is alterity that makes it impossible to assert one's freedom. Or, as he puts it in *Totality and Infinity*, "My freedom does not have the last word; I am not alone" (101). It is not the overcoming of loneliness, as a decisive feature of the free will, that leads to freedom, according to Levinas. The subject is never really autonomous. Alterity is more primary than the subject's existence—being is being with. My freedom always includes others, and in this sense the free will is only ever a distortion of this primary ontological relation. Freedom is enacted by resisting this distortion of the free will. Hence, the recognition of an unsurpassable alterity undoes every attempt to achieve a free will. The radical critique of ontology entails the ethico-political conclusion that one is free only in relation to others. This point is made forcefully by referring to alterity as one's "Master": "My freedom is . . . challenged by a Master who can invest it" (101). The other masters the I, producing a sense of ethical freedom that is more primary than the free will. And again: "[The Other] reveals himself in his lordship" (101). This mastership or lordship of the other does *not* entail a loss of one's freedom—since this would be tantamount to asserting that an ideal freedom, a pure autonomy, is possible. The lordship of the other entails that I can only be free when my being is not silent and alone. I can only be free in resisting my disembodiment entailed by the isolation of the free will. Or, in positive terms, I can only be free in the relations that I forge with others, which preserve my being in the world and my embodiment. This move describes the Levinasian freedom whereby the ontological and political aspects of freedom are provided with an ethical support.

Ethical Laughter: The Nature Theater of Oklahoma

It is important to turn at this point to the final chapter of *Amerika*, which presents the Nature Theater of Oklahoma.[10] There are two interrelated reasons for this. First, this chapter can be read as Kafka's assertion of a redemptive vision. I cited the following statement from Walter Benjamin's notes on Kafka in chapter 1: " 'I imitated because I was looking for an exit, and for no other reason,' said the ape in his 'Report to an Academy.' This sentence also holds the key for the place of the actors of the Nature Theatre. 'Right here' they must be congratulated, since they are allowed to play themselves, they are freed from imitation. If there is in Kafka something like a contrast between damnation and salvation, it has to be searched for entirely on the contrast between the world theatre and the Nature Theatre."[11] I have dealt with Benjamin's reading elsewhere, but I need to provide here a reading of Kafka's chapter too.[12] The contrast between "damnation and salvation" can be read as the assertion of a separation of a world of idealized freedom and a Fallen world of suffering and unfreedom. Can we discover in the final chapter of *Amerika* a mechanism that resists such a separation? Second, it is all the more urgent to turn to the final chapter of *Amerika* because of its status in the history of Kafka's reception. This chapter has been presented as Kafka's theological statement par excellence, and hence as thoroughly imbued with the tradition of metaphysics that Levinas attacks in *Totality and Infinity*. Is it possible, then, to discover in "The Nature Theater of Oklahoma" the Levinasian lesson of the indispensable role of the ethical in the construction of ontology and politics? In both cases, it is Kafka's laughter, as I will show, that provides a resolution.

It is commonplace to say that "The Nature Theater of Oklahoma," the last chapter of *Amerika*, is a unique moment in Kafka's work. When Karl Rossmann arrives at the Nature Theater, he seems to achieve absolute freedom—indeed, this is the single scene in Kafka approximating redemption or an admission to heaven. For such an absolute freedom to be represented, Karl Rossmann had to arrive to America like a convict in a penal colony, to quickly be rejected by his uncle, and then to be ensnared in one situation after another.[13] From this gigantic prison that spans the continent, Karl escaped to the Nature Theater where everyone is absolutely free—one is "allowed," as Benjamin puts it, "to play themselves." One can read then—as Brod suggests and as many an interpreter follows suit—the novel as culminating in a point of salvation from the Fallen world of suffering and unfreedom. In other words, the Nature Theater of Oklahoma comes to symbolize redemption as the achievement of a state of absolute freedom.

Howard Caygill complicates this picture in an important article, titled "The Fate of the Pariah: Arendt and Kafka's 'Nature Theatre of Oklahoma.' "[14] He points out that a whole generation of critics were misled by a number of editorial decisions by Brod, which cumulatively led to raising the status of the final chapter of *Amerika* to this special position in Kafka's oeuvre as the point of redemption, and hence as a theological moment.[15] These editorial decisions include the publication of *Amerika* after the publication of *The Trial* and *The Castle*, thereby reversing the order of composition. The first edition of Kafka's works does not make this reversal clear, generating the impression that Kafka's "last word" in a major work is the chapter "The Nature Theater of Oklahoma," that is, a redemptive moment, a "frail moment of hope," and "a hope of future happiness."[16] Caygill demonstrates how this anachronistic order of publication influences Hannah Arendt's interpretation of Kafka. Further, Brod corrected Kafka's spelling from "Oklahama" to "Oklahoma." This correction is unfortunate, because the misspelling reveals, as Caygill convincingly argues, Kafka's source for the Nature Theater. This is Arthur Holitscher's picture book *Amerika Heute und Morgen*, published in 1912. It contains a photo whose caption uses the misspelling "Oklahama" and that depicts two blacks who have been executed for racist reasons hanging from the trees, while white spectators inspect the spectacle.[17] Caygill draws the following inference: "Far from being the utopia believed by Brod [and subsequently influencing the entire initial reception of Kafka] . . . the 'Nature Theatre of Oklahama' begins to appear as a site of execution, one inextricably tied to the history of slavery and racism in the United States."[18] Far from being a redemptive moment, then, "The Nature Theater of Oklahoma" is the culmination of the critique of that land—Amerika—which functioned in Kafka's time as a metonymy for freedom but was in fact, in Kafka's depiction, a land of oppression.[19]

Caygill's important reading throws significant doubts on the status of the final chapter of *Amerika*—and yet it fails to also acknowledge one significant "fact": that this "site of execution," which records a history of racial oppression, is actually depicted as the site of absolute freedom. If the Nature Theater is an ironic allegory of racism and violence, then are not the means of depicting this irony also important—that is, the presentation of an absolutely liberated world? I contend that the means of presentation are just as important. Without paying attention to *how* Kafka adumbrated his critique, the Nature Theater will appear merely as a "j'accuse" whose value is only historical or sociological. After all, if the last chapter does depict an execution, as Caygill argues, the most important aspect for the interpretation of this scene is not the misled history of its reception, but rather the virtuosity with which Kafka depicts such an execution as a joyous festival of absolute liberation. Absolute freedom leads to execution—to disembodiment. This point resonates strongly with Levinas's critique of freedom in *Totality and Infinity* and his own reformulation of freedom in ethical terms—that is, in terms that seek to retain embodiment through the relation between the subject and its others.

To recall Levinas's turn of phrase in describing the presupposition of alterity in the isolation and silence propagated by the free will, laughter about the ethical possibilities of freedom is lurking perfidiously in the description of the Nature Theater of Oklahoma. This laughter culminates in the very last paragraph, which, just as in the case of "The Judgment" and the *Metamorphosis,* can be seen as the apotheosis of laughter, as the punchline of the joke. After the completion of the recruitment for the Nature Theater and a festive meal, the new recruits take the train to Oklahoma completely unencumbered, without even any luggage (296/416). It is as if they have been ridden of anything that binds them to the Fallen world, and they are now totally liberated.[20] On the carriage, Karl is initially excited with his friend Giacomo, riding "carefree [*sorgenlos*]" across America (296/416). Soon, however, their conversation dries up and the interaction with the other passengers, also actors of the Nature Theater, becomes uninteresting. "Everything that went on in the little compartment . . . remained unnoticed in front of what one could see outside [*Alles was sich in dem kleinen . . . Coupee ereignete vergieng vor dem was draußen zu sehen war*]" (297/418). The actors are finally absolutely free. They have departed from the Fallen world and they are liberated. And yet, what sets in is boredom. They have nothing to say to each other, they cannot even look at each other. Those who embody absolute freedom are not worth looking at, and the gaze is diverted to the outside.

But the reverted gaze has another, deeper and more remarkable effect. Suddenly, the landscape outside appears much more captivating than the sight of absolute freedom: "[B]road mountain streams appeared, rolling in great waves down on the foothills and drawing with them a thousand foaming wavelets, plunging underneath the bridges over which the train rushed; and they were so near that the breath of coldness rising from them chilled the skin of one's face [*der Hauch ihrer Kühle das Gesicht erschauern machte*]" (298/419). These are the last words of the chapter on the Nature Theater as well as the conclusion of the novel. Without forewarning, a single sentence announces that the members of the Nature Theater, those who have been liberated and have reached absolute freedom, appear boring, while the landscape outside becomes fascinating. Even more emphatically, the final metaphor of the text referring to the stones' breath suggests that the mountains are animated whereas the actors are petrified, they are frozen in a kind of rigor mortis. Whence the unexpected petrification of the newly freed actors? Kafka is making a similar point to Levinas. Free will and its corollary, the notion of absolute freedom—the freedom enjoyed by Gyges when he found the magic ring—lead the subject to loneliness and silence. From that point of view, absolute freedom and absolute imprisonment cannot sustain their separation. Instead, they transpire to be the obverse sides of the same coin. They both lead to the same result: a loss of embodiment, the eradication of singularity. Gyges's invisibility and the actors' petrification belong to the same ontological trajectory that condemns the individual to lose its embodiment.[21]

As already intimated, Kafka laughs at the complete separation of freedom and imprisonment—in other words, he laughs at the free will. But this also means that the complete separation of freedom and imprisonment is necessary for laughter to figure. Kafka laughs at the illusion of such a separation. The new recruits of the Nature Theater are no more free than stones, inanimate matter for which the question of freedom cannot even arise. Their freedom leads to silence, to invisibility—and Kafka mischievously laughs with them as he turns his gaze to the animated nature outside the train window. This laughter allows for a recuperation of the singularity and embodiment that the Kafka characters lose in their search for absolute freedom.

The destruction of limitless or absolute freedom in Kafka's works does not merely require a demonstration of the philosophical weight of Kafka's prose, as if a political message were separable from the literary work.[22] Rather, it first requires showing the destruction of the free will in Kafka, while noting that this does not eliminate freedom but radically reworks it so that freedom and imprisonment are not governed by a relation of absolute separation. Second, it requires showing how freedom from the free will makes possible a notion of embodiment so that the singularity of the subject is not squandered in the promise of a future redemption or in the illusion that one is already precluded from such freedom. Third, it requires identifying the means of the presentation of the kind of embodiment made possible by this new kind of freedom, which consists of paying close attention to Kafka's laughter—this is the literary quality of his work, and hence can only be discovered through a close reading. All the above three points require, at the same time, that the free will and the metaphysical armature it carries be only an effect of something more primary: the effect of an ethical freedom showing that subjective identity is produced by one's interaction with its others. I will take up the broader importance of this effect in the last section. But we can infer at this point that by asserting such an ethical freedom, Kafka's laughter is also an ethical laughter.

As I argue in my reading of the Nature Theater of Oklahoma, then, the means of presentation are crucial for discovering Kafka's laughter. His technique consists of presenting the separation between absolute freedom and imprisonment, but for laughter to show that there is another, more primary freedom contained within it or presupposed by it. I will turn now to two short stories by Kafka—"A Report to an Academy" and "A Hunger Artist," to demonstrate two ways in which this primacy of ethical freedom is asserted through the technique of laughter. I will show, in other words, how the separation of absolute freedom and imprisonment and the free will are effects of ethical freedom.

The choice of "A Report to an Academy" and "A Hunger Artist" is not arbitrary. They both present the separation of freedom and imprisonment, which is necessary for laughter to figure in such a way as to undo the disembodiment propagated by the free will. The separation of freedom and imprisonment moves in opposite directions in the two short stories. Whereas in "A Report to an Academy" the ape is imprisoned seeking freedom, in "A Hunger Artist" the artiste feels free in his cage while abstaining from nutrition only for this freedom to dissolve in a sense of imprisonment. Nevertheless, despite the different directions of the relation between freedom and imprisonment in the two short stories, it will be instructive to discover that they both lead to disembodiment and the loss of singularity. The laughter in the face of this loss figures as a response to the separation of freedom and imprisonment, thereby asserting the freedom from the free will and the affirmation that singularity cannot be eliminated. This regained embodiment makes Kafka's laughter ethical.

Regaining the Power to Say "One": "A Report to an Academy"

"A Report to an Academy" relates the story of an ape, Rotpeter, who is captured in Africa and transported by boat to Europe. He relinquishes his animal nature to escape the cage where he is held as captive.[23] Starting from a sense of absolute imprisonment, an idealized freedom is posited. Freedom and imprisonment are completely separated. Such a positing of freedom is, however, nothing but a ratiocination, or the operation of reason characteristic of the human. The animal can only achieve an ideal freedom if it already thinks like a human. It can only escape to the human nature if it is already trapped in human nature, imprisoned in a nature other than its own. This creates a double movement throughout "A Report to an Academy." Initially, imprisonment is seen as a deplorable state from which the ape seeks to escape. The ideal toward which the ape strives is freedom. But the second movement reveals that this striving is already a human characteristic, so that in striving for such a freedom the ape is already trapped in a different nature, resulting in the loss of the ape's embodiment.

The title, "Ein Bericht für eine Akademie," registers this double movement. It does so through the ambivalence of whether the "*ein*" and "*eine*" are indefinite articles or numerical adjectives. Is it "*a*" report to "*an*" academy, or "*one*" report to "*one*" academy, or "*one*" report to "*an*" academy, or "*a*" report to "*one*" academy? An animal can only desire something specific, while the human can yearn for abstract ideals such as freedom. Just as a dog could only say "I want this one bone in front of me," the transcendence of animality can be indicated by the ability to say "I want a something"—not necessarily now, but as a general, abstract proposition. So long as Rotpeter speaks in numerical adjectives, he remains tied to the animal desire that is linked to the here and now. His escape from the cage has not been accomplished. The movement of the short story is from the adjectives to the indefinite articles that show the human capacity for abstract thought and ratiocination. Rotpeter's report wants to suggest that he no longer says "one" report to "one" academy, but rather "a" report to "an" academy. And yet, the use of the indefinite article means that Rotpeter is encaged in a nature that is not his own, he is trapped in human nature. There is, on the one hand, the desire to escape from imprisonment in order to find freedom, but, on the other hand, the fulfillment of that desire presupposes the entrapment in a different nature, which is an even more pervasive or sinister form of imprisonment than the cage Rotpeter had found himself in. It is more pervasive or sinister because Rotpeter thereby loses his embodiment, he is trapped in the abstraction of the indefinite, he puts himself in the cage of reason. Kafka traces this movement throughout the short story and ultimately shatters this cage through the figuration of laughter.

The pivotal term around which the whole report is structured is "*Ausweg*," meaning exit or way out. As Rotpeter explains, when he found himself trapped in the cage on the ship's deck, he realized that he needed to copy the manners of his human captors in order to join them outside the cage. Thus the imitation was not an end in itself. "There was no attraction for me [*es verlockte mich nicht*] in imitating human beings; I imitated them because I was looking for an exit [*einen Ausweg suchte*] and for no other reason" (257/311, trans. modified). Rotpeter says that it was not alluring to him—he had no uncontrollable, animal desire—to imitate the humans. His only goal was to find an exit. "No, freedom was not what I wanted [*Nein, Freiheit wollte ich nicht*]. Only an exit: right or left, or in any direction. . . . To get out, to get out! [*Weiterkommen, weiterkommen!*]" (253–54/305, trans. modified). Even though Rotpeter says that "I did not think it out in this human way [*Ich rechnete nicht so menschlich*]" (255/307), still the structure of the sentences that describe his conception of the exit unmistakably indicate that in his cage he was already thinking like a human. It is not only that he is searching for *an* exit, any kind of exit, an exit with an indefinite article, nor is it only that he can conceptualize the play-acting of being human as the means to the goal of achieving such an abstract exit, that suggests he has already been calculating like a rational human.[24] Further, this exit is conceived as a "*weiterkommen,*" that is, as a movement away from the cage but also as a progress, as a bettering of one's state through calculation. Thus, Rotpeter can only assert that he was looking for *an* exit so long as he was already human in some way. There is an absolute separation between the animal and the human that corresponds to the absolute separation between imprisonment and freedom—the ape is locked up in the cage while the humans are free outside. Rotpeter strives to become human to find himself in the space of freedom outside the cage. He thereby renounces his singular being in the world. His being is now an imitation, a calculated hypocrisy.

At the same time, in a remarkable passage, Rotpeter denies that this hypocrisy, which is necessary to appear as—to *be*—human and to escape the cage, leads to anything that resembles human freedom. Although he steps outside the cage to join the humans, his exit and human freedom are categorically different: "I fear that perhaps one does not quite understand [*man nicht genau versteht*] what I mean by 'exit.' I use the expression in its fullest and most popular sense. I deliberately do not use the word 'freedom.' I do not mean the great feeling [*große Gefühl*] of freedom on all sides. As an ape, perhaps, I knew that [*Als Affe kannte ich es vielleicht*], and

I have met men who yearn for it. But for my part I desired such freedom neither then nor now" (253/304). He rejects explicitly the "great feeling" of limitless, unconditioned freedom—"freedom on all sides." That's the freedom desired by mankind but experienced concretely by apedom. Even though Rotpeter can grasp what a human in the abstract ("*man*") can or cannot understand, his rejection of that great feeling differentiates him from the humans. But this is not merely to assert that the sense of freedom is different for humans and apes. It further enacts a *reversal* whereby the exit that the ape is searching for appears more primary than the freedom the humans are yearning for. In other words, the reversal halts the oscillation of the two movements—human or animal, free or captured—that can be found in "A Report to an Academy."

This reversal is configured as laughter. Rotpeter continues immediately after the previous citation:

> In passing: may I say that all too often men are betrayed by the word freedom. And as freedom is counted among the most sublime feelings, so the corresponding disillusionment can be also sublime. In variety theatres I have often watched, before my turn came on, a couple of acrobats performing on trapezes high in the roof. They swung themselves, they rocked to and fro, they sprang into the air, they floated into each other's arms, one hung by the hair from the teeth of the other. "And that too is human freedom," I thought, "self-controlled movement." What a mockery of holy Mother Nature! Were the apes to see such a spectacle, no theatre walls could stand the shock of their laughter. (253/304–05)

The ape's laughter is directed against the humans. Rotpeter says that the humans' idea of freedom—that is, the idea of freedom of those whose manner of thinking he has adopted in order to find his exit—is laughable. This is a laughter that Rotpeter directs against Kafka as well—or maybe Kafka directs that laughter against his fellow humans, given that the scene described by the ape resembles the scene from the short story "Up in the Gallery."[25] Even though Kafka often uses scenes from the circus or variety theaters, still this resemblance is significant given that "Up in the Gallery" was published as the third story in the collection *A Country Doctor* that also contains "A Report to an Academy" as its concluding story. The two-paragraph story presents two different scenes of acrobatics—one of abjection and the other of exaggerated sublimity—that deeply affect a spectator. An ape could never be affected like that because it does not yearn for such lofty or great feelings of freedom on all sides. If there is such a freedom, the animal has already tasted it. Limitless freedom is a concrete reality for the ape. Therefore, it finds the human attempts at grasping such a freedom mere idealizations—they are futile, even ludicrous. So, even though Rotpeter can only look for an exit if he is—and the "is" is ontologically strong here—already a human, his rejection of freedom indicates a position that is more primary than the human, or, more accurately, a position that is more primary than the human understood as completely separate from the animal, and human freedom as completely separate from imprisonment. The ape's exit requires the passage through the human but is, at the same time, the enactment of a reversal figuring as the laughter that destructs the illusion that governs the human ideal of freedom.[26]

Deleuze and Guattari arrive at a similar conclusion about the laughter in Kafka: "Only two principles are necessary to accord with Kafka. He is an author who laughs with a profound joy, a *joie de vivre*, in spite of, or because of, his clownish declarations that he offers like a trap or a circus. And from one end to the other, he is a political author, a prophet of the future world."[27] Kafka's laughter and the political import of his writings are inextricable. Deleuze and Guattari explicitly address this connection in "A Report to an Academy" as a line of flight: "for Kafka, the animal essence is the way out, the line of escape, even if it takes place in place, in a cage. *A line of escape and not freedom*."[28] This line of escape or exit is indeed a freedom irreducible to an idealized notion of freedom that is positioned as solely human as well as completely separated from imprisonment. But the idea of the reversal expressed as Kafka's laughter can be better articulated by slightly reformulating Deleuze and Guattari's assertion about Rotpeter: the animal essence is the way out, the line of escape—not simply "even if" but more emphatically—*only because* it takes place in place, in a cage. In other words, the ape has to be captive in order to search for the exit. The ape has to traverse the separation of freedom and imprisonment as well as the separation of the human and the animal, it has to pronounce the humanizing indefinite articles—"a" report to "an" academy. The ape has to humanize itself and thereby lose its singularity and embodiment, lose its animality.[29] Only by going through this terrain that allows for a conception of an idealized freedom, or what Levinas calls "an-archic" freedom, is it possible to show that there is something more primary, namely, a freedom understood as *Ausweg*. This exit or way out is not absolute, it is not unconditional. In fact, it can only be an exit *from*, a way out *from*—a freedom *from*. Without the cage, such a sense of mediated or conditioned freedom is impossible.

When the reversal is registered in the form of laughter, the ape can reclaim the numerical adjective—"one" report to "one" academy. But regaining the capacity to say "one" no longer refers to a single entity standing on its own. Starting from within the cage, the ape pronounces the indefinite article "a," it passes through the human, it includes the other. So, the ability to revert back to the "one" also asserts that Rotpeter is liberated from the free will, and its corollary, the separation between freedom and imprisonment, that produces loneliness, isolation and disembodiment. Regaining the ability to say "one" is then both an act of freedom more primary than the free will and an ethical act in that it includes the other, the human, in its illusion of absolute freedom.

The Other's Laughter: "A Hunger Artist"

The term *Hungerkünstler* was not unusual in Kafka's days.[30] As Peter Payer has shown, hunger artists performing exhibitions were common in Central Europe.[31] The most famous of these exhibition hunger artists was Giovanni Succi, whose career was the direct inspiration for Kafka's short story.[32] The successor of these exhibition artists is David Blaine, who, in September 2003, enclosed himself in a transparent cage next to the Thames and abstained from food for forty-four days. Alongside the exhibition artists, fasting has a venerable history in religion. The religious significance of severe food deprivation is profound.[33] For instance, the Orthodox Hesychast movement of the fourteenth century used techniques that included fasting to achieve *theosis*, or deification.[34] There are, of course, physiological reasons why fasting leads to visions.[35] Regardless, those who can sustain themselves without nutrition for a long period exercise an unmistakable fascination. Whether they are thought to experience a vision of the divine, or whether their exhibition has a "pulling" power, the hunger or fasting artist is regarded as moving beyond the humanly possible, and consequently as a venerable individual endowed with special powers. Kafka's *Hungerkünstler* treads on the line between the exhibition hunger artist and the fasting saint. What is absent in Kafka's story is the fascinated gaze of others on the *Hungerkünstler*. Instead, it is the artiste himself who exhibits an unwavering self-belief in his practice—in his greatness—all the while remaining oblivious both to whether he is performing a religious or a commercial function, and whether others even notice this ambiguity.[36] He regards himself as most free when he is alone in his cage, unhindered in his abstinence.[37]

Even though the cage with the iron bars is common to both "A Report to an Academy" and "A Hunger Artist," it functions in different ways. In the former, the cage indicates a sense of absolute imprisonment from which the ape seeks to escape. In the latter, the cage is *the* site of absolute freedom for the artiste. The hunger artist is happy in his cage, "paying no attention to anyone or anything" (268/334). And his "happiest moment [*am glücklichsten*]" is when those watching him overnight to make sure that he eats nothing are served "an enormous breakfast" in the morning (269/336). This instills in him a sense of superiority. It is as if he is apart from his fellow men. Alone in his cage he is happy and free. Indeed, he is so separated from the others that, in reality, he is "the sole completely satisfied spectator of his own fast" (270/337). Thus, although "A Report to an Academy" presents the cage as enforcing complete imprisonment, and "A Hunger Artist" as leading to freedom and happiness, still the two share an important common characteristic: both require a clear-cut separation between freedom and imprisonment. As already shown, this separation characterizes the Western philosophical tradition that seeks the fulfillment of human existence in the free will. As Levinas argued, however, the fulfillment of this ideal can only lead to the loneliness and silence of "an-archic" freedom. The hunger artist fulfills this image—his freedom belongs to the same category as the invisibility of Gyges and the petrification of the actors of the Nature Theater.

Through Levinas's description of the presupposition of the Other in "an-archic" freedom, it was possible to argue for an ethical kind of freedom that indicates a liberation from the free will. Absolute freedom can never be actualized because it is impossible to sustain the separation between freedom and imprisonment. The border collapses through the intervention of the others. This effect is registered in this short story through the commercial aspect of fasting: "The longest period of fasting was fixed by the impresario at forty days, beyond that term he was not allowed to go, not even in great cities, and there was good reason for it, too. Experience had proved that for about forty days the interest of the public could be stimulated by a steadily increasing pressure of advertisement, but after that the town began to lose interest" (270/337–38). As an exhibition artiste, his freedom is conditioned by the audience's interest. This exasperates the hunger artist. "He had held out for a long time, an illimitably long time, why stop now, when he was in his best fasting form, or rather, not yet in his best fasting form?" (271/338–39). He wanted his fasting to be "beyond what is possible to conceive [*ins Unbegreifliche*]" since his fasting abilities were limitless (*denn für seine Fähigkeit zu hungern fühlte er keine Grenzen*) (271/339). It is this desire toward the inconceivable and the limitless that, on the one hand, separates him from the other humans, raising him to a higher physico-spiritual level, and, on the other hand, impedes him from fully enjoying his status given the externally imposed commercial restrictions.

The waning of public interest in exhibitions of fasting is, consequently, a relief for the hunger artist. The public represents an other that figures merely as a constraint, a contingent limitation. Seeking a contract with the circus that allows him to fast indefinitely, the artist thinks that he is on his way to greatness. It is immaterial that the circus management does not put him at the center stage of the orchestra, since ultimately his quest is not commercial but spiritual: he wants to fast beyond the limits of reason. The scene of freedom that takes place in the circus recalls "Up in the Gallery" as well as the reference to the acrobats in "A Report to an Academy." In both these cases, the sublime, great feeling of freedom is represented in the orchestra. This, of course, would have provoked the boisterous laughter of the apes. But the hunger artist's mission is no longer to exhibit his achievement for all to see. He is indifferent to the exhibition value of the orchestra. Instead, it is a personal quest, and the audience passing his cage on the way to the menagerie is only an added bonus. The hunger artist is left there to fast alone, without hindrances, without limits. It is this loneliness, and the silence that accompanies it, that characterizes the freedom of the will and leads to disembodiment—as we will discover very soon.

In this story, too, the Kafkaesque laughter can again be heard, and it is once more the effect of the absolute freedom, the effect of the separation between freedom and imprisonment. A long time passes and the hunger artist is forgotten. One day the circus personnel notice the cage. Poking in the straw, they discover the hunger artist's emaciated body and they ask him, surprised, whether he is still fasting. With hardly any strength left, the hunger artist whispers: " 'Forgive me, everybody' " (276/348). This is not a message to the onlookers. It is, rather, a soliloquy. The hunger artist admits to himself that he has failed to achieve a feat that is beyond human reason and that transcends the limits of Fallen human existence. This failure is *not* due to his imminent demise. Rather, it is because " 'I have to fast, I can't help it . . . because I couldn't find the food I liked. If I had found it, believe me, I should have made no fuss and stuffed myself like you or anyone else' " (277/348–49). It is not merely the death following this admission that robs the hunger artist of his embodiment. He had lost his body long before that. The reason is that, instead of a spiritual quest that would have allowed him to transcend the other humans and reach a higher level of happiness and freedom, in fact the hunger artist was determined by a baser instinct—revulsion for food. Even though he presents fasting as a higher human quality, he is in fact trapped in an animalistic desire—a desire that says "I don't want this *one* food, nor this *one*, and so on." His fulfillment of complete freedom was the loss of his human body in the body of the animal, the other that can never be spiritually enlightened and free.[38] The reversal that was discovered in "A Report to an Academy" operates here as well. The hunger artist's greatest moment of liberation is in fact his most profound moment of submission. The hunger artist is neither a performer nor someone who fasts for religious transcendence. Instead, he is someone who has lost this human embodiment in the other, the animal body, a body like the panther's, who occupies the cage after the hunger artist's death.

The laughter in "A Hunger Artist" is different from the laughter in "A Report to an Academy." The ape's laughter arises because it has traversed human freedom, escaped from the cage, and regained its embodiment in being able to say "one" again. The initial position within imprisonment allowed him to achieve a freedom from the free will after it destroyed the human illusion that imprisonment is completely separate from freedom. The hunger artist, on the contrary, starts from a position of freedom. His cage is his paradise, the equivalent of the stage of the Nature Theater of Oklahoma. And, like the actors of the Nature Theater, the hunger artist has no means of escaping. His actions to enhance his freedom in fact push him further into a state of disembodiment, the loss of his singularity in the inconceivable and the limitless. Unlike the ape, the hunger artist does not have a chance, because the prison of absolute freedom is stronger than the prison of an actual cage.

Correspondingly, the laughter in the two stories is different. In "A Report to an Academy," the reversal leads back to imprisonment, albeit changed, an imprisonment that is in fact a liberation from the free will because it reverts to corporeality or materiality. Consequently, the laughter there is mischievous, exuberant, celebratory—this is a *joyous* laughter and it is a *joyous* reversal.[39] In "A Hunger Artist," the reversal does not lead back to the cage and the illusion of spiritual freedom. Instead, it leads to the other, the animal that is excluded as unspiritual, as unworthy of the grand quest that the artiste sets for himself. It is through the other that laughter figures:

> The panther was missing nothing. The food he liked was brought him without hesitation by the attendants; he did not seem to miss his freedom even once [*nicht einmal die Freiheit schien er zu vermissen*]; his noble body, furnished almost to bursting point with all that it needed, seemed to carry freedom around with it too [*dieser edle . . . Körper schien auch die Freiheit mit sich herumzutragen*]; somewhere in his jaws it seemed to lurk; and the joy of life [*die Freude am Leben*] streamed with such ardent passion from his throat that for the onlookers it was not easy to stand the shock of it. (277/349, trans. modified)

The freedom of the panther consists in being content within its own "noble body." The freedom that it holds in its jaw is also a smile at the previous occupant of the cage, whose body was held captive by an illusion of absolute freedom. Just as in the end of *Amerika,* that which by definition lacks freedom, the inanimate matter, the stone, is suddenly animate, and it is as if it grins to the petrified actors of the Nature Theater; similarly, here it is the other—the animal that is content in its own body so long as the body is fed—that grins to the hunger artist. The laughter that results from an initial position of freedom is more delicate, less discernible, because Kafka cannot find here the redeeming quality of reverting back to the cage. This is a *lugubrious* laughter since the reversal does not lead back to singularity.[40] Still, even though the hunger artist fails to gain his singularity, the laughter is still related to it, since it is registered on the face of the panther in a cage, where freedom is neither missed nor absent. This is the laughter of the other that the hunger artist sought to suppress but did not manage to.

"The fall is the proof of our freedom"

The establishment of an ethical freedom that retains the subject's embodiment by putting the subject in relation with others appears in Kafka as an effect. *Discursively*, the effect is the establishment of a sense of freedom from. This entails that Kafka rejects two related positions. The first is that imprisonment can be reduced to the empirical and hence given steadfast limits—for instance, the walls of the cage that the ape is placed in. There is no Fallen world—the particularity in which the human is imprisoned. The second is that freedom can be limitless—for instance, the freedom of restrictions for the actors of the Nature Theater or the unhindered fasting of the hunger artist. To put this the other way, ethical freedom establishes, first, that the borders of imprisonment are porous—the ape is not freed when it steps outside the cage—and second, that freedom is conditioned or mediated, it is always a freedom *from*—for instance, freedom from the entrapment of the ape in human nature or the freedom of the panther from the unrestricted freedom of the hunger artist. Discursively, these two perspectives from which ethical freedom can be understood could be summed up by saying that they designate the freedom *from* the free will. This is a mediated or conditioned freedom—never an absolute freedom separated from an absolute imprisonment.

Textually, the effect is the laughter that arises as a response to the free will and its accompanying separation between freedom and imprisonment. Denying ethical freedom entails that imprisonment and freedom be seen as opposites that are completely separate. However, this separation cannot be sustained because in fact it presupposes that being relies on alterity. The ape is not free when he starts acting out as a human, nor is the hunger artist free when he enacts his instinctual revulsion to food. Kafka's texts sustain for as long as possible the illusion that freedom and imprisonment can be separated. As a result, the laughter in his texts is easily overlooked. But to notice that laughter is to recognize the political significance of his writings. In other words, it is to recognize that the textuality of Kafka's prose is inextricable from the discursive issue of ethical freedom. This means that the laughter registers alterity: the ape laughs at the human's illusion of absolute freedom, the panther laughs at the hunger artist's illusion that a spiritual freedom would liberate him from his animal instincts.

The question then arises: If ethical freedom, both discursively and textually, is enacted as an effect, then what's the cause of that effect? It is here that Kafka provides a Spinozist answer in the dialogues recorded by Janouch: "'Accident is the name one gives to the coincidence of events, of which one does not know the causation. But there is no world without causation. Therefore in the world there are no accidents, but only here . . .'

Kafka touched his forehead with his left hand. 'Accidents only exist in our heads, in our limited perceptions. They are the reflection of the limits of our knowledge. The struggle against chance is always a struggle against ourselves, which we can never entirely win.' "[41] Just like Spinoza, Kafka proposes a certain determinism by saying that there are no accidents. But the main point is, rather, that just as accidents are "in our heads," so is also the chain of causes and effects. Final causality is merely a human fiction. Conversely, to "struggle against chance" means to struggle against the egoism of the self that looks for final causes—causes whose aim is, for instance, to lead to "an-archic" freedom. The cause for Kafka, as for Spinoza, is immanent, that is, it is only present in its effects that consist in the struggle against the self's representations.[42] In other words, ethical freedom is ungrounded. To the extent that it cannot be fully defined, it is not even a concept. Instead, it appears only as the resistance to its opposite—as the destruction of limitless freedom. And yet, this destruction is productive, since it gives rise to freedom *from* the free will as it is enacted in one's relation to others.

The productive aspect of ethical freedom entails that the effect figures as a means. It is the discursive means whereby mediated freedom arises and the literary means that structure the textuality of Kafka's works. At this point, the notion of the reversal attains its full significance. The reversal is crucial for two reasons. First, it allows for—it is the means for—the unfolding of the relations of ethical freedom as an effect. These are formal relations—they concern ways that freedom and imprisonment relate to each other. They are relations between neither existent entities nor concepts. It is the *task of criticism* to unfold these relations, and the relations are potentially singular to every text—or, rather, to every critical reading of the text. Two such types of relations have been discussed, and many more could be discovered through a textual analysis of Kafka's short stories. The first reversal discussed above showed that the ape imprisoned within the cage could find an exit only so long as it was already a human and hence had already joined the men outside his cage. But this humanization of the ape is reversed through the way the ape laughs at the illusion of unlimited freedom. The second reversal started in the same setting—a cage—but from a different position, since the hunger artist is contending to be happy and free in his cage. In fact, however, the hunger artist was trapped in an instinctual revulsion that made a mockery of his spiritual quest for limitless freedom. The laughter here is registered through the panther who replaces the hunger artist in the cage and who is truly happy and content in its own body, it feels free so long as it is well-fed. The first aspect of the reversal, then, allows for an interaction between the discursive and the textual elements of the text so that the text becomes a story—it acquires a meaning.

Second, the reversal allows for—it is a means of—the *possibility of judgment*. Judgment depends on the presupposition of alterity, or recognizing ethical freedom. This depends on whether singularity has been attained. In the case of the ape, for instance, the starting point of imprisonment enabled Rotpeter to traverse the position of the human and its imprisonment in limitless freedom in order to regain the power to say "one." That power consisted in finding again his own singularity. Conversely, the hunger artist was lost in the limitless space of freedom as he envisaged it alone in his cage. He shunned the baser drives, such as the commercial aspect of his exhibitions, in favor of a spiritual quest. At the end, however, it was only the panther who retained its embodiment in the cage and who could grin at the fate of the cage's previous occupant. A final but significant note is required here. The reversal can allow for judgment about whether singularity is retained because the judgment is related to the effect of ethical freedom. As such, singularity or embodiment cannot possibly be understood either as a collapse to the empirical—that's the notion of imprisonment as limited, as a Fallen world—nor as an abstraction—that's the notion of limitless, absolute freedom. Singularity is the way that the empirical and the limitless are held in a productive and yet unresolvable suspension. They are mediated, they condition each other, they are formed *from* the possibility that neither usurps the other. Thus, the possibility of judgment and singularity is tied up with the freedom from the free will.

Kafka was fully aware of the power of the reversal in general and of its importance for the development of a notion of freedom in particular. For instance, in the *Conversations*, Kafka says to Janouch: " 'Men can act otherwise. The Fall is the proof of their freedom.' "[43] Kafka does not believe in salvation—or, more accurately, he deconstructs the idea that there is a limitless freedom where one can be free alone. Nor can freedom take place within the Fallen world, if that world is separated from a world of absolute freedom. Rather, "the Fall is the proof of our freedom" only so long as we are in this world, that is, only so long as we renounce the illusion of an otherworldly, absolute freedom. Only then is it possible to be embodied. And this also entails that we need to act. We can "act otherwise" in coming into relation with others, when we are not alone and isolated in a silent space. So long as we have freedom from the free will, we have embodiment, and this places on us the ethical imperative to relate to others. Thus, Kafka asserts here the ineliminable connection between the freedom from the free will and its ethical implications.

This thought is expressed in yet another succinct way in another conversation that Janouch records: "'Anyone who grasps life completely has no fear of dying. The fear of death is merely the result of an unfulfilled life. It is a symptom of betrayal.'"[44] This recalls Spinoza again, Proposition 67 of Part IV of the *Ethics*: "A free man thinks death least of all things, and his wisdom is a meditation of life, not of death." Freedom is understood in contrast to both the actual fact of empirical death and the fear of a death that would have spurred the establishment of the space without fear, a space of absolute freedom. Freedom is the attainment of singularity so long as freedom is understood as mediated by this dual impossibility—an impossibility that figures in Kafka's cages. The illusion of the separation between absolute freedom and imprisonment is the effect of this impossibility, and as such it is the effect of ethical freedom.

4

The Law of Freedom

Reading *The Trial* through Spinoza

A Cage without Walls: Kafka and Biopolitics

Hannah Arendt's re-evaluation of Kafka persistently defines his works in terms of what they do *not* stand for—Kafka is not amenable to religion or psychoanalysis, he is neither a realist nor a surrealist, and so on. In the midst of this "negative exegetics," the following assertive statement suddenly appears: "Kafka's laughter is an immediate expression of the kind of human freedom and serenity that understands man to be more than just his failures."[1] Arendt is intuiting here the point that I have been making explicit all along in the present book: that the different presentations of encagement and confinement in Kafka's writings are not the indication of a mere failure for his characters. Rather, Kafka sets up these cages to generate laughter. Laughter is a response to the sense of absolute imprisonment that his characters are presented as undergoing. In this way, comic elements become the technical means for presenting a revamped notion of freedom. Instead of an idealized freedom that can never be reached, thereby leading to a sense of human failure, Kafka proposes a sense of ethical or mediated freedom that consists, above all, in freeing oneself from that idealized notion of freedom. Arendt points precisely to the same nexus between laughter and freedom in Kafka's work.

We have thus far seen how Kafka's cages lead to a revamped notion of freedom as the state of being free from the free will. This takes place in a variety of ways, which in turn raise different concerns. Thus, we discovered this idea in his early writings, such as "The Judgment" and *The Metamorphosis*, which were written in the first big burst of creative energy in the latter part of 1912. From the perspective of Kafka's cages, the main feature of these texts is that laughter undermines subjective autonomy and thereby disturbs the boundaries of the topography of the free will, according to which there must be a clear and sharp separation between a space of idealized freedom and a space of confinement. We further saw how the presence of alterity is also instrumental in dismantling the structure upon which the free will relies. Reading "A Report to an Academy" and "A Hunger Artist"—two stories written in the later stages of Kafka's career, after he contracted tuberculosis—we saw how the dismantling of the separation between absolute freedom and imprisonment is crucial in retaining our embodiment, and how a conception of ethical freedom is presupposed by any conception of the free will. In the early writings, the laughter making possible the recognition of a freedom more primary than the free will was presented through the function of sexuality, which disturbed distinct identities. In the later, shorter fiction we discovered the interplay of a movement, either from absolute encagement to freedom as in "A Report to an Academy," or from absolute freedom to encagement as in "A Hunger Artist." Laughter distorted the seeming unidirectionality of this movement, introducing ethical freedom.

There is, however, a special period in Kafka's life that may seem to challenge the picture painted thus far. This period occurs after the first significant burst of writing in 1912 but before the onset of his illness. It starts, roughly, after the broken engagement with Felice Bauer in July 1914 and lasts until January the following year. This is the second period of incessant writing, which is also the reason that Kafka appears more at ease—one may even say happy and content with himself.[2] In this period, several stories are written—including "In the Penal Colony," which we will examine in chapter 5—as well as the last chapter of *Amerika* on the Nature Theater of Oklahoma that we looked at in chapter 3. But the major work of this period is undoubtedly *The Trial*. So how does the work of this period—and *The Trial* in particular—challenge the argument about the manner in which the Kafkaesque laughter can perform a liberation from the free will?

What characterizes the writings of this period is the presentation of such an all-encompassing authority that it appears as if the possibility of an ideal freedom completely evaporates. It no longer appears as if an idealized freedom can exist in the world of *The Trial*—it is now as if there is nothing but imprisonment.[3] The cage is paramount and impermeable—precisely because its walls have evaporated. In *The Trial* Kafka describes a generalized sense of encagement by the law. *The Trial* presents a man, Josef K., ensnared by an all-pervasive law. As the novel famously opens: "Someone must have slandered Josef K., for one morning, without having done anything wrong, he was arrested" (3). This is a similar beginning to the *Metamorphosis*. A man wakes up to find himself completely trapped. Josef K., like Gregor Samsa, is also in his room. There is the image of the narrow street outside the window as well, although here the outside intrudes because the neighbors from across the road spy on Josef K. The main difference from *The Metamorphosis* is telling: whereas Gregor is confined in his room throughout the novella, Josef K.'s entrapment by the law disperses over his entire milieu. Josef K. enjoys freedom of movement, but everywhere he goes everyone seems to have already judged him as guilty for something indistinct, unexpressed, unknown. In other words, Josef K. can exercise his free will, but this takes place within a cage—a cage without walls in which any vestige of ideal freedom is impossible.[4]

This poses a challenge to the idea that laughter is a response to the separation between an ideal freedom and imprisonment. If there is no longer a notion of ideal freedom, then how does laughter figure? And in the context of the present study—which posits the mutual implication between the free will and the separation between an ideal freedom and a world of imprisonment—the above question can also be reformulated thus: If there is no separation between an ideal freedom and imprisonment, is there any vestige of the free will left? The stakes are high, for if there is no longer a trace of free will, then how could the notion of the freedom from the free will figure? Ultimately these questions amount to asking: Is laughter possible in a cage that flouts, by its very constitution of pervasive encagement, the very notion of ideal freedom?

As we know, laughter does figure in *The Trial*. I am quoting here again the famous passage from Brod's biography of Kafka that I cited in the "Preamble": "[We] laughed quite immoderately when he first let us hear the first chapter of *The Trial*. And he himself laughed so much that there were moments he couldn't read any further."[5] My contention about the writings of this period is that Kafka performs an extraordinarily counterintuitive move: He shows that there is no contradiction at all in presenting an operative free will in the midst of the most terrible and pervasive encagement. Even when it is a diffuse and pervasive cage that precludes ideal freedom as the telos that animates and legitimates the freedom of the will, still Kafka manages to find ways in which his characters are presented as exercising their free will. The maneuver whereby he presents the free will without an ideal freedom is to show that the ideal is retained but it is now solely a matter of personal choice—or, one might say: delusion. From the perspective of social and political relations, there is no ideal freedom. Thus, whereas Josef K. stubbornly clings to the hope of shaking off his guilt so as to be free, still his milieu is like a giant cage without walls. Encagement usurps the ideal while also dominating the quotidian—and yet Josef K. still harbors a belief in an ideal that dictates the choices that he makes toward attaining his freedom. There are two spheres in particular where we can discern this move—in relation to the function of the law and to the operation of power in Kafka's writings. I will deal with the law in the present chapter and tackle power in the next one.

The situation described—an impermeable cage within which free will can still thrive—here has a significant resonance within the context of contemporary political philosophy. The move described here is paradigmatic of biopolitics. In general, biopolitics is the folding of the political into the social and the biological. As a variety of thinkers have theorized, this leads to a dispersal of power in every aspect of life. The idea of a diffuse power controlling life is a common denominator for otherwise diverse thinkers such as Foucault, Negri, Agamben, and Esposito. In *Sovereignty and Its Other* I argue that this diffuse power can best be described as the operation of an instrumentalism that *seems to* lack ends. There is supposed to be no end or ideal dictating the various means that power has at its disposal to exercise control. This insight directly links Kafka's writings from this second period of extraordinary creativity—and *The Trial* in particular—with biopolitics.[6] The elimination of ideals includes the elimination of the ideal of freedom. Freedom, as a political ideal, is liquidated as soon as the political folds into the social and the biological.

Significantly, the elimination of freedom as an ideal does not spell the end of the free will. Such a diffuse biopower suffocates any conception of ideal freedom within an interpersonal context, but the free will can be retained on a personal level. As Foucault has shown, for instance, in his lectures in *The Birth of Biopolitics*, the idea of a kind of apolitical freedom, which is at the same time linked to the freedom of the individual in specified spheres of activity such as the economy, is fundamental in the operation of neoliberalism—the regime of power that Foucault directly associates with biopolitics. The crucial distinction that allows for such an operation of the free will, according to Foucault, is the ambiguity between freedom understood as right and freedom from the perspective of government.[7] This distinction may recall Isaiah Berlin's own distinction between negative and positive freedom. But there is one crucial difference, which can be described from two perspectives. As I showed in chapter 1 when discussing Berlin's essay, his distinction relies on a certain moral substratum that allows for judgments about freedom within particular historical circumstances. Such an ideal substratum is absent from Foucault's analysis. There is no ideal regulating the distinction between a freedom understood from the perspective of rights and a freedom understood from the perspective of government. This same differentiation also records a historical typology for Foucault. Freedom according to right belongs to the juridical tradition of constituted power, which Foucault defines as predating biopolitics. The introduction of the idea of freedom as government transforms the older, juridical principle. Freedom now is transfigured into economic freedom, which has essentially subordinated within it the entire juridical system that includes not only the individual right to be free but also the traditional notion of sovereignty.[8]

In this context of governmentality that characterizes biopolitics, freedom becomes an instrument of regulation and control. And this means that biopolitics both needs to renounce any political ideal of freedom and simultaneously to retain the free will: "The new governmental reason needs freedom therefore, the new art of government consumes freedom. It consumes freedom, which means that it must produce it. It must produce it, it must organize it. . . . The formula of liberalism is not 'be free.' Liberalism formulates simply the following: I am going to produce what you need to be free. I am going to see to it that you are free to be free. . . . Liberalism must produce freedom, but this very act entails the establishment of limitations, controls, forms of coercion, and obligations relying on threats, et cetera."[9] The biopolitical formula that Foucault describes is simple enough: Neoliberalism does not tell the individual "be free." The reason is that neoliberalism does not contain within its conception of the social any vestige of ideal freedom. Rather, individuals are given the means—which Foucault identifies with consumption and the "free" market—to exercise their free will, but the expression of this free will is organized, regulated, and normalized by government. Thus, the free will afforded by biopolitics is nothing but one of the means that biopower has at its disposal for dispensing its authority. If the diffuse power of biopolitics operates as a giant social and biological cage without walls within which the individual is incarcerated, still this is only possible because the individual is afforded—nay, demanded and prescribed to exercise—a free will. Biopolitics eliminates ideal freedom from any interpersonal relation and returns it squarely back to the individual—but now this individual free will is so implicated in the function of biopower that it appears as nothing but an illusion.

It would be too easy and hasty to argue that Kafka's *The Trial* presents the construal of freedom that we find in the theories of biopolitics. It may be analogous to the biopolitical freedom in the sense that freedom is no longer an ideal and yet the free will is retained. For instance, it is striking that all the courts described in *The Trial* are set in private places: It appears as if the political and social aspect of the juridical process cedes its place to a law that remains private and at the same guarantees the accused's freedom of movement—the exercise of free will. But there is also one fundamental difference. The control exercised by governmentality, according to Foucault, is incommensurate with the law. Foucault is not simply concerned with describing the operation of biopolitics in the various test cases he includes in his lectures. In addition, and more broadly, Foucault uses the evacuation of the juridical as a—perhaps, *the*—distinguishing feature of biopolitics, as opposed to the juridical power of classical sovereignty. Thus, governmentality for Foucault is essentially antinomian. This feature is further accentuated in subsequent thinkers—virtually producing a *sensus communis* about the separation of the law from the operation of biopower.[10] The consensus is that biopolitical operations unfold in a sphere that is essentially distinct from state power and hence from the law. This is not the case with *The Trial.*

There are various readings of *The Trial* from the perspective of biopolitics, and I will discuss Giorgio Agamben's reading in the last section of the present chapter. The most readily available example to demonstrate that *The Trial* is not amenable to the antinomianism that biopolitical readings, in accordance with the internal logic of biopolitics, ascribe to it, is the often-cited dialogue between Josef K. and the painter, Titorelli. According to Titorelli, who is the "official" painter of the court and as such seems to have access to legal knowledge that a common lawyer does not possess, there are three possible outcomes for the trial: "actual acquittal, apparent acquittal, and protraction" (152). Now, the first option is not available, since no actual acquittal has ever eventuated—the cage is impermeable. The other two options are similar in that they strive for indefinite deferral of the trail. Titorelli describes apparent acquittal thus: "Our judges, then, lack the higher power to free a person from the charge, but they do have the power to release them from it. When you are acquitted in this sense, it means that the charge against you is dropped for the moment but it continues to hover over you, and can be reinstated the moment an order comes from above" (158). And protraction: "protraction is when the trial is constantly kept at the lowest stage" (160). The upshot of all these different options is that Josef K. should relinquish the hope that he will ever free himself from the law that placed him under arrest and that he should enjoy his freedom of movement within the constraints imposed on him by this charge. Differently put, there is no absolute freedom from the law, but Josef K. can still exercise and enjoy his free will. Titorelli's message amounts to saying that it is a delusion to think that there is a space outside the law. The law is everywhere and all powerful, especially when its statutes, its judges, and their judgments are invisible and inaccessible. This is an important difference from the antinomianism of biopolitical theories, which define the impermeable cage without walls of biopower precisely as pointing to the limits and the exteriority of the law. In *The Trial*, there is a cage without walls because the law has no exteriority, whereas in biopolitical theories there is a cage without walls only because the law can be excluded. (We will see later how Agamben interprets the parable "Before the Law" on this principle, by emphasizing the messianic dimension of the shutting of the gate at the end of the story.)

Despite the similarities with the theorizing of biopolitics, therefore, Kafka does not seem to have a taste for antinomianism in *The Trial*. Here, it is not governmental control, but rather the law that produces the prison without walls eliminating any vestige of an ideal freedom. In *The Trial*, the law is omniscient, omnipotent, and omnipresent.[11] This is fundamentally different from the idea that nonjuridical forms of regulation spread throughout and completely overlay the social and biological spheres. As I will argue in the next chapter, the reason for this difference from Foucault—and implicitly from the theorization of biopolitics in general—is Kafka's different conception of power. I will argue that "In the Penal Colony" demonstrates a mutual support between the different functions of sovereign power, which means that these functions cannot be separated into distinct logics—such as Foucault attempts to do by distinguishing, for instance, classical sovereignty, which for him is essentially juridical power, from biopolitics, which is governmental power. I mention this since power and law are intimately connected. Here, however, I will not be focusing on the conception of power presented in Kafka's writings any more than is necessary to highlight his conception of the law, and in particular the anti-antinomianism that characterizes *The Trial* and the writings about the law in that creative period from August 1914 to the beginning of the following year. I want to pay particular attention to the Kafkaesque law that challenges the biopolitical conception of freedom.

The questions that organize my thoughts are the following: How is this—may I call it "philonomianism"?—conducive to a freedom from the free will? And how does laughter figure in this pervasive law? These questions entail a further one: Why is the law omniscient, omnipotent, and omnipresent in *The Trial*?

Spinoza's Ethical Laughter: The Empty Law of the *Tractatus Theologico-Politicus*

The reason for the law's omnipresence, omniscience, and omnipotence in *The Trial* is that the law is empty. As the lawyer Huld explains to Josef K., "the proceedings are not public. . . . As a result, the court records, and above all the writ of indictment, are not available to the accused and his defense lawyers" (113). Josef K. is accused of something, but he is not allowed to know what the accusation is or the law on which the accusation is based. The proceedings of the courts, as well, are never made public: "The final verdicts of the court are not published, and not even the judges have access to them" (154). The impossibility of finding the content of the law takes a humorous twist when Josef K. does manage, after a lot of effort, to get hold of the law books of an abandoned courtroom, but they turn out to be nothing but dirty books: "They were dog-eared books. . . . K. opened the book on top, and an indecent picture was revealed. A man and a woman were sitting naked on a divan" (57). The book of statutes turns out to be a pornographic illustrated novel.[12] If the law is understood as a proscription—"you shall not do this or that"—then the pornographic content of these law books seems conversely to preach promiscuity.[13] So, not only is the sole law book seen by Josef K. devoid of actual laws, its content is incompatible with the law as such. Such a law devoid of content is, as Patrick J. Glen avers, an "empty norm."[14] This emptiness is what makes the law all the more omnipresent, omniscient, and omnipotent. Thus, the key to understanding how free will operates in the law that creates a cage without walls, and how mediated freedom figures, is to examine the notion of the empty law.

Prior to having a close look at the emptiness of the law in *The Trial*, it is necessary to contextualize this figure of the empty law—or, rather, to show how it has been conceptualized within a philosophical context that is not antinomian. I will do so with reference to Spinoza's *Tractatus Theologico-Politicus*, for several reasons.[15] First, in the manner in which Deleuze emphasizes the laughter in both Spinoza and Kafka, we can say that there is an intellectual affinity, even kinship, between the two.[16] This does not consist only in the determination to counter any ideals, to undermine any universals, with a trenchant insistence on materiality. In addition, it articulates with Spinoza's own philonomianism, which is of immense importance in the philosophical tradition.[17] Second, the *Tractatus Theologico-Politicus* is concerned with the problematic of freedom, and the law is presented therein as empty, as pure obedience.[18] Thus, Spinoza's empty law is related to the problem of freedom, just as in *The Trial*. Third, the law's emptiness in Spinoza signifies its liberatory potential.[19] Hence, the detour via Spinoza will provide us with indications of how to identify, in Arendt's words, the "laughter" as the "expression of freedom" in the world of *The Trial* that is dominated by the omnipotent, omniscient, and omnipresent empty law.

The affirmation of the emptiness of the law is best articulated by Spinoza in chapter 14 of the *Tractatus*. This chapter bridges the analysis of the Bible offered in the previous thirteen chapters and the analysis of power and freedom propounded in the rest of the book. This is done with reference to the law. Spinoza writes that "the aim of Scripture is simply to teach obedience. . . . Moses' aim was . . . to bind [his people] by covenant" (515). Spinoza avers that the Mosaic law is purely functional. Its function is solely to instill obedience as a means of securing a "covenant," or the creation of a Jewish state. Articulating Spinoza's conception of the empty law in terms of existence, we can say that law as a means toward pure obedience corresponds to the modality of necessity. The law is necessary for the creation of a state, and that's the only function that the law performs. "Moses, by his divine power and authority, introduced a state religion . . . to make the people do their duty from devotion," writes Spinoza in chapter 5 (439). The discussion of the handing of the Ten Commandments to Moses in chapter 1 of the *Tractatus* may appear curious since it concentrates on the question of whether Moses actually heard the voice of God.[20] But this is thoroughly consistent with Spinoza's aim to describe the law as purely necessary. The content as such of the commandments is irrelevant. All that matters is that the commandments will be binding, and this requires that they be perceived as necessary by the people in need of a legal framework to form a state. In other words, all that matters is the functionality of the law—the fact that the law is a means. Thus, even though the Ten Commandments might have been written on stone, their content is secondary compared to the modality of necessity they enabled to be perceived as God's law—a necessity required in order to allow Moses to introduce a "state religion." The voice of God, as described in chapter 1 of the *Tractatus*, is precisely that modality of necessity that leads to unquestioned obedience.[21]

The modality of necessity that characterizes Spinoza's empty law is accompanied by the modality of contingency. This is related to the fact that the law is conceived by Spinoza as constitutive to the building of sociality. In chapter 14 of the *Tractatus*, shortly after arguing that the sole purpose of the Mosaic Law was obedience, Spinoza writes: "the entire Law consists in this alone, to love one's neighbor. . . . Scripture does not require us to believe anything beyond what is necessary for the fulfilling of the said commandment" (515). We see here again that the law is conceived as empty. The function of the empty law—its necessity—consists solely in the love of one's neighbor, insists Spinoza. This neighborly love becomes the constitutive element of "state religion." In other words, it is indispensable for the creation of a community. Spinoza refers here to Paul's assertion in Romans (13.8–10) that "Thou shalt love thy neighbor as thyself. . . . [L]ove [is] the fulfilling of the law." However, just as in the case of the Mosaic Law and the Ten Commandments, here Spinoza again significantly reinterprets—I am tempted to say, "subverts"—Paul's meaning. In the standard interpretation, the love of one's neighbor is the fulfillment of the law in the sense that it points to a universal sense of justice.[22] Spinoza uses neighborly love to refer to contingency instead. When discussing in chapter 3 the universal importance of the Mosaic Law, Spinoza insists that Moses's law was written to suit the specific—that is, contingent—needs to the law-maker/prophet and the people he was addressing at that particular place and time. Or, if law is understood as means, then the law must be adaptable to the given circumstances in which the law is to function. At that point, Spinoza turns to Paul's Romans. He interprets the epistle as arguing that "to all men without exception was revealed the law under which all men lived" (423). If there is a "universality" to the law, then that "universality" never belongs to one people and is never expressed in one way. Rather, it is a materialist universality, expressed always in contingent terms, related to the living conditions of the people to whom the law applies. Later, when Spinoza addresses explicitly the command to love one's neighbors in chapter 12, he prefaces that by saying that one cannot expect to find "the same markings, the same letters and the same words" in the laws of different people (508). The law of Scripture is empty since its content is changeable and it can only be expressed under the modality of contingency. Thus, all written laws are nothing but "letters that are dead," since statute depends on the contingent circumstances of the community (521). So, whereas Paul presented love as such to identify it with universal or divine justice, Spinoza emphasizes instead a love *for*—a love that requires an object that is only ever transient, aleatory, contingent.

The reconfiguring of both the Mosaic Law and the sense of legality in the New Testament are to be understood together. There is, according to Spinoza, a mutual dependency between necessity—the fact that the law's only purpose is obedience—and contingency—the expression of that obedience according to the given, accidental circumstances. The law is empty because it is both necessary and contingent. Or, as Spinoza puts it, "since obedience to God consists solely in loving one's neighbor . . . it follows that Scripture commands no other kind of knowledge than that which is necessary for all men before they can obey God according to this commandment and without which men are bound to be self-willed, or at least unschooled to obedience" (511). The contingent expression of the love toward one's neighbor is the fulfillment of the necessity of the law that consists in nothing else than the fact that the law is to be obeyed. Defining the law in terms of such contingency and necessity makes the law a means—a pure functional element. This co-presence of necessity and contingency denominates "state religion" and the "theologico-political" in the title of Spinoza's treatise.

Further, the co-presence of the modalities of necessity and contingency indicates that the emptiness of the law presupposes something more primary. Or, more precisely, there is an element that arises out of the emptiness of the law that cannot, however, be contained by it. This element is associated with rebellion: "faith requires . . . dogmas [that] move the heart to obedience; and this is so even if many of those beliefs contain not a shadow of truth, provided that he who adheres to them knows not that they are false. If he knew that they were false, he would necessarily be a rebel" (516–17). The moment that an excess is perceived in obedience, it is no longer possible to rest content with its dictates, especially if they are false. This overcoming of falsity introduces an instability in the obedience that characterizes the coordination of the necessity and the contingency of the empty law. The emptiness of the law—unquestioned obedience, pure authority—is paradoxically premised on the power of rebellion. "No body politic can exist without being subject to the latent threat of civil war ('sedition'). . . . This is the cause of causes," as Étienne Balibar puts it.[23] Rebellion exceeds the political theological nexus of necessity and contingency, but in such a way as to underlie "state religion." Rebellion is more primary than state constitution.[24] But this simply means that the law as means has no end. No matter what specific content the law has, that content is always changeable. There is no telos that defines what a state should look like or what a state should proscribe its citizens.[25]

The rebellious countering of the falsities of obedience is associated by Spinoza with the truth-making function of philosophy: "The domain of reason . . . is truth and wisdom, the domain of theology is piety and obedience" (523). Truth is excessive of the necessity and contingency that characterize the Mosaic and Pauline laws of "state religion." Or, differently put, truth shows that the means lack an end—there is no teleology in nature, as Spinoza makes clear in the preface to Part IV of the *Ethics*. The introduction of truth leads to the third and last modality of existence, namely, possibility. This is expressed in the *Tractatus* as the theory of power or *potentia*, and it is introduced in chapter 16 in terms of a theory of rights.[26] According to Spinoza's conception, rights are the expression of one's possibilities: "each individual thing has the sovereign right to do all that it can do; i.e. the right of the individual is coextensive with its determinate power" (527). The search for truth is not an abstract activity, but rather is embedded in existence. It is linked to the exercise of one's right to realize their power. The notion of right in Spinoza is incompatible with liberal notions of right, according to which rights point to universal human values. Rather, right for Spinoza is precisely the possibility to rebel when truth interrupts the nexus of necessity and contingency, that is, when truth interrupts the emptiness of the law. Or, differently put, right as power is excessive of, and interrupts, "state religion."

At the same time, it is important to note that Spinoza does not lapse into a utopian vision of a world that, having eliminated the empty law, could be absolutely free—a vision that is characteristic of political theology. There is no pure expression of power.[27] Rather, the expression of power requires the presence of the empty law. It is the rebellion against the empty law that allows for the expression of power and hence for freedom.[28] In this sense, freedom for Spinoza is the freedom *from* the empty law.[29] Thus, freedom in Spinoza requires the two modalities of necessity and contingency. Freedom is the breaking of the hold of obedience that they institute—a breaking that is enacted through the introduction of truth. Truth, then, forges the connection with the third modality of existence, possibility, giving rise to Spinoza's theory of power that allows for a conception of freedom not as absolute but rather as mediated—a freedom from the free will.

Spinoza's adumbration of the empty law, then, indicates how the nexus of potentiality and truth points to the possibility of freedom. The emptiness of the law relies on the way that the modalities of necessity and contingency are co-present. Within this context, the excessive elements of rebellion and truth point to the modality of possibility. Thus, the emptiness of the law indicates that a political being can in fact be conceived otherwise. Freedom consists in retaining this "otherwise"—the possibility of resistance and change. Politics is never finalized. There is no universal determination of the right political value that would determine a telos to the state and its laws. Truth is not an abstract thesis or inference valid forever. Rather, it is the enactment of that "otherwise"—the possibility of resisting the current political arrangement. According to Deleuze, this possibility—this power—to arrange human relations "otherwise" constitutes Spinoza's "ethical laughter." Deleuze contrasts that laughter to the irony and mockery that characterize the tyrant, whose purpose or telos is to remain in power. Such mockery is "another way of saying that human nature is miserable," whereas the affirmation of life and materiality makes Spinoza's laughter joyful—a laughter that affirms the possibility of change.[30]

Empty Law without Truth: The Priest's Discourse and Existential Torment

The empty law of *The Trial* can be understood in Spinozan terms. Specifically, it is possible to understand the emptiness of the law as the conjunction of necessity and contingency. The best place to examine the description of the law's emptiness in terms of necessity and contingency is the dialogue between Josef K. and the priest after the latter narrates the parable "Before the Law." The parable and the ensuing dialogue are contained in the chapter "In the Cathedral."[31] An attentive reading shows that the priest accepts the entirety of Spinoza's conception of the empty law, except for the function of truth. This rejection is what makes resistance to the law impossible and hence turns the law into a theological concept. In addition, rejecting the possibility of truth as linked to resistance eliminates any vestige of freedom other than as a free will that fully submits itself to the theologized notion of the law.

Josef K. goes to the cathedral to meet a customer of his bank. The customer does not turn up. Nevertheless, Josef K. meets a priest who narrates the parable. It is the story of a "man from the country" who wants to be admitted to the law. A gatekeeper does not so much prohibit him from crossing a first gate on the way to the law, as warn him that there are more gates guarded by increasingly ferocious gatekeepers, so it may be better for him to wait for admittance. The man from the country waits for many years, but to no avail. His pleas with the gatekeeper fall on deaf ears. He grows old, his strength and eyesight weaken, and as a matter of fact he is about to expire, when a strange thought crosses his mind: How come no one has striven to reach the law all these years, even though everyone wants to have access to it? The gatekeeper responds: " 'No one else could gain admittance here, because this entrance was meant solely for you. I'm going to go and shut it now' " (217). This conclusion to the parable fits perfectly the Spinozan framework of the emptiness of the law. We can identify here the necessity and contingency that characterize empty law. There is no proscription against entering the first gate toward the law—the man from the country is free to do so, but he is warned against it because of the ferocious gatekeepers that he is bound to encounter farther down the road. He does not enter the gate, then, for functional reasons. This functionality determines necessity. Contingency is also present when the gatekeeper asserts that the entrance to the law "was meant solely for you." From this perspective, the law articulates itself through its contingent relation to the subject. The law is not universal but rather suited to the specific circumstances of the man from the country. The combination of necessity and contingency delineates an empty law in the parable that is amenable to the Spinozan conception of empty law.[32]

The affinity with Spinoza is complicated, however, when at the end of the exchange with the priest the question of truth arises. Josef K. avers that it is not possible to understand everything that the gatekeeper is saying as true. The priest objects that the category of truth is inappropriate: " 'you don't have to consider everything [the gatekeeper says] true, you just have to consider everything necessary.' " Josef K. can be read as conceding the point to the priest when he says that, as soon as truth is separated from necessity, "'Lies are made into a universal system'" (223)—although I will return to this assertion in the following section to explore a different interpretation that retains a Spinozan possibility of resistance.[33] The gatekeeper's articulations determine the law as both contingent and necessary—they determine the law as empty. The separation or disengagement of truth from the empty law creates a dualism, which entails that, in Spinoza's terms, the possibility of mediated freedom is eliminated. The man from the country is presented as being absolutely obedient. Without recourse to truth, he has no recourse to any methods of resistance to the contingent and yet necessary pronouncements of the gatekeeper. Separating the emptiness of the law from truth leads to a different understanding of truth than what we discovered in Spinoza. Truth no longer resists teleology. Or, differently put, truth no longer points to the possibility that the political can be configured "otherwise." Therefore, the way that the empty law is construed as disengaged from truth has repercussions for how the third modality, possibility, can be understood. Possibility is inscribed here as the impossibility of searching for the truth, and hence the impossibility of resistance. Spinoza's rebellious stance is excluded from this construal of power. The fact that the law is empty means that the law is inaccessible, and therefore the representative of the law speaks with a necessity that has absolute authority.

The empty law that relies on a necessity without truth can take three guises: a theological, a biopolitical, and a moral one. I discuss these three categories as the three modalities of sovereign power in my book *Sovereignty and its Other*. From this perspective, the priest affirms a sovereignty that is not amenable to the freedom from the free will. I will examine the different articulations of sovereign power here only schematically, and only to the extent that they bear on the relation between freedom and the empty law—but I will return to a more detailed discussion of power in chapter 5. I will examine these three ways in which the law is severed from truth in turn.

The incontestable authority of a law devoid of truth can spawn a theological reading of *The Trial*, because such a law in *The Trial* draws its power from the fact that it is both invisible and thoroughly pervasive. The invisibility and all-encompassing nature of the law in the *Trial* has often been given a theological interpretation.[34] Passages like the following do seem to allow for such a reading: "'[Everyone is] in agreement . . . that the court, once it brings a charge, is convinced of the guilt of the accused, and that it is difficult to sway the court from this conviction.' 'Difficult?' asked the painter [Titorelli], throwing one hand in the air. 'The court can never be swayed from it. If I were to paint all the judges in a row on this canvas and you were to plead your case before them, you would have more success than before the actual court' " (149). The judges can be understood as metonymies of the divine that, as Augustine demonstrates in his *Confessions*, never responds despite the appellant's pleas.[35] Or, one can understand the judges' absence in negative theological terms, as the absence that makes the presence of their universal judgment possible.[36] What such readings have in common is the supposition that there is a universal dimension to the law that is visible in the universal ascription of guilt. We have here a fallen world because of an original sin. The law is legitimated through such a universalized guilt. And yet, we have already seen that the law's emptiness requires the contingent. How can the law be both contingent and universalized?

The answer is simple enough, and it leads from a theological to a biopolitical construal of authority.[37] It is not the content of the law that is regarded as universal. Rather, the emptiness itself of the law is universalized. For instance, no one knows the content of the law that has Josef K. arrested. In the absence of content, everyone in the novel becomes a guardian of the law.[38] Thus, when Titorelli says that the judges are invisible, this is not because the judges are hidden and their judgments assume a universally true content, but because they are everywhere and their judgments are arbitrary. Everyone is a judge, everyone condemns Josef K. from the very first moment of his arrest without charge. In the absence of any justification or legitimacy based on a sense of legality, their judgments are capricious, contingent on their mood. And yet, their judgments are simultaneously all the more uniform and universal—they all pronounce Josef K. guilty. The effect of this universalization of contingency is that the law is dispersed and all-encompassing—it is omnipresent and omnipotent. Here, everyone is a proxy to the law, everyone is a legitimate judge. Such a dispersal of the law is seeking to take control of the everyday characterizes biopolitics, according to the last lecture of Foucault's *Society Must Be Defended*. Foucault expresses this idea in one of his examples: "Ultimately, everyone in the Nazi State had the power of life and death over his or her neighbors, if only because of the practice of informing."[39] The dispersal of an empty law makes judgment legitimate, and yet also completely arbitrary and thus an instrument of the exercise of unlimited authority. Law's emptiness—the absence of a content to the law—can become the ultimate trick that authority plays, namely, dissimulating a denial of content only so that everyone is forced to supply arbitrary content every instant anew, and yet always with the same result—ascription of guilt. The emptiness of the law is universal, but in biopolitics this is understood as the license for everyone to pass an arbitrary judgment—that is, a judgment without concern for truth. In this sense—and leaving aside the caveat about the function of the law in theories of biopolitics and in Kafka, which I highlighted earlier—the prison without walls represented in *The Trial* can be viewed as the perfect depiction of the repressive emptiness of the law. This pure authority of the empty law is only possible because the law is dissociated from truth.

There is a final turn to the mechanism that disengages law from truth, thereby foreclosing the possibility of mediated freedom. This consists in the introduction of morality as the law beyond or above the legal system.[40] As it has already been shown, the universalization of the law's emptiness means that the judgments passed are arbitrary—everyone regards Josef K. as guilty, even though none relies on a definite content of the law. There is no process whereby guilt is tested by evidence—there is no "natural justice"—and hence the very idea of a state law becomes dubious. Maybe, then, we are not dealing here with law as statute but rather with law as an unwritten moral imperative. Immanuel Kant describes such a moral imperative in the *Groundwork of the Metaphysics of Morals*.[41] He defines a categorical imperative that can never be given any steadfast content, but is rather the principle that should determine action "as if" one knew at any time what that content were. It is this "as if" that gives the empty moral law its universal dimension. In *The Ethics of Reading*, J. Hillis Miller examines this empty law by analyzing one of Kant's examples, namely, the proscription against making empty promises—the proscription against lying.[42] Miller shows that Kant cannot determine whether the proscription articulates this empty law through a contractual agreement between humans or through reference to a transcendent law. Both possibilities are necessary, and yet they contradict each other.[43] Or, in the terminology used earlier to describe Spinoza's position, an empty moral law is caught in a double bind that is called to decide between contingency and necessity—and yet, it cannot make that decision without annulling its emptiness. Miller compares this Kantian conundrum to Josef K.'s assertion that "Lies are made into a universal system," and infers that "Whether I intend to lie or do not intend to lie I lie in any case."[44] The separation of truth from the empty law indicates a space of judgment and law beyond the legal system—it signifies morality. Nevertheless, the incapacity of that morality to decide between contingency and necessity articulates itself as a lie, thereby contradicting its own moral proscriptions. In other words, the empty law without truth of morality appears as nothing other than a persistent lying. It would be easy to infer at this point that such lying creates a "world order" that represents a lamentable existential condition.

The theological, the biopolitical, and the moral interpretations of Kafka's law can combine to create the image of an empty law but without truth. The priest's discourse performs precisely this combination. The upshot of this combination is despair and a profound sense of failure. It presents Kafka as the most tortured of tortured authors, the most sublimely tragic figure. Guilt is inescapable, there is no possibility of resistance, and everything turns into a lie. There is nothing more foreign to Kafka's laughter than condemning the human to such a fallen world with a dispersed power of control and a moral law that exists only as a lie. Further, the combination of these three modalities of sovereignty establishes a fallen world without an idealized counterpart that can offer consolation. As soon as we realize that the three modalities combine to create an empty law without truth and hence devoid of the possibility of resistance, the individual is free to act and to exercise free will, but can only ever do so condemned to a generalized confinement. This free will within a context of absolute confinement is the fodder of existential despair. Such an existential despair is a direct result of separating empty law from truth, which produces a dualism that can be articulated in different yet complementary and mutually supportive ways that lead to a pervasive sense of confinement wherein the operation of the free will is an instrument of encagement.[45]

Deleuze and Guattari note that *The Trial* presents "the law as pure and empty form without content."[46] They describe this emptying of content as the law's transcendence that posits "a necessary connection of law and guilt." They continue: "Guilt must in fact be the a priori that corresponds to transcendence. . . . Having no object and being only pure form, the law cannot be a domain of knowledge but is exclusively the domain of an absolute practical necessity." They point to the priest's separation of necessity from truth as the presentation of such a transcendent law.[47] The transcendent law that cannot be known, the law that cannot be related to truth, is absolutely necessary because it ensnares the individual in perpetual guilt. As opposed to this lamentable condition of humanity, Deleuze and Guattari insist on a different possibility. They argue that the discovery of Kafka's laughter leads away from dualism and the ensuing despair—and even leads toward the discovery of a promise of freedom in Kafka's writings.

The Laughter of Truth: Josef K.'s Hesitation

The possibility of such a promise of freedom through laughter can only be discerned by remaining attentive to how truth figures in *The Trial*. We need to return to the separation of the empty law from truth, as it is expressed at the end of the exchange between the priest and Josef K. Citing the passage in its entirety is required so that an alternative interpretation can emerge that no longer leads to despair:

> "The man has only arrived at the Law, the doorkeeper is already there. He has been appointed to his post by the Law, to doubt his dignity is to doubt the Law itself." "I don't agree with that opinion," said K., shaking his head, "for if you accept it, you have to consider everything that the doorkeeper says as true. But you've already proved conclusively that that's not possible." "No," said the priest, "you don't have to consider everything true, you just have to consider everything necessary." "A depressing opinion," said K. "Lies are made into a universal system [*Die Lüge wird zur Weltordnung gemacht*]." K. said that with finality [*abschließend*] but it was not his final judgment [*Endurteil*]. (223/302–03)

As seen in the previous section, truth can be separated from the empty law because truth is understood as something universal, unrelated to the possibility of resistance and of seeing the world "otherwise." A different understanding of truth starts arising by noting that the distinction between "finality" and "final judgment" in Josef K.'s assertion introduces a sense of interruption. Josef K. says that lying is a universal principle in conclusion (*abschließend*), but this is not his final judgment, since that would have implied an endless guilt of the human who, after shedding the yoke of a repressive content to the law, is now even more repressed than ever. This leads inexorably to a lament for human suffering in the state of lying. But by not articulating his final judgment (*Endurteil*), Josef K. interrupts that ceaseless lament, refuses to see humanity as being in a state of perpetual suffering, and hence does not seek consolation from the priest.[48]

This interruption is the first move toward retaining a notion of the truth. In fact, such a notion of truth can be gleaned from what Josef K. says about lying. The crucial move is to resist the interpretation that lying—as it is expressed by Josef K.'s formula that "Lies are made into a universal system"—points to the separation of truth from the empty law. In other words, the notion of lying suggested in Josef K.'s statement should not be seen as an apposition to the priest's assertion that what the gatekeeper says is necessary but has nothing to do with truth. When lying is seen as related to truth, then lying leads back to the possibility of resistance and the mediated freedom that we discovered in Spinoza.

So, how does truth re-inscribe itself through the figure of lying so as to assert the possibility of freedom? The first point to note is that Josef K.'s statement can be taken to denote a process. "*Die Lüge wird zur Weltordnung gemacht*" does not simply mean that lies are becoming a universal principle, but that the process of lying is such a principle. Understanding lying as a process is important because it opposes the presupposition of the priest's previous statement, according to which the gatekeeper's articulations do not pertain to truth but only to necessity. The priest presupposes—and that is what the rejection of the link between necessity and truth amounts to—that truth is universal, or that truth needs to be understood in terms of an assertion of a universally true content. Josef K. responds that lying, as a process, describes how the world is. Understanding lying as a process amounts to rejecting the premise that truth is to be defined in relation to content. Instead, Josef K.'s statement allows for an understanding of truth as that which is allowed—that which is *possible*—in relation to the lying that pervades the world. In other words, lying is understood as the untruths of the contingent expression of empty law—as the falsities against which, as Spinoza insists, rebellion is necessary.

Understanding lying—and hence truth—as a process affects the way the relation between contingency and necessity is understood. When the gatekeeper tells the man from the country that this entrance to the law is only for him and that he will now shut it, the gatekeeper, as already intimated, affirms the contingency of the law as it is applied to the man from the country. But what exactly does the shutting of the entrance mean? From the perspective that seeks to separate the empty law from truth, the entry to the law is barred because the law is empty and it is this emptiness that is universalized. In other words, even though the entrance is solely for the man from the country, still the shutting of that entrance pertains to the guilt that is ascribed to everyone. That is why, also, there is no process here—Josef K. was judged as guilty from the moment of his arrest because everyone is guilty ab initio. Conversely, allowing for a relationship between the lying or untruth of the law's articulation and truth highlights the impossibility of eliminating process. The relation between contingency and necessity is not resolved—or, dissolved—in a universalized state that is separated from truth. Rather, it is a relation that is infinitely negotiable, continuously evolving, and transformable. It is a relation pregnant with possibilities. There is an agonistic stance articulated as the opposition to any form of occlusion. In this construal, the gatekeeper does not guard access to the law as such—if such a thing exists—but rather to the solidification of the law. The gatekeeper suspends access to the law so that the law can remain open and transformable in its contingency. He shuts the entrance to the law so as to avoid any misunderstanding that the empty law can be attributed to a telos. From this perspective, the gatekeeper functions as Spinoza's figure of the philosopher, whose role is to resist blind obedience to the law. It is as if he is telling the man from the country to stop hanging around the gate, submissively waiting for an entrance to the law, urging him instead to rebel. Such a rebellion should be understood in Spinozan terms, namely, as the admonition to stop seeing the empty law as a tool that leads to absolute obedience.

This agonistic stance can be seen as a rebellion against universality. It will be recalled that the universalization of the emptiness of the law is a defining characteristic of the empty law without truth, and it results in arbitrary judgments. According to biopolitics, since the law is empty, then everyone can pass judgments, even though such judgments are completely arbitrary. The shutting of the gate is a different form of judgment. It is a judgment that is no longer arbitrary. Rather, it interrupts the process that makes judgment arbitrary. It does so by severing the link between necessity and universality. Or, it is a judgment that insists that a sense of truth is possible, even only as the process of agonism against untruth, against obedience, and against an empty law whose transcendence creates universal guilt. To express this in yet another way, the judgment here inscribes itself as the interruption of occlusion, and hence as the interruption that allows for process to continue.[49]

The possibility of such a sense of judgment is the form that power takes in its agonistic opposition to empty law without truth. Kafka presents Josef K. as arriving at this sense of power, but also as being unable to recognize it. (I will describe shortly the Kafkaesque laughter arising from Josef K.'s inability to recognize the possibility of such a sense of judgment even though he has already arrived at it.) At the end of the dialogue with the priest, Josef K. asserts that "*Die Lüge wird zur Weltordnung gemacht.*" The way that the world is organized consists in lying, avers Josef K. here. The corollary of this assertion is that truth is not universal, or even more emphatically, that there is no universality as such in the world order. Josef K. says this in conclusion to the conversation (*abschließend*) but not so that he makes it into a final judgment (*Endurteil*). Recall that, according to the interpretation that separates the empty law from truth, this concluding remark does not arrive at a final judgment in the sense of an incessant lament for the ineliminable guilt of a "humanity" faced with a transcendent law.

But this conclusion to the conversation can be read in a completely different way. It can also be taken as the reiteration of the gatekeeper's gesture of shutting the door in the face of the man from the country. The remark that lying is the order of the world is, literally, a shutting up, an *Abschließen.* Josef K. asserts the possibility of an interruption of this process—this dialogue—so that he is not led to the final conclusion that the possibility of judgment (*Urteil*) has ended and is substituted instead by lament. It is a shutting up that allows for the continuation of the process. This process continues because the shutting up affirms an agonistic stance against a final judgment—a judgment about the universalization of contingent necessity that eliminates truth. At the point that Josef K. stops the process that is intended to suspend all process, at the moment that he interrupts the disempowering gesture that separates truth from necessity in order to universalize arbitrary judgment, Josef K. asserts his potential, assumes his power and responsibility. In Spinozan terms, Josef K.'s observation about the pervasiveness of lying is an assertion of his power (*potentia*), an act of resistance against an empty law devoid of truth.

Such an assertion of power is not a sense of freedom as the opposite of the imprisonment in guilt that is the outcome of a transcendent law. Rather, it is a freedom from the free will, it is mediated freedom. It is, as Deleuze and Guattari put it, a "line of escape and not freedom."[50] In other words, it is a sense of freedom that operates in a register that is different from that of a law without truth. In fact, it is a liberation precisely from that false promise of freedom contained in transcendent law. This is not an absolute freedom from imprisonment and guilt, but a freedom that is *mediated* by its agonistic relation to that illusory sense of absolute freedom. Josef K. liberates himself *from* the universalization of empty law. He is free *from* the illusory promise of free will that the empty law without truth offers.

If such a potential has been reached, if Josef K. has discovered the possibility that he has at his disposal in order to adopt an agonistic stance against omniscient, omnipotent, and omnipresent biopolitical power, then how can we explain the fact that Josef K. does not grasp that possibility, does not realize that potential? Why does he not recognize this mediated freedom? I will show that this lack of awareness by Josef K. is in fact conducive to the Kafkaesque laughter that functions as the means to the attainment of this mediated freedom. This is typical of Kafka's technique, which often contains at the end a reversal that upsets the entire narrative. This is also a typical technique of narrating a joke. The punchline is always at the end. We can discern—I will show—the Kafkaesque laughter at the very end of the dialogue in the cathedral, when Josef K. fails to recognize that he has discovered a way to escape the existential torment that the priest's discourse generates.

There are two crucial aspects to answering why Kafka does not present Josef K. as aware of being free from the unknown accusation that ensnares him. The first aspect is Kafka's own circumspection. Kafka is cautious to pre-empt any illusion that a sense of idealized freedom is still possible when the empty law is separated from truth. There is no theological sense of enlightenment that discloses a spiritual freedom, nor is there a sense of universalized freedom that conforms to the biopolitical paradigm, nor, finally, an individual freedom within the confines of a moral law. What all these senses of freedom presuppose is the separation of an empty law from truth. Obedience to the law is always seen as a lack of freedom, as an instance of absolute obedience that curtails the individual. Presenting Josef K. as liberated from the unknown accusation that an omnipotent, omniscient, and omnipresent law leveled against him would have run the danger of appearing as if a sense of absolute freedom from the empty law can be achieved. That would not have been merely a utopian conclusion. Further, by accepting the presuppositions of the separation of empty law and truth, it would have affirmed the primacy of that separation itself—thereby asserting the priest's position, according to which the empty law is separated from truth. Absolute freedom is not the opposite of the absolute imprisonment that characterizes transcendent law. Rather, absolute freedom and absolute imprisonment operate within the same dialectic of transcendence that produces an empty law devoid of truth. Kafka wants to avoid any confusion between such a notion of absolute freedom and the mediated freedom that is the immanent expression of freeing oneself from the guilt induced by transcendence.

Besides wanting to resist any misconception that such an absolute sense of freedom can be achieved, there is a second aspect of why Josef K. is not presented as aware of being liberated. As already indicated, Josef K. has already reached a sense of freedom different from the absolute—and thus unreachable—freedom presupposed by the separation of the empty law and truth. We saw the discovery of that sense of freedom in the conclusion to the conversation with the priest. The finality of his conclusion to the exchange, his *Abschließen*, it will be recalled, is a form of interruption, like the gatekeeper's shutting of the door. What this interrupts precisely is the universalizing impulse that requires an understanding of truth, no less than of freedom, as absolutes. Josef K. concludes without a final judgment, resisting occlusion in such absolutes. Such an interruption posits a sense of freedom *from* the discourse that understands both freedom and truth as absolutes. And yet, Josef K. remains unaware of it. Like the man from the country, he appears on this occasion, when he finds himself before the empty law, a bit naive, a bit unsophisticated, a bit too obedient to recognize that authority can always be challenged—indeed, that the possibility inherent in making judgments that stake a claim to truth is precisely the challenging of the necessity of authority. Josef K.'s ignorance of what he has achieved is an expression of Kafka's humor.

Kafka laughs with Josef K. by presenting him as having arrived at the conclusion but without being able to recognize it. The entire novel then appears as a joke at the expense of Josef K. The joke is that Josef K. constantly strives toward complete liberation—to be granted "complete acquittal," in the vocabulary of *The Trial*—and yet he never realizes it because such an acquittal is unattainable. But the reason is simply that he is looking for the wrong thing—namely, absolute freedom. Everybody is warning him that "complete acquittal" does not exist. Absolute freedom is the chimera that imprisons the subject. Josef K., the bank manager who dresses up like a city dandy—someone who aspires to a high social and economic status—acts like the man from the country, an unkempt buffoon with dark nasal hair.[51] We have, on the one hand, someone who is meant to be "in the know," and on the other, someone who is meant to be ignorant of the ways of the world. They form a comic pair because they are set up as complete opposites, and yet they ultimately appear not dissimilar. They are not only presented with the same task—the attempt to comprehend their relation to the law—they also both fail to see that their relation to the law points to action and truth. They fail to see that there is no inner sanctum of the law that can be reached. There is no absolute freedom. Rather, it is the enacting of their relation to absolute freedom that is a liberation *from* that sense of freedom. Their task is to liberate themselves *from* the emptiness of the law devoid of truth. They both arrive at this conclusion and yet they both fail to see it—until it is too late. The sentence of Josef K. to die "like a dog" recapitulates the erasure of the distance that separates him from his comic pair—the dandy banker lapses into animality and to country ignorance, he descends from his lofty position and thereby meets the animal or a representative of the lowest stratum.[52]

Arendt's assertion discussed at the beginning of the chapter makes perfect sense from this perspective. Arendt noted that Kafka's laughter points to a sense of freedom that "understands man to be more than just his failures." Josef K. has indeed failed to recognize his liberation from transcendent law. But this failure is articulated as laughter. Kafka's humor is *immanent* in Josef K.'s failure. This takes two guises. First, it is immanent in the sense that it points to a sense of being that is not reliant on transcendence. One cannot laugh when one is confronted by transcendent ideals—a heroic endeavor toward something lofty and ideal is never funny. Indeed, laughter is a physical symptom, a bodily expression, that does not point to anything high, anything transcendent. No wonder that it has always being associated with "low" literature.[53] Kafka embraces that low literature—or what Deleuze and Guattari call "minor literature"—that is meant to provoke laughter in the reader.

The second aspect arises when it is recognized that, even if a heroic deed that aspires toward transcendent ideals is not meant to be funny, it can still appear laughable. In other words, the failure to live up to transcendence can be the subject of laughter.[54] In fact, as we have already seen, Deleuze calls Spinoza's laughter "ethical" precisely because it is an opposition to forms of transcendence that constitute attempts at imprisonment. Deleuze and Guattari raise an equivalent point when they discuss Kafka. They argue that even though Kafka presents an empty, transcendent law that is absolutely necessary in *The Trial*, still "the humor that he puts into it shows an entirely different intention."[55] In fact, Deleuze and Guattari argue that the empty law without truth is "a superficial movement" in Kafka's work that is needed because it "indicates points of undoing, of dismantling."[56] What is being dismantled is the structure of transcendence that separates necessity from truth, thereby leading to absolute authority. Laughter performs such a dismantling, or "even . . . a demolition," as Deleuze and Guattari emphatically put it.[57] In other words, laughter leads to an empty law that is conceived in terms of its immanent relation to whoever is before it. Thus laughter functions as the *means* for the expression of a freedom from the empty law without truth. In Kafka's world, laughter is the conduit to mediated freedom. The one who laughs at Josef K.'s perennial guilt is Spinoza's necessary rebel who interrupts the nexus of contingent necessity by recognizing its falsity.

Agamben's Antinomianism: The Biopolitical Return of Theology

We have now reached a point where it is necessary to return to the biopolitical discourses that claim Kafka as a biopolitical author. As I argued in the first section, biopolitics and *The Trial* share a number of crucial characteristics. The most notable are: the expansion of power to create a cage without walls, the—seeming—elimination of the ideal, and the retention of the free will of the individual now at the services of the machine of confinement. I argued, in addition, that there is a crucial difference. Whereas biopolitical theories tend to posit a space outside the law—I called this the "antinomianism of biopolitics"—Kafka creates a world in *The Trial* where the law is omnipotent, omniscient, and omnipresent—I called this "philonomianism." Further, this expansive and diffuse law is empty, and yet it presupposes something more primary, a sense of rebellion that unsettles its authority, as we saw in Spinoza.

We need to return to this distinction between biopolitical theories and Kafka because it is commonplace to designate their antinomianism as the emptiness of the law.[58] This gives rise to the following problematic: How does Kafka's empty law in *The Trial* differ from biopolitical theories? Has their difference been overplayed? I do not think so. And to demonstrate that, I will now turn to Giorgio Agamben. As Carlo Salzani persuasively argues and documents, Agamben does not simply make extensive use of Kafka in a variety of texts. In addition, and more importantly, "Kafka's diagnosis becomes one of the cornerstones of Agamben's analysis of modernity. Kafka's legal world unveils in fact, for Agamben, the true nature of the law."[59] Given that modernity for Agamben is precisely biopolitical, given that Agamben's description of the law is exactly as an empty norm, it is apt to look at Agamben to draw the distinction between the function of the empty law in his theory of biopolitics and Kafka's *The Trial*. I will concentrate on his discussion of *The Trial* in *Homo Sacer* because it summarizes all the crucial moves Agamben makes in his reading of Kafka.[60]

The discussion of Kafka occurs at a strategic junction in *Homo Sacer*. Agamben's interpretation of *The Trial* occurs in the chapter titled "Form of Law," which is the last chapter of Part 1, titled "The Logic of Sovereignty." Agamben summarizes and concludes the entire logic of sovereignty—or the "biopolitical ban," as he names it—that he has developed thus far. In addition, and more importantly, he closes the chapter with the description of a Messianism that transcends the biopolitical logic of sovereignty. Further, the premise of this redemptive potential is the thesis that Kafka's work has a privileged access to the logic of sovereignty. The chapter opens with the following statement: "In the legend 'Before the Law,' Kafka represented the structure of the sovereign ban in an exemplary abbreviation" (49). Given that "[e]verywhere on earth men live today in the ban of a law" (51), the stakes for the interpretation of Kafka are high. The conception of the law in *The Trial* is positioned as a—even *the*—cipher for the condition of humanity in the era of biopolitics.

What exactly does this logic of sovereignty, this ban, consist of? Agamben describes this as the state of exception, which is constitutive of the operation of biopower and which leads to an empty law. The state of exception is the separation of the human into two parts, one of which is included within the law and the other of which is excluded from the law. This excluded remainder of the human is given a variety of different names by Agamben, depending on the historical and conceptual context. The most famous are perhaps zoe (with reference to Aristotle), homo sacer (as a figure of Roman law) and the Muselmann (from the Nazi concentration camps). The man from the country in Kafka's parable "Before the Law" is also such a figure to whom the ban applies: "According to the schema of the sovereign exception, law applies to him in no longer applying, and holds him in its ban in abandoning him outside itself. The open door destined only for him includes him in excluding him and excludes him in including him. And this is precisely the summit and the root of every law" (50). This continuous operation of exclusion and inclusion is the "root of every law," or, as the title of the chapter puts it, the form of the law. I would like to point out here the first element of the biopolitical antinomianism I have been referring to. Note how the ban operates by reserving an extra-legal region. This is precisely the place where the man from the country stands: before the law and yet also outside the law.

The empty law in Agamben is a product of the ban and hence of the antinomian conception of an extra-legal region. "Seen from this perspective [i.e., from the perspective of the ban], Kafka's legend presents the pure form in which law affirms itself with the greatest force precisely at the point in which it no longer prescribes anything—which is to say, as pure ban" (49–50). The form of law is the positing both inside and outside the law. The ban is not a proscription, but rather this position, both inside and outside. The operation of the law does not rely on its content because the law is "pure ban," that is, the law is empty. The chapter "Form of Law" describes how the emptiness of the law can assume two guises. Following, first, Scholem's interpretation of the law in Kafka, Agamben describes the emptiness of the law in linguistic terms as "a force without significance" (53). And recording, second, Benjamin's riposte in a letter, the empty law is presented as "indistinguishable from life" (53). Further, the emptiness of the law does not diminish its force. On the contrary, "law is all the more pervasive for its total lack of content" (52). The emptiness of the law intensifies its power over life.

The ultimate point of the biopolitical crisis consists of the intensification of the ban: "Law that becomes indistinguishable from life in a real state of exception is confronted by life that, in a symmetrical but inverse gesture, is entirely transformed into law" (55). To translate Agamben's point in the terms used in the present study, the emptiness of the law is responsible for a sense of pervasive imprisonment—an imprisonment that Agamben describes as the incessant exclusion and inclusion from the law. But as the ban intensifies, the two senses of the human—the one included in the law and the other excluded—become indistinguishable, and at this point law and life themselves mutually transform or morph into each other. With this mutual transformation of law and life, Agamben may appear to rescind his antinomianism. This is not in fact the case. Agamben continues: "Only at this point do the two terms distinguished and kept united by the relation of ban (bare life and the form of law) abolish each other and enter into a new dimension" (55). Jessica Whyte describes the move performed here with great clarity. Whyte shows that in Agamben "catastrophe . . . precede[s] redemption" and that "disaster presages redemption." And she clarifies a few pages later: "The possibility of redemption . . . is premised on our ability to 'render inoperative' . . . the empty forms of past social and political orders, in order to make possible a life that is freed from both sovereignty and the apparatuses of government."[61] The redemptive potential is, as Whyte correctly observes, freed from the sovereign ban, that is, freed from the operation of the law. The biopolitical crisis presses for a resolution that is only forthcoming, in Agamben's schema, by intensifying antinomianism. Agamben demonstrates this with his interpretation of "Before the Law."

Agamben presents the man from the country not as a buffoon but as a cunning strategist and a messianic figure.[62] His brilliant action, in Agamben's reading, consists of "a complicated and patient strategy to have the door closed in order to interrupt the Law's being in force" (55). And he succeeds because at the end "the door of the Law [is] closed for ever" (55). In other words, the man from the country succeeds because he has placed himself in anomie—access to the law is forever barred. Agamben describes the messianic task in the following terms: "The messianic task of the man from the country . . . might then be precisely that of making the virtual state of exception real, of compelling the doorkeeper to close the door of the Law. . . . For the Messiah will be able to enter only after the door is closed, which is to say, after the Law's being in force without significance is at an end" (56–57). There is a beyond or an overcoming of the empty law. Antinomianism here returns in full force. It is the cipher of political action in the present as well as of the vision of a community without biopolitics in the future. Thus, the man from the country is presented—paradoxically—as the supreme strategist in the liberation from the biopolitical chains clapped on humanity by the sovereign ban.

This vision presents an ambiguity that stems from its antinomianism: How are we to understand this move beyond the empty law? Whence does this overcoming originate? What causes it? Agamben does not tackle this problematic explicitly, but it is nascent in the structure of his thought as well as in his vocabulary: Agamben is envisaging an "after" of the ban and sovereignty that arrives only after the operation of the empty law is "at an end." Thus there is clearly a connection between the before and the after. Two answers are possible. The connection between the before (the empty law) and the after (the beyond biopolitics in a new, revamped antinomianism) is either a causal or a noncausal connection. Its cause can either be the crisis of the biopolitical ban that precedes it, or there is no causality at all as this anomie is entirely sui generis. Differently formulated, either the empty law is the source of the messianic end to itself, or the messianic end to the law is totally discontinuous with and separate from the ban. Both of these two options are riddled with difficulties.

If we entertain the first alternative, then we are perilously close to the discourse of the priest in the cathedral. As long as the empty law is the cause of its own overcoming, then the empty law is also the precondition of any politics beyond biopolitics. But, then, how different would such a politics be in the end? If it is a reaction to the interplay of inclusion and exclusion from the law, then would it not forever remain dependent on this ban for its existence? From this perspective, the priest's judgment appears prescient: what the gatekeeper says is purely necessary. In fact, from this perspective the man from the country is thoroughly dependent on the gatekeeper as the representative of the law to somehow close the gate to the law and exclude the law from the new politics outside the ban. Moreover, even if we manage to think of a way to return the responsibility for the strategy and the achievement to close the door of the law back to the man from the country, it is notable that this "feat" is achieved only at the moment of his death. Does not the death of the man from the country reproduce the desubjectification characteristic of the ban—after all, as Agamben's reminds us earlier in the book, the homo sacer is the body that can be killed with impunity. The first option, according to which the ban is the cause of its overcoming, does not accord with Agamben's line of argument, so I propose to reject this reanimation of the priest's discourse. The empty law cannot be the cause of the messianic antinomianism because then no real break with the empty law is possible.

And yet, the second option is even more fraught with difficulty. There are two significant difficulties in embracing a complete rupture with the biopolitical empty law as a noncausal relation. The first consists of the seemingly miraculous overcoming of the biopolitical ban. Agamben's interpretation of the man from the country is symptomatic of this. The expression "a man from the country" denotes a person who is not streetwise and does not exhibit any particular brilliance. Agamben's reading presents him completely transformed. He is now a master strategist who manipulates the gatekeeper and the law to achieve the final liberation from the biopolitical ban. But this still does not explain how the biopolitics is overcome. There is no explanation other than the abrupt rupture effected by the man from the country. His achievement then appears as a creation out of nothing. The man from the country appears as if he has created the condition for the readjustment of the entire biopolitical world, which, as Agamben constantly reminds us, is mired in the state of exception. This is more akin to a rekindling of the theological conception of the second coming than a political interpretation. And if Agamben were to reject such an eschatology, the Christian logic still persists. For instance, Agamben might have countered that this "after" that puts "an end" to the law arises from the contrast between the most low and the most high exemplified in the man from the country—both naïve and a Messiah. But then we have nothing but a return to Christology. The man from the country now exemplifies in an even more radically Christian gesture the body of Christ, which can be sacrificed on the cross, but which cannot be killed as it is the divine itself and as it resurrects itself in a promise to transform the world. Just like Christ, the man from the country is the efficient cause of the transformation of the world. From this point of view, the antinomianism that takes us beyond biopolitics is a contemporary variation of a Christian logic and there is no real discursive support for this position, other than a belief in a man from the country who can effect a radical rupture of cosmic proportions.

But let us assume—*concesso non dato*—that Agamben finds a way to disentangle the poor man from the country from all this Christology. Maybe Agamben has a way to show that the radical eschatology that he is proposing here is not, somehow, Christian. Maybe, after all, the man from the country is not an efficient cause for overcoming biopolitics. Then a further intractable problem remains, which is a direct result of the mirroring of antinomianism in the biopolitical ban and beyond it. The logic of the ban, the logic of the inclusion of the body to the law through its exclusion, requires a double region, a topography of the inside and the outside. Granted, this is not the same as the topography described in chapter 2, since the crisis of the empty law is, as we saw Agamben argue, the coincidence of law and life and the erasure of the topography of the inside and the outside. But is not the subsequent, the messianic antinomianism, a mirror image, a replica, of exactly the same logic? We first have the separation of the biopolitical from that which—whatever that may be—comes after it, at the end of the law. The antinomianism of this move also creates a topology of that which is subject to the empty law, and that which is beyond it. At the same time, the line of questioning that we are pursuing here about the source and the origin of this move beyond the biopolitical makes the distinction between biopolitics and its beyond precarious, even indistinct. Thus, both the biopolitical ban and its transcendence are determined by a zone of indistinction of what is inside and what is outside the law. At best, the biopolitical and the eschatological antinomianisms are mirror images.[63] At worst, they are exactly the same logic and it is only an illusion that they are distinct.

If Kafka had been a reader of Agamben, he may have opted for the latter possibility. The reason is that it presents Agamben as one of Kafka's own characters who is unaware of the illusion that he is suffering. Kafka would have laughed with a man from the country that saw himself as the Messiah, who, through a sheer act of his will, can have the door of the law shut once and for all. And he would have laughed—as we have seen him laugh time and again in this study—with the antinomian idea that there is a region beyond the law that provides humanity a space of idealized freedom.

Let us at the same time recall Kafka's own position, delineated with recourse to Spinoza's philonomianism. According to this position, there is nothing beyond the empty law. Neither Kafka nor Spinoza is a prophet of what comes after the end of a cage without walls. Their point is quite different. As the reading of the necessary rebel in the *Tractatus Theologico-Politicus* and of Josef K.'s assertion that lying is the universal system of the world demonstrated, for them there is an excess to the empty law that is more primary. The rebel is the condition of the possibility of obedience, according to Spinoza, and the condition of the inscription of truth and potentiality is contained within the law's necessity and contingency, which are nothing but a lie.

We saw this move in chapter 2 as resolving the conundrum between the two competing interpretative strategies in Kafka. It appeared then that the strategy highlighting the laughter at the free will is presupposed by the alternative readings. And we saw the same strategy in chapter 3, when the ethical—the presence of alterity—appeared as the presupposition of any attempt to conceive of absolute freedom. We encounter this move here again: the empty law presupposes something more primary, a potentiality that disrupts the smooth operation of necessity and contingency. This move, in all three cases, is registered as the eruption of laughter in Kafka's writings.

The move that I have described Spinoza and Kafka as making is much less exuberant than the eschatological "after the end of the law" that Agamben envisages. Despite its modest character, Spinoza and Kafka's move affords them the possibility of laughing in the process of conceiving a sense of freedom from the free will. Their mediated freedom is not compatible with any attempt to separate a beyond to this world, even though it affords the possibility of conceiving of this world otherwise. I regard this philonomianism as providing much more robust possibilities for a radical politics than the antinomianism that characterizes much of biopolitical theory. The reason is that their philonomianism challenges the view that the cage without walls can only be overcome in a beyond, which is instituted through the sheer will of a genius master strategist. The laughter in the face of this genius is much more radical than any eschatological horizon, given the transformation that such a laughter can effect on a whole series of ontological, ethical, and political terms.

5

Executing Violence

The Drama of Power in "In the Penal Colony"

Two Executions: The Spectacle of Power

Elias Canetti's book *Kafka's Other Trial* is characterized by a measured tone. Canetti is attempting to demonstrate the influence of the broken engagement with Felice Brauer on Kafka's second productive period, from August 1914 to the beginning of the following year. In this measured text, one statement stands out: "Of all writers, Kafka is the greatest expert on power. He experienced it in all its respects, and he gave shape to this experience."[1] This is high praise indeed from someone who was steeped in questions of power.[2] But whereas Canetti makes this assertion by reading the diaries and Kafka's letters to Felice, I will demonstrate here Kafka's extraordinary sensitivity to questions of power with reference to a short story from the same period, "In the Penal Colony."

The reasons for turning to this short story, written in the same period of the second half of 1914, are threefold. First, after discussing the law in *The Trial*, it is important now to turn to the concept of power. The two concepts are interconnected, and turning to power will enhance the previous description. In particular, I left unresolved in chapter 4 the issue of the relation between different types of power. I will take this up here explicitly. Second, "In the Penal Colony" is concerned with how power makes itself visible. The presentation of power will allow us not only to discover the critique of power in Kafka's text, but also to note those dramatic—in the sense of theatrical—elements that make this a genuinely comical story. Third, with the eruption of laughter, we are back in the territory of freedom. An analysis of the Kafkaesque laughter of "In the Penal Colony" will allow us to return one final time to a point I have been stressing throughout the present study, namely, the *relation* between the notion of mediated freedom and the free will presented through Kafka's laughter. As I have been arguing throughout the book, mediated freedom is not simply the overcoming the free will. We do not have, in the manner in which I showed Agamben attempting, a redemptive move whereby the human triumphs over the free will. Instead, I have been arguing all along that the freedom from the free will is more primary than the free will itself. I have demonstrated this idea on the exegetical level (chapter 2), in terms of ethics (chapter 3), and in the legal sphere (chapter 4). This analysis also requires addressing the issue of power.

For the question of power in "In the Penal Colony" to come to the fore, we need to pay particular attention to the way that power is presented in the short story. How does it appear? Essentially, I am proposing to read "In the Penal Colony" as setting up a theater play of and about power. The play of power is revealed in the way that the execution is carried out in Kafka's short story. To understand what kind of play we are dealing with, and what kind of presentation of sovereign power we have, we can start by juxtaposing the description of two executions—one cited by Michel Foucault to establish a break between different regimes of power, and the other in Kafka's "In the Penal Colony." I will cite here the two long descriptions of the executions, since the entire chapter consists, in a sense, in teasing out the differences between these two passages.

The first passage is Bouton's account of the execution of Robert-François Damiens in March 1757, which is cited at the beginning of Michel Foucault's *Discipline and Punish*. Damiens was condemned as a regicide because of his—failed—assassination attempt against Louis XV. His sentence was to be quartered by horses:

> The horses tugged hard, each pulling straight on a limb, each horse held by an executioner. After a quarter of an hour, the same ceremony was repeated and finally, after several attempts, the direction of the horses had to be changed. . . . Finally, the executioner, Samson, said to Monsieur Le Breton that there was no way or hope of succeeding, and told him to ask their Lordships if they wished him to have the prisoner cut into pieces. . . . After two or three attempts, the executioner Samson

> and he who had used the pincers each drew out a knife from his pocket and cut the body at the thighs instead of severing the legs at the joints; the four horses gave a tug and carried off the two thighs after them, namely, that of the right side first, the other following; then the same was done to the arms, the shoulders, the arm-pits and the four limbs; the flesh had to be cut almost to the bone, the horses pulling hard carried off the right arm first and the other afterwards. When the four limbs had been pulled away, the confessors came to speak to him; but his executioner told them that he was dead, though the truth was that I saw the man move, his lower jaw moving from side to side as if he were talking. One of the executioners even said shortly afterwards that when they had lifted the trunk to throw it on the stake, he was still alive.[3]

The second passage comes from Kafka's "In the Penal Colony." We are presented here again with the practice of a death penalty, this time conducted by an elaborated execution machine. Just like Damiens's execution, this one also does not quite go according to plan, since the execution machine breaks down:

> Because it was working so silently the machine simply escaped one's attention. The explorer observed the soldier and the condemned man. The latter was the more animated of the two, everything in the machine interested him, now he was bending down and was stretching up on tiptoe, his forefinger was extended all the time pointing out details to the soldier. This annoyed the explorer. He was resolved to stay till the end, but he could not bear the sight of these two. "Go back home," he said. The soldier would have been willing enough, but the condemned man took the order as a punishment. With clasped hands he implored to be allowed to stay, and when the explorer shook his head and would not relent, he even went down on his knees. The explorer saw that it was no use merely giving orders, he was on the point of going over and driving them away. At that point he heard a noise above him in the Designer. He looked up. Was that cogwheel going to make trouble after all? But it was something quite different. Slowly the lid of the Designer rose up and then clicked wide open.

> The teeth of a cogwheel showed themselves and rose higher, soon the whole wheel was visible, it was as if some enormous force were squeezing the Designer so that there was no longer room for the wheel, the wheel moved up till it came to the very edge of the Designer, fell down, rolled along the sand a little on its rim, and then lay flat. . . . This phenomenon made the condemned man completely forget the explorer's command, the cogwheels fascinated him, he was always trying to catch one and at the same time urging the soldier to help, but always drew back his hand in alarm, for another wheel always came hopping along which, at least on its first advance, scared him off. . . . But at that moment the Harrow rose with the body spitted on it.[4] (164–65/243–45)

It is not uncommon to draw similarities between Foucault's famous opening of *Discipline and Punish* and Kafka's short story.[5] What unites both passages is an external description. There is no residue of emotionality, there is no insight into the observer's thoughts. In addition, the two passages about the administration of a death penalty speak about sovereign power.

There is, however, at the same time a quite different kind of description. There is a hysterically comical element in Kafka's depiction of the execution that is totally absent from the description cited by Foucault. The divergent manner of description entails a discursive dissonance between the two executions. They seem to presuppose different ways in which sovereign power can exercise its violence. The effect of this dissonance is that whereas Foucault uses description to separate classical sovereignty from biopower, Kafka's laughter mixes distinct forms of power. This entails divergent ways of conceptualizing sovereign power. We need to start with a clear delineation of the main elements of sovereign power to be in a position to draw inferences about the distinct dramas enacted in the description of the two executions.

The Death Penalty and Sovereignty

The death penalty, as Foucault himself remarks, is a hallmark of the exercise of the sovereign prerogative of life and death. The cold, impassioned description of the execution of Damiens does not so much describe the death of a human being, but rather the destruction of a body by the sovereign power. Violence is dispensed with in its pure, unadulterated self-justification. It is justified violence because the right over life and death is legitimately exercised, according to the sovereign logic, against whoever threatens the sovereign. In discussing Machiavelli's *The Prince*, Foucault points out two important characteristics of classical sovereignty—or what I prefer to call "modern" sovereignty. These are the fact that the end of power is nothing other than the exercise of power, and that the sovereign has a discontinuous relation to his principality.[6] Taken together, these two characteristics point, on the one hand, to the immanent operation of power. Thus, it is not surprising that sovereign power is applied directly to the body of the one who affronts the sovereign. On the other hand, the absolute sovereign—and here "absolute" retains its Latin meaning of *absolutus*, that is, separated—retains a mystical element. This is not exactly the doctrine of the king's two bodies, since in historically accurate terms this doctrine is not present on the Continent—or at least it does not have the same determinative influence that it has had in the British Isles.[7] Rather, the prince or sovereign is posited as the end of the justification of violence. This explains the violence directed against Damiens. His assassination attempt, according to this logic, was not directed simply against another individual human being. Rather, he had offended against the sovereign, who personified the body politic. As such, corporeal punishment is the means deemed appropriate to repay the offense against the mystical body that holds the state together. The exercise of this violence justifies the end—the preservation of the sovereign body politic.

At this point, I need to make a detour to the theory of sovereignty that I develop in my book *Sovereignty and Its Other*.[8] This is needed not only to highlight some differences from Foucault's position and to introduce some terminology that I will have recourse to later, but to outline the conceptual framework within which I read "In the Penal Colony." I argue, then, that there is a sovereign logic that underlies a rationalized instrumentalism of violence. Sovereignty takes place whenever violence is exercised in a justified manner. Or, more simply, sovereignty is justified violence. At the same time, this logic can have different variations, depending on how the justification is accomplished. The instrumentality is understood differently according to how justification operates, even though the two are inseparable. This allows for the distinction between three forms of sovereignty, or, more accurately, between three modalities of the justification of violence. Specifically, in modern sovereignty the means of the exercise of sovereign violence justify their end—which of course is nothing else than legitimizing the perpetuation of sovereignty itself, as Foucault recognized in his delineation of Machiavelli's position, described a moment ago. Damiens's execution, as described in *Discipline and Punish*, conforms to this modality of justification: his dismemberment justifies the affirmation of the king's absolute power in France. What I call "ancient sovereignty" is the reverse justification, whereby the end justifies the means of the exercise of violence. And the third modality of justification, the biopolitical one, operates through dissimulating the lack of an end, as a violence immanently applied to the regulation of the population's life. For the moment, I just want to introduce this vocabulary. I will further elaborate on the operation of the ancient and biopolitical modalities of the justification of violence in my reading of "In the Penal Colony" in due course.

Let us return now to the second execution. The presentation of a death penalty is ipso facto a political statement. And such an execution accords with the operation of what Foucault calls "classical" and what I call "modern" sovereignty. Despite the terminological differences, at its most general, a depiction of an execution, such as in "In the Penal Colony," gives the short story a decidedly political flavor.[9] We can also point to specific and contextual references to politics. To start with, the story is written in October 1914, that is, at the start of the Great War, which deeply affects Kafka. In the wider, both political and literary context, the model for the short story is Octave Mirbeau's *The Torture Garden*—a source whose importance has not been fully explored, as I will argue later. Mirbeau's novel is a riposte to the Dreyfus affair. Dreyfus was sentenced to the Devil's Island, a French penal colony in the Atlantic Ocean.[10] Kafka would also have been aware of the various descriptions of European penal colonies around the world.[11] The influence of all sorts of psychiatric apparatus for various treatments is also present in the description of the execution machine in "In the Penal Colony." In describing the apparatus, the officer states: "You will have seen similar apparatus in hospitals" (143).[12] In this direct political context within which Kafka's story is composed and to which it responds, we discover, then, the colonial and the racial marks of violence, as well as the torture machines whose therapies on the body Foucault himself so powerfully describes under the rubric of disciplinary society.

The Tragedy of Modern Sovereignty and the Existential Drama of Biopolitics

And yet, besides these similarities due to the political concerns introduced by the death penalty, there are also obvious differences between the two scenes of execution. These stem from divergent articulation of sovereign power presupposed by the two texts. We can outline these differences by paying attention to the description of the execution and especially to what each observer notices.

The execution of Damiens is carried out in Paris in front of a big crowd of fascinated spectators—it is a spectacle, the opportunity for entertainment. Following this spectacular logic, Bouton only has eyes for the gruesome dismemberment—and these eyes do not shy away from precise details, such as that the executioners cutting the body at the thighs instead of at the ligaments. Bouton does not glance sideways to the gathered crowd. His eyes are fixed—even fixated—on the spectacle of the exercise of violence. The execution described by Kafka is only witnessed by three people, and yet the gaze of the observer can hardly focus on the actual execution. Instead, it is distracted by the antics of the secondary characters. Kafka's fascination with these antics, or "allotria," as Stanley Corngold calls them, is thoroughly absent from Bouton's account.[13] This may appear as an insignificant, epiphenomenal difference. I contend, on the contrary, that the different registers of what is visible—of what can be seen and recorded—are symptomatic of the conceptualization of sovereign power entailed in each description.

Let us start with the register of visibility in the execution from *Discipline and Punish*. The first point to note is that Foucault himself uses Damien's execution to draw a distinction between two different ways in which constituted power is exercised—what he calls the "classical" and the "disciplinary" models.[14] Shortly after the clinical description of Damien's dismemberment, Foucault provides a long citation from Léon Faucher's rules for young inmates. The rules are described in an equally clinical manner, but in a way that seems to invert dramatically the images of the administration of the death penalty. It is as if we have two different dramas: after the royal tragedy to which Damiens's execution belongs we encounter a dystopian drama of pervasive control. It was such a dystopia that I described in chapter 4 as the existential drama mobilized by the priest's discourse. (I will actually contend later that this is only a seeming difference, since they both participate in a politics that privileges death over life.) Faucher's manual consists of a detailed daily schedule that does not seek to destroy the body, but rather to discipline it. The schedule accounts for the entire day of the young inmates, from their early morning rise to the early retirement into the cells. Foucault explains this as a redistribution of the economy of punishment.[15] Torture disappears as a spectacle and in its place arises the codification of behavior as a form of punishment. If the classical form of sovereign power directed its violence against the body to the point of its utter devastation, the new, disciplinary form is corrective—it directs its violence in such as a way as to manage and control the body in its various daily movements. Foucault generalizes this point in *Discipline and Punish* with references to Bentham's panopticon. The Greek etymology of the term is accurately descriptive: it is a compound of *pan*, meaning everything, and *opsis*, meaning sight. The panopticon is the condition of totally visibility. Such a visibility—as Zamyatin's *We* dramatizes it—is also a condition of surveillance and hence unfreedom.

The year following the publication of *Discipline and Punish*, at the last lecture of his course "Society Must be Defended" at the Collège de France, delivered on March 17, 1976, Foucault uses for the first time the word "biopolitics" to describe the spread of constituted power to include and regulate potentially every aspect of life. Biopower is presented as a quantitative intensification of disciplinary power. Foucault notes that biopolitics reverses the old sovereign right "to take life or let live," which now becomes the biopolitical right "to make live and let die."[16] The contrast between the death penalty and the incarceration manual in the first few pages of *Discipline and Punish* can be read as presentations of the two different rights of constituted power that Foucault describes in his subsequent lectures—the prerogative of life and death characteristic of absolute sovereignty and the biopolitical right that essentially consists of the regulation and normalization of the life of a population.

There is another way to express the difference between classical sovereign power and biopower, which highlights the differences between the two citations at the beginning of *Discipline and Punish*. Sovereign power is spectacular. This explains the presence of the large crowd that has come to witness the execution of Damiens. Conversely, there is nothing spectacular about the administration of inmates—or of the panopticon effect in general. The dismemberment of a body is a special occurrence, while management, control, and regulation are everyday, banal, otiose activities. Keeping in mind these two different orders of visibility, it is instructive to ponder why Carl Schmitt is a thinker of modern sovereignty but not of biopolitics. For Schmitt, the political defines a specific sphere of activity, which is distinct from society, culture, and the economy. Specifically, Schmitt understands the political as the spectacular confrontation with the enemy—the entity that threatens the existence of the sovereign.[17] The political consists in a visible, bloody struggle, which may include executions such as Damiens' described in *Discipline and Punish*. Conversely, the exercise of biopower is diffuse. There are no identifiable enemies in biopolitics, because everyone is subject to regulation and management, everyone is policeable, and hence everyone is an enemy—or, treated as such. Michael Hardt and Antonio Negri capture this idea in *Empire* by identifying "omni-crisis" as a constitutive feature of biopolitics.[18]

We can also formulate this difference from the perspective of the opposition between freedom and confinement. Modern sovereignty exercises itself by asking whether and when one will be subjected to the justified violence of the sovereign—that is, whether or when one will be subject to the right of life and death. Conversely, with biopolitics, one is always already in the sight of biopower. Hence, it is no longer relevant to ask the "whether" and "when" questions. Instead, biopolitics is about how and to what extent one is subjected to the sovereign violence in the guise of surveillance, control, management, and regulation. In the former case, the subject may lose its freedom in certain instances—whether and when it opposes sovereign power. In the latter case, the subject is always encaged by the increasing multiplication of mechanisms of normalization. In modern sovereignty, imprisonment is envisaged as a special case, whereas in biopolitics encagement is the norm. In the previous chapter, I referred to this generalized imprisonment in biopolitics as "a prison without walls."

The Economy of Substitution: Death and the Free Will

The spectacular dismemberment of Damiens' body places his execution squarely within the ambit of classical sovereignty as understood by Foucault. The conditions of visibility and speculation are radically different in the passage from "In the Penal Colony." Essentially, this means that the execution scene as described by Kafka conforms to the order of visibility for both forms of power identified by Foucault, thereby problematizing their separation. Compounding this problematic, Kafka introduces a third way of justifying the administration of violence—the kind that I describe as ancient sovereignty in *Sovereignty and Its Other*. Therefore, the initial effect of "In the Penal Colony" is to disturb the neat divisions between separate orders of power and their corresponding orders of visibility.

This is a complex operation, so let us see how it is carried out by focusing in this section only on one sentence from the passage about the execution in Kafka's "In the Penal Colony" cited at the beginning of the present chapter: "The explorer observed the soldier and the condemned man." The most striking feature of this sentence is that the condemned man is not the one who is being executed. Instead, the officer, the one in charge of the executions, voluntarily—through the exercise of his own free will—submits himself to the apparatus. There is an exchange or substitution. This substitution does two things at once: It introduces the free will as the voluntary self-execution of the officer, and this economy of substitution of the bodies also entails a substitution or exchange between distinct orders of power.[19] Let us see how the substitution—both as a register of the free will and as the manifestation of an economy of sovereign power—works by turning to "In the Penal Colony."

There are four characters in the story, two "main" ones and two "secondary." The main ones are the officer and a traveler or explorer.[20] The secondary ones are the condemned man and the soldier guarding him. The short story starts at the site where the execution of the condemned man is about to take place. The focal point is the execution apparatus. The officer shows it off to the explorer, explaining how it works and that it was designed by the previous Commandant. According to the officer, the organization of the colony under the former Commandant was complete (*die Einrichtung der Kolonie . . . in sich geschlossen ist*). The old Commandant is presented in such a manner as to approximate the mystical figure of the king. He was the law-giver and the judge of the island community, the person with the greatest, incontestable authority as well as the most startling inventor, as the apparatus demonstrates. The torture apparatus was invented to protect this authority and this perfect organization of the colony. Any threat to the figure of this authority was punished by the public execution of the offender on the apparatus. Back then there were "hundreds of spectators . . . all of them standing on tiptoe as far as the heights there" (153). Even children were vying for the best position to view the execution. That was the old days, during the reign of the former Commandant, whose description conforms with Foucault's outline of the classical sovereign—that is, the figure that all violent actions of constituted power seek to preserve. Simultaneously, a radical temporal rupture seems to be announced.[21] The situation in the present time—the time of the narration—is drastically different. At the site of the execution that the traveler is about to attend, there is no audience. The execution is no longer a spectacle. Only the four characters directly involved in one way or another are present.

The situation is drastically different in more ways than simply a lack of spectators. If the apparatus is the symbol of the sovereign's right over life and death, the condemned man is nevertheless not arrested because he somehow offended or threatened the mystical body of authority. Rather, his offence is to have fallen asleep. The officer explains to the explorer: "A captain reported to me this morning that this man, who had been assigned to him as a servant and sleeps before his door, had been asleep on duty. It is his duty, you see, to get up every time the hour strikes and salute the captain's door" (145–46). Saluting the closed door on the hour is not a duty that serves or protects a sovereign authority. The condemned man is not even a sentry, but only a servant. The mindless duty is simply a way of controlling and managing his behavior. Such a duty could have come out of a detention manual for incarcerated juvenile delinquents. In fact, the condemned man is described more as a brute than as a young and inexperienced man—he looks, writes Kafka, "like a submissive dog" (140). The mindless duty of saluting the door in the middle of the night is not, then, an oppressive order against an individual but like the training of one who represents a kind of population—those who are dumb like dogs—to perform a task every time the clock strikes the hour, not because the task in itself has any intrinsic value, but only so that they learn to obey and act according to the given rules. The condemned man's offence is not comparable to Damiens's attempt to kill the king. But it resembles the breaking of the rules of an incarceration manual, such as the one by Faucher cited by Foucault. Therefore, the justification of violence against the condemned man is biopolitical—regardless of the fact that the means of his punishment is an instrument associated with classical sovereignty.

All the more startling, then, that this "dog" of a human being is substituted by the officer in the execution. If the conviction of the condemned man has all the characteristics of a biopolitical exercise of power, the substitution is not as straightforward. Ostensibly, the officer decides to execute himself since he realizes that the days of the apparatus are over. His last chance is the explorer, whom he tries to enlist in his attempt to protect this ritualistic administration of the death penalty from the new Commandant's modernizing ways. When the explorer flatly refuses to cooperate, the officer decides to execute himself as a form of justice toward the old Commandant. Such a sacrifice—just like any sacrifice for one's country or king—is a symbolic affirmation of the old Commandant's status as the absolute sovereign of the penal colony. The death of the officer is meant to be, then, a final affirmation of the greatness of the mystical power of the old Commandant. In this regard, the substitution is the affirmation of modern absolute sovereignty. The sacrifice/self-execution is the means that justifies the old Commandant's political authority.

And yet, the substitution of the condemned man demonstrates in addition something else—namely, the spread of the constituted power's violence, which is now applicable to anyone and everyone. The substitution shows that sovereignty no longer—or more accurately, not *only*—exercises its violence as a means of self-protection, but rather the exercise of violence is the means whereby power appears as such. Differently put, the substitution shows that the spread of justified violence entails that it is no longer a matter of whether and when one will be stricken by sovereign violence, but rather how and to what extent violence will strike. Thus, the substitution is *both* an affirmation and a celebration of modern absolute sovereignty, *and* the transition to the dispersed and all-intrusive biopower. At the same time, this "both/and" also means that the substitution is a symbol or hallmark of *neither* absolute sovereignty *nor* biopower, since the distinction between the two now waivers and becomes porous.

As if this porosity between modern and biopolitical justifications of violence is not destabilizing enough, the Christ-like qualities of the officer's sacrifice introduce a third form of justified violence and hence a third way of understanding the exercise of sovereign power. Christ sacrifices himself both as the son of God whose body is immortal, and as a human being who dies on the cross—a favorite Roman apparatus of execution. The self-imposed martyrdom of the officer as the "son" of the old Commandant and as the subject to a generalized violence, which administers his death, reproduces the split we find in the figure of Christ. "In the Penal Colony" conveys this split in two closely connected ways. First, the officer describes his position as law-maker, prosecutor, judge, and executioner in the aftermath of the old Commandant's death. There is no inkling of natural justice here. Instead, the law remains an invisible, but omnipresent, omniscient, and omnipotent force. Since it is invisible, the law is not a state law, referring back to a sovereign authority understood either as modern or as biopolitical. Rather, this is a different law, whose source is itself forever withdrawn, inaccessible to sight and thus protected from both the spectacular visibility of absolute sovereignty and the generalized surveillance, the diffuse visibility, of biopower. The articulation of this invisible law through the calligraphy of the needles of the apparatus on the condemned man's back is after all indecipherable to the spectators. Neither the condemned man nor the spectators can see the invisible law, which thus becomes, by its very invisibility, akin to the divine law—the paradigm of the law's invisibility.[22]

This invisible law is also reminiscent of the prison without walls that characterizes *The Trial*, as we discussed in the previous chapter. After all, the officer's assertion that his "guiding principle" is that "guilt is never to be doubted" could well have been a line copied straight from *The Trial*. There are extrinsic reasons for this similarity: "In the Penal Colony" is written in October 1914, while Kafka is in the midst of the writing of *The Trial*.[23] There is, however, an important difference from *The Trial*, which constitutes the second way in which the divine-like sacrifice of the officer is conveyed. This consists in the ultimate aim or end of the apparatus, which provides a third justification for its operation. It concerns the moment of enlightenment enjoyed by the executed after the prolonged torture and just before expiring. The officer insists on this moment, as a—perhaps, *the*—constitutive feature of the executions carried out by the apparatus:

> how quiet he [i.e., the one being executed] grows at just about the sixth hour. Enlightenment [*Verstand*] comes to the most dull-witted. It begins around the eyes. From there it radiates. A moment that might tempt one to get under the Harrow oneself. Nothing more happens than that the man begins to understand the inscription, he purses his mouth as if he were listening. You have seen how difficult it is to decipher the script with one's eyes; but our man deciphers it with his wounds. To be sure, that is a hard task; he needs six hours to accomplish it. By that time the Harrow has pierced him quite through and casts him into the pit. (150/219–20)

The apparatus executes the condemned man by inscribing on his back his sentence, which he does not otherwise know. The deciphering of this inscription on the body leads to a mystical moment of understanding

(*Verstand*). But this is an understanding of something that the naked eye cannot see, namely, an understanding of the invisible law that determines his fatal submission to the apparatus. This moment of enlightenment or understanding was the feature that most fascinated the spectators in the olden days:

> It was impossible to grant all the requests to be allowed to watch it [i.e. the enlightenment or *Verstand*] from nearby. The Commandant in his wisdom ordained that the children should have the preference; I, of course, because of my office had the privilege of always being at hand; often enough I would be squatting there with a small child in either arm. How we all absorbed the look of transfiguration [*Verklärung*] on the face of the sufferer, how we bathed our cheeks in the radiance of that justice, achieved at last and fading so quickly! (154/226)

Let the children come—declares Christ.[24] And they do come to see this transfiguration in the face of the martyr subjected to the apparatus. The children come to the officer/"son" to witness in his arms the perception of the imperceptible, the understanding of the invisible—and hence divine—law. The parallels with the Christian narrative of the sacrifice are not trivial. They are fundamental in that they indicate a third way in which justification operates. Here, the end—this *Verklärung* or transfiguration that collapses the distance between a brute of a criminal, a dull-witted individual, and the invisible or divine law—it is this mystical end, which justifies the means of the exercise of violence. The *Verklärung* justifies the exercise of violence by the apparatus. The end justifies the means, thereby reversing the modality of justification characteristic of modern sovereignty, which, as you recall, operates when the means of the exercise of violence justify the end. This reversed justification I call "ancient" sovereignty.

So, "In the Penal Colony" is a political work, and in particular a short story concerned with sovereignty. The split between a past time and a present time seems to mirror the split between the classical sovereignty and biopower as extrapolated by Foucault.[25] It is as if the old form of power is substituted with the new one. There is, however, a more important, more fundamental substitution, namely, the substitution of the condemned man by the officer in the execution apparatus. If we accept that sovereignty entails the various modalities of the justification of violence, then this substitution presents within itself all three possible modalities of justification. Ancient, modern, and biopolitical sovereignty all surface through this substitution. What inferences can we derive from this coimplication of the three modalities of justification—of the three forms of sovereignty? I describe in *Sovereignty and Its Other* two main effects of this, which are also valid for our short story here:

First, sovereignty is not simply, not even primarily, concerned about the justification of violence in a particular modality, but rather for the justification of violence in all three different modalities. Differently put, sovereignty is the exchange between ancient, modern, and biopolitical justifications of violence. This cosupponibility of the different modalities of justification presents sovereignty as an economic function. A particular articulation of sovereign power can be accurately described and understood only by asking the question about the relations of exchange between ancient, modern, and biopolitical articulations of the justification of violence. Sovereignty is an economic concept and praxis.[26]

Second, this economy entails that sovereignty persists in a process of dissolution. Derrida names this the "autoimmune" process whereby the assertion of sovereignty's power is simultaneously its weakening.[27] I prefer to refer to it as the process whereby the cosupponibility of the different modalities of justification both institutes the autoreferential movement that characterizes sovereignty, and simultaneously inaugurates the process of its dejustification, since the three justifications contradict each other and cannot accommodate each other. Deleuze expresses a similar idea in discussing *The Trial*: "Kafka, already standing at the point of transition between the two kinds of society [i.e., disciplinary society and society of control], described in *The Trial* their most ominous judicial expressions: apparent acquittal (between two confinements) in disciplinary societies, and endless postponement in (constantly changing) control societies; these are two very different ways of doing things, and *if our legal system is vacillating, it is itself breaking down*."[28] I am not concerned here with the distinction between a disciplinary and a control society in Deleuze's text any more than to point out that these two societies point to different structures of power. Deleuze points out that Kafka's strategy consists of showing a vacillation between these two systems—a vacillation that puts the system of power into a self-destructive trajectory.[29] Deleuze is already writing a "postscript" in the sense that the societies he describes are in a process of dissolution—their death is announced by the pernicious vacillation that destroys their distinction. I am describing something similar as taking place in "In the Penal Colony." Sovereign power is presented as the circulation or economy between three different ways in which the justification of violence is carried out. These three different modalities both support each other, and yet they also contradict each other.

To construct sovereignty as an instrumental rationalization and as an economic function, sovereignty must be unstable and in a process of dissolution. Kafka depicts the dissolution of sovereign power as the officer's failure to achieve transfiguration. As the traveler is removing the officer's cadaver from the apparatus, "almost against his will" he looks at the face of the corpse. But in that face "no sign was visible of the promised redemption." The malfunction of the apparatus expedited the execution to just a few minutes—instead of twelve hours—thereby depriving the officer of "what the others had found in the machine." His substitution fails to celebrate the sovereign authority of the old Commandant, and the transfiguration that promises the collapse of the distance between the human and the divine has not transpired. The abrupt and violent transition to death also contradicts the diffuse operation of biopower.

This failure of sovereignty, which results from the two effects of the cosupponibility of the three sovereign justifications of violence, discloses at the same time its highest achievement, namely, that the exercise of its power is a thanatopolitics: The description of what the officer sees in the substituted body that has just been self-executed reads: "the lips were firmly pressed together, the eyes were open, with the same expression as in life, the look was calm and convinced, through the forehead went the point of the great iron spike" (166). The body on which sovereign power exercises—in a rapid movement—all its various modalities of violence is a body that is both alive and with an "iron spike" through its forehead—which means neither dead nor alive. The sovereign economy needs this body to be alive so as to exercise its violence, thereby killing it. This thanatopolitical ambiguity regulates the physical expression of the sovereign economy.

And, finally, let us not forget that this thanatopolitical ambiguity, which sets in motion the sovereign economy and its dissolution in "In the Penal Colony," is instigated by a simple, voluntary act, an act of the free will: the substitution of the prisoner by the officer in the apparatus. The free will then is steeped in this thanatopolitics—it is a will to death.

Generalized Violence as Ontology: Mirbeau's *The Torture Garden*

What are we to make of the inscription of thanatopolitics in the scene of substitution? What are we to make of Kafka's depiction of the operation of sovereign violence? More emphatically: what does violence signify in this short story? It is necessary at this point to turn to Octave Mirbeau's *The Torture Garden* (*Le Jardin des supplices*, 1899). It is well known that Mirbeau's novel provided the literary model for "In the Penal Colony."[30] I would argue, however, that this has nothing to with the actual depictions of violent acts. Rather, the influence is felt as the foregrounding of the problematic of violence in Kafka's short story.

The obvious point of comparison between Mirbeau's novel and Kafka's short story is the depiction of torture. This similarity, however, does not significantly promote progress in interpretation. For instance, we can agree with Anderson that they indicate art nouveau aestheticism, but this does not advance our inquiry into the question about the copresence of different forms of sovereignty within the scene of substitution that characterizes the execution.[31] A comparison with *The Trial*, the novel Kafka was writing while he composed "In the Penal Colony," will also be of limited exegetical value if it is confined only to the visual depictions of torture and execution. *The Trial* also bears the marks of Mirbeau's novel in "The Flogger" chapter. And it concludes with the ritual execution of Josef K., who is "killed like a dog" by having his throat cut. A comparison with *The Trial* merely on the use of torture falls short of addressing the problematic of violence in its full scope.

A comparison with *The Trial* is useful when the issue of violence—not simply the depiction of torture—is brought to the foreground. Violence is certainly present in *The Trial*, even though it appears to be restricted to the diffuse law, which haunts Josef K. everywhere. Conversely, "In the Penal Colony" is set in a constitutively violent place. If Josef K. can find some relief from the oppressiveness of the law in the arms of Leni, the penal colony is ipso facto a place of generalized violence. The rule of the old Commandant, with his invention of the apparatus, contributes to and accentuates the sense of a pervasive violence. Where *The Trial* presents a generalized prison without walls, "In the Penal Colony" presents a locale where violence is so generalized that it has become the norm.

This generalization of violence is underscored by locating the story on a remote island. The theme of the island, or of the remote and isolated enclave, is a dominant motif to describe the human condition. The standard example in literature is the early eighteenth-century novel *Robinson Crusoe* by Daniel Defoe. Stranded on an island after a ship wreck, Crusoe becomes the sovereign of this island, whose authority both reproduces and comments on the structure of civilized societies.[32] In philosophy, in *The Critique of Pure Reason* Immanuel Kant describes the correct use of reason as an isolated island, surrounded by the stormy waters of all those activities that go beyond, and thus disturb, rationality.[33] Both Mirbeau and Kafka operate under the same conventional use of the metaphor. The remote locale in which they set their stories is not a utopian fantasy but a discursive presentation of violence.

It is not in the depictions of torture but rather in this conception of social being or human interaction in general under the guise of an omnipresent violence that Mirbeau's influence is most acutely felt in "In the Penal Colony." This idea is pivotal in Mirbeau's text. Let me substantiate this with just a few indicative references. Mirbeau dedicates what he calls "these pages of Murder and Blood" to "Priests, Soldiers, Judges."[34] Mirbeau then links the practice of murder with the Christian culture and the various forms of power that European articulations of sovereignty have developed under its influence. Mirbeau does not mince his words: "Europe and its hypocritical, barbaric civilization is a lie."[35] At the same time, the framing of the novel suggests that violence is not confined to the Christian religion and the European civilization but is part of the human condition. There is a gathering of friends. After dinner, a discussion commences when one notes that "murder is the greatest human preoccupation."[36]

> The need to kill is born in man with the need to eat, and merges with it. . . . This instinctive need, which is the mainspring of all living organisms, is developed by education instead of being restrained, and is sanctified by religion instead of being denounced. Everything conspires to make it the pivot upon which our admirable society revolves. As soon as man awakens to consciousness, we instill the spirit of murder in his mind. Murder, expanded to the status of a duty, and popularized to the point of heroism, accompanies him through all the stages of his existence.[37]

It is this idea of the generalized condition of violence characteristic of the human, or, as Mirbeau puts it, "that vast slaughter-house—humanity," which is the main topic of the novel.[38] And it is this idea that is decisive for Kafka's "In the Penal Colony"—an idea that is not foregrounded in *The Trial*, despite the strong resonances between the short story and the novel.

This idea would not have been unfamiliar to either progressives or conservatives of Mirbeau's and Kafka's times. We can situate, for instance, both Carl Schmitt's definition of "the political" as the identification of the enemy, and Georges Sorel's assertion about the central role of violence in historical development, within the purview of this idea. Walter Benjamin's famous essay on the "Critique of Violence" belongs here, too.[39] It is also noticeable that in all of these three famous cases, as well as in Mirbeau's novel and in Kafka's short story, violence is intimately connected with the operation and determination of sovereign power. But if violence and its political expression constitute the generalized condition of humanity, then power and ontology converge. The question of violence indicates a politico-ontological nexus. Power can only be approached via this nexus—which simply means that power is not a matter of abstract principles as to how violence is justified, but is also related to existence and living.

So we can reformulate the questions at the beginning of the present section thus: Is the sovereign economy to be translated into a general economy of violence? Or broadening the scope, given that violence here is presented as a general condition of existence, we can refine the question thus: Does the sovereign economy of violence necessitate an ontology in which being is understood as inherently violent? Is the human existence a being in, for, and through violence? Is violence the source of human ontology?

The articulation of sovereignty—in all its three modalities of the justification of violence—will concur with the constitutive role of violence in the being of the human. The economy of sovereignty presupposes an ontology of originary violence. We can list here some of the main characteristics of originary violence as they are articulated in the three forms of sovereignty—ancient, modern, and biopolitical—as a historical support for this position. I am thinking of characteristics such as the just war theory, first expounded by Augustine and refined by Aquinas; or the theory of the state of nature as the violent human condition whose overcoming legitimates the juridical definition of sovereignty; or the generalized state of "civil war" that theorists such as Foucault, Negri, and Agamben identify as central to biopolitics. Thanatopolitics is the political articulation of this originary ontology of violence presupposed by sovereignty. It is worth noting that the execution apparatus as the symbol of the thanatopolical machine of sovereignty in "In the Penal Colony" begins its operation as soon as the voluntary substitution we described in the previous section takes place. The officer freely wills to take the place of the condemned man. This articulation of the officer's free will sets in motion all three modalities of the sovereign justification of violence in our short story. Thus, the free will is complicit in the thanatopolitics of sovereignty.

The economy of sovereignty and its thanatopolitical articulation unify the sovereign operation of the three modalities of justification. I describe in *Sovereignty and Its Other* this connection in terms of immediacy.[40] This consists in the immediate connection between the originary violence and justification of violence. Sovereignty justifies its violence as fighting against the originary violence—hence the plethora of discourse about protection and security. At the same time, this immediate connection between an ontology of violence and its thanatopolitical articulation aims to disguise and cover up the circulation of justification between its three distinct modalities. The coherence of the structure depends on justification, and yet the three justifications contrast with each other. There is a circularity in the way that the three justifications are mobilized, and yet the immediate recourse to the originary violence as something dreaded that is to be avoided at all costs disguises this contradiction. Thus, the originary violence is crucial not only for the thanatopolitical positioning of the subject within the ambit of sovereignty, but also for securing justification by disguising the fact that there are three modalities of justification that support each other.

The Theater of Laughter: Secondary Characters Center Stage!

If the disguise of the cosupponibility of the three modalities of justification is crucial for the operation of sovereignty, then what happens when their cover is blown and they are presented in the circularity—as happens in the execution scene in "In the Penal Colony"? Does Kafka's condensed presentation of all forms of sovereignty present the sovereign "without his clothes on"? And how does that affect the immediate connection between originary violence and sovereignty? How does it affect the conception of an ontology of originary violence? Perhaps it is even possible to discover an alternative ontology—which no longer finds its source in violence—through Kafka's uncovering of the substitutions of the economy of sovereignty.

To tackle the problematic about the exposure of how the disguise of the justification of violence is removed, we are led back to questions of visibility and presentation. It becomes crucial, then, to describe the drama unfolding in front of the explorer. It is important to remember here that the execution befits a particular order of visibility. As outlined earlier, Damiens's execution presents this human drama like a theater play. Bouton's clinical description of the unfolding drama recalls a critic who is reporting the happenings on the proscenium of a royal theater. The spectacle of sovereignty befits a tragedy in which death is writ large. Thus, Damiens does not die simply as a human being, but as an actor in the sovereign drama, according to which violence is the natural condition of humanity and the source of the human being's condition in the world. The drama of ancient, modern, and biopolitical sovereignty may be different. For instance, the drama that aims at transfiguration characteristic of ancient sovereignty is one of suffering and martyrdom. The modern drama may entail the violence exercised to protect sovereignty. And the drama of biopolitics could result from the existential angst that anyone can find themselves at the execution machine. Nevertheless, one thing remains constant in all these dramatic presentations—the presence of an originary violence. It is this violence that gives this sovereign drama its tragic character.

Kafka presents a different kind of play. It is impossible to understand the execution in his story as amenable to the script of a sovereign tragedy—in any of its possible forms. The site of the execution in "In the Penal Colony" is described from the beginning as a stage. But this is no longer the proscenium arch of a royal theater, but rather "a deep hollow" (140) reminiscent of makeshift theatrical performances.[41] On the island of the penal colony, which stages the condition of humanity, this sunken stage puts the spotlight—"the glare of the sun in the shadeless valley" (142)—on violence. But here, at the climax of the drama, at the moment of the execution, the two main characters—the officer and the explorer, who may well have been characters in a sovereign tragedy—are no longer the focus of attention. Instead, the secondary, lowly characters, especially the condemned man, enact all the movements on the stage. The secondary characters attract all the attention of the narrative voice, and they demand our gaze. The secondary characters are suddenly center stage! Let us look closely at the passage cited at the beginning of this chapter.

The shift away from the center of attention in the scene of execution is first signified by the sentence we examined earlier: "The explorer observed the soldier and the condemned man." The observer's eye moves away from the execution—that is, from the action that presents the justification of violence and hence the human condition as constitutively violent. This lateral gaze is quickly fixated on, and incapable of diverting itself from, the antics of the condemned man, who in an animated state runs around the machine, inspecting it while gesticulating wildly. The gaze is no longer on kings and sovereigns but on a slapstick comedy. The explorer, writes Kafka, "could not bear the sight"—not of the execution apparatus but "of these two." He asks them to go home, "but the condemned man took the order as a punishment." The condemned man was almost impervious to the punishment that he was going to receive on the execution apparatus, but perceives the order to leave the execution site as unbearable. Could there be a funnier contrast than this twisted response to punishment by the condemned man, who remains impervious to the thanatopolitics of sovereignty as he is about to receive punishment, but is devastated to miss out on the spectacle offered by thanatopolitics? This theater of laughter is presented through a play of gestures. The condemned man's exaggerated gestures in reaction to the explorer's command to go away are pure slapstick: "With clasped hands he implored to be allowed to stay, and when the explorer shook his head and would not relent, he even went down on his knees." Gestures such as these explain Walter Benjamin's fascination with the gesture in Kafka's works.[42] Their importance in this particular scene is that they contrast with the "serious tragedy" of the execution. Even at the point when the apparatus is malfunctioning, ready to savage the officer, the comedy persists unabated: "This phenomenon [i.e., the malfunctioning apparatus] made the condemned man completely forget the explorer's command, the cogwheels fascinated him, he was always trying to catch one and at the same time urging the soldier to help, but always drew back his hand in alarm, for another wheel always came hopping along which, at least on its first advance, scared him off." If we take "In the Penal Colony" as a tragedy, which is meant to accord with the thanatopolitical script of sovereign violence, then the play goes off the rails at this juncture. Conversely, if, hard as it may be, we divert our gaze from the apparatus to the secondary characters and laugh at their slapstick antics, then we see a comic play in which the characters, who would have been secondary in a tragedy, now emerge as the real protagonists of the play.

As we have already seen, when Kafka read his stories at the literary salon in Prague, laughter was the usual response. There is, however, an account of Kafka reading "In the Penal Colony" at Munich in November 1916, which may appear as an exception:

> As he spoke his first words, a stale smell of blood seemed to fill the room, and a strangely stale and pallid taste crept over my lips. His voice may have sounded apologetic, but his images cut into me like a razor. . . . Inside, confusion in the hall, a lady was carried out unconscious. Kafka continued reciting his text. Twice more, his words made people swoon. The ranks of the listeners began to thin out. Some fled at the last moment before the vision of the author overwhelmed them. Never have I observed an effect of spoken words like this. I stayed to the very end.[43]

This account is usually dismissed as unreliable, and probably inaccurate.[44] And it would indeed be an overly exaggerated reaction if the audience was reacting to the depictions of violence as such. After all, the violence of accounts of executions such as Damiens' are unquestionably more bloody than anything that can be found in Kafka's story, not to mention that the reading takes place during World War I, while violence is the order of the day.

But what if the audience was not affected by the presentation of violence as such, but rather by the contrast between violence and the large, comic gestures of the "minor" characters? Kafka himself, as well as his Munich audience, may have come across large, comic gestures such as those that characterize this scene at the movies or in performances of Yiddish theater.[45] If the audience were prepared either for a spectacle of sovereign violence, or for the gestural play of a comic theater, they may nevertheless have been totally unprepared for Kafka's idiosyncratic combination of the two. Maybe the images of "In the Penal Colony" cut "like a razor" because the tragedy of the human condition, which according to the sovereign logic represents the being of the human as inherently violent, is here presented as a comedy. Maybe what was unbearable, in the midst of World War I, was the transfiguration of the secondary, comic characters into the real protagonists of the drama in the penal colony.

This laughter exposes the disguise of the cosupponibility of the various justifications of violence and undercuts the notion of originary violence. The laughter presents something more primary than the thanatopolitics of the logic of sovereign violence. Maybe, then, positioning the secondary characters center stage made the audience feel "seasick on earth," as Kafka puts it in "Description of a Struggle." Maybe what made the audience swoon was the presentation of the economy of sovereignty, which in "In the Penal Colony" moves rapidly from ancient, to modern, to biopolitical sovereignty. And, maybe they felt even dizzier from the totally unexpected gesture of using this rapid circularity of sovereignty to subordinate sovereign power to laughter.

Of course, we will never know with any certainty exactly what took place during that reading in Munich.[46] Nevertheless, we have now reached a position to draw some inferences from the elevation of the secondary characters to the protagonists of the comic play. In fact, I want to draw three inferences from this theater of laughter. All of them concern the outline of a different ontology that results from this laughter.

Toward an Ontology of Laughter: An Agonistic Economy of Freedom

How does the theater of laughter reconfigure the ontology of originary violence into an alternative ontology? This question essentially returns to the point about the primacy of mediated freedom over the free will. I have described this primacy in various ways thus far—as ontological with recourse to the Zürau aphorisms, in exegetical terms with reference to "The Judgment," as ethical freedom in the two stories about cages, and in the juridical context of *The Trial*. This question, then, essentially, asks: What is the relation between the ontology of generalized violence that characterizes the logic of sovereignty and the ontology of laughter that characterizes the elevation of the secondary characters to center stage? Or, how can mediated freedom be presented as more primary in the context of the nexus of power and ontology?

First, the laughter in the midst of the execution registers an opposition to sovereign power. The operation of the death penalty is the starkest assertion of the sovereign justification of violence. Laughter in the midst of this operation becomes a tool or technique to unravel justification. Laughter dejustifies the violence performed by the apparatus in the name of sovereign authority. This has a historical element. Laughter has been used to challenge authority and even to confront various forms of sovereign power. Mikail Bakhtin reads Rabelais in precisely this manner. His laughter is seen as a response to power. The hierarchies of power are flattened out by Rebelais's laughter.[47] And it also performs a political function. Kafka's comedy does not say that violence is a laughing matter. Rather, what is laughable is that there is an authority that assumes it can justify its own violence. What is laughable is the self-justification of sovereignty that it can fight an originary violence with a rationalized instrumentalism—that is, essentially, with more violence.[48]

Both this historical confrontation with sovereignty and the immanently political role in deconstructing the assertion of justified violence are not meant to eliminate violence tout court. Laughter does not eliminate violence; Kafka is not proposing a *pax risi*. Violence does exist. After all, the condemned man narrowly escapes the needles of the apparatus, only for the officer to then willingly submit himself to the execution machine. Rather, laughter challenges the conception of a human ontology as constitutively violent. "In the Penal Colony" assumes the idea of a generalized violence as the condition of humanity, only to laugh in its face. The elevation of the condemned man to the lead role in the drama of being is the demotion of those characters who represent violence as originary for the being of being human.

Second, and in addition to the dejustification of sovereign violence, the comic characters assert a different ontology, which transforms justified violence into agonism. There is indeed something "violent" in diverting one's gaze from a horrific execution. And the antics of the condemned man on the side of the operating apparatus are also "violent" in the sense that they contrast with, and thus criticize and deconstruct, the justified violence represented by the execution. But this is no longer the violence that is justified with recourse to a rationalized instrumentalism. It is no longer an originary violence that justifies violence. Instead, it is a "violence" against violence—it is a comportment of being that is agonistic against any attempt to justify violence.

This agonistic attitude also, and significantly, exhibits a love for life. This is its distinguishing feature from the thanatopolitics of justified violence. The antics of the condemned man stem from an insatiable curiosity about the operation of the apparatus. The condemned man is attuned to his environment and relishes living, while the officer submits himself to the execution machine, thereby condemning himself to the death penalty.

Whereas the officer conforms to the thanatopolitics of sovereignty, the laughter and curiosity of the condemned man articulate themselves as this constant movement, this incessant desire to act and participate in the process of living. Thus, laughter has the capacity to lead to an ontology of the living.

I argue in *Sovereignty and Its Other* that these two characteristics—the dejustification of violence and the ontology that privileges living—are constitutive of an ontology that translates politically as democracy. In this sense, democracy is the opposite of thanatopolitics.[49] Kafka does not explicitly arrive at an affirmation of democracy at the conclusion of "In the Penal Colony." Some may say that this is because the institution of modern literature is linked to the emergence of the bourgeoisie and capitalism, thereby being antidemocratic.[50] And yet, "In the Penal Colony" subverts the registers of visibility that govern the administration of the death penalty to such an extent that its dejustification of sovereignty and its affirmation of life already take us into the terrain of a democratic ontology. Others may point out Kafka's deep dissatisfaction with the ending of "In the Penal Colony," to conjecture that it stemmed from his inability to conceptualize the democratic implications of writing. Tempting though such a suggestion might be, we should also not forget that Kafka—with the exception of "The Judgment"—is always dissatisfied with the endings of his stories. With this dissatisfaction in mind, it is perhaps more important to note what presents as a potential: The dissatisfaction—amply registered in his diaries and letters—prompts Kafka to keep on trying to write. Writing becomes his response to the "failed" stories. Instead of the mortification of a perfect ending that may exhaust the story, the imperfect conclusion demands further work—it calls for more writing. As such an activity that affirms living, maybe writing is Kafka's starkest and clearest affirmation of an ontology of the human who is a being of living and life—a democratic comportment to the world.

An important question remains: What is the relation between the two ontologies that we have outlined? On the one hand we have an economy of sovereign justification, which is premised on a generalized constitution of violent being. On the other hand we have an ontology that both laughs at sovereignty's justifications and constructs a conception of being that affirms living. So, what is the relation between the two? As I showed at the end of chapter 1, this ontology of the living is more primary than the ontology of transcendence. We need to show how this move is carried out also in terms of power.

Significantly, the problematic about the relation between the two ontologies also has profound implications for how we understand freedom in Kafka's "In the Penal Colony." There are two clear, contrasting acts of freedom, which correspond to the sovereign and the democratic ontologies. They are both encapsulated in one sentence: " 'You are free,' said the officer to the condemned man" (160). There is, on the one hand, the voluntary decision by the officer to substitute himself for the condemned man. The officer exercises his free will to execute himself on the apparatus when the explorer declines to help him preserve the apparatus despite the new Commandant's reforms. There is, on the other hand, the liberation of the condemned man from the execution machine and hence from the thanatopolitics of sovereignty. What is the relation between these two freedoms?

The questions about the two different ontologies of power and the two different conceptions of freedom overlay each other. As I show in the present book, the key feature of the conception of the free will is that it posits a separation between an ideal freedom and a state of unfreedom, submission, oppression, and imprisonment. This separation is registered in the sovereign instrumentalism of violence. The end of the justification of violence encapsulates an ideal—be that a heavenly cashing-out of one's moral worth in ancient sovereignty, or the security and obviation of fear that the transference of one's rights to the sovereign effectuates in modern sovereignty, or the preservation of some kind of notion of the health and vigor of the society and the population, as the biopolitical modality of the justification of violence would contend. We have also discovered an alternative freedom in Kafka: a freedom from the free will and from any ideal. This is a freedom conditioned by the circumstances that one finds oneself in, and it is mediated by one's interactions with others. It is an ethical freedom that privileges living. The instrumentalism of sovereignty recuperates the separation of ideal freedom and unfreedom through the interplay between justification and violence, while the ontology of laughter flattens out this hierarchy into ethical and mediated freedom.

So—what is the relation between these two senses of freedom? There seem to be three alternatives. First, they can exist side by side, in a kind of mutual toleration. Second, one can prevail over the other. And, third, one of them is more primary than the other, or one entails the other as its effect. The only possible answer to the problematic about the relation between sovereignty and democracy—and correspondingly about the two conceptions of freedom—consists of choosing the third alternative. The inference that needs to be drawn is that mediated freedom is the cause of the free will. The separation of an ideal freedom and a Fallen world of suffering is the aftereffect of mediated freedom. I can propose two main arguments to support this assertion. They are both relatively straightforward, so long as the description we have developed thus far of the relation between free will and freedom from the free will, as well as the two ontologies of sovereignty and democracy, are kept in mind.

First, we can approach the problematic by pointing out that relation is an economic concept. We then face the possibility that one conception of freedom can substitute for the other. The two exist in a state of mutual toleration, and the human agent can chose either the one or the other. However, this is precisely the logic of substitution that we saw to be operative in the officer's self-execution. Choosing to die or not to die—this is a translation into the vocabulary of the human agency of the sovereign prerogative of life and death. It simply reproduces in the guise of the free will the sovereign economy of substitution. Voluntary thanatopolitics—that's sovereignty's ideal enactment of the free will. We can also express the idea that the relation is economic in ontological terms. We will then have mutatis mutandis the same argument. If one ontology is to prevail over another, then that prevailing itself will be an enactment of violence. It is the assertion of a sovereign authority that prevails over how being is conducted and how freedom is understood. Prevailing entails an economy of violence and hence requires an originary violence. The first argument, then, leads to the conclusion that if such a relation is to take place, it cannot take the form of an economy of substitution, because then such an economy will completely subsume laughter and democracy.

Second, we also need to point to a different economy, one that is conflictual. I call this economy "agonism." The distinctive difference between agonism and the economy of sovereignty is that agonism does not rely on substitution. Rather, agonism asserts the necessity of the relation between ontology and the political, while also insisting that the relation is unresolvable. There is always a conflict between being and its political articulation—not an originary violence that resolves itself in a particular political formation. Democracy is this conflict between being and politics. This means that democracy neither tolerates nor prevails over sovereignty. Instead, sovereignty is understood as the futile attempt to resolve the connection between being and politics in a relation of immediacy. Sovereignty is the illusion that being can be immediately articulated in the political realm. This economy of immediacy and substitution persists in an agonistic relation to laughter and the persistence of living. Democracy is the persistence of this relation—of this agonism—which means that democracy can never be solidified in a constitution or in a set of normative values. Rather, democracy is the enactment of this conflict.

Having described the relation between the two ontologies of power, we need to turn now to the relation between the two conceptions of freedom. What would it mean that the free will is an aftereffect of mediated freedom? What does it mean that conditioned freedom is the cause of the separation of an ideal freedom and the fallen world of unfreedom? Freedom from the free will entails that one is free when one's life is not fully justified or justifiable. Freedom is the freedom from justification. But this is not a libertine license to do "whatever." Rather, this freedom from the free will is agonistic, which means that it is always responsive to the various forms that the free will and sovereignty might assume. It requires vigilance against the economy of substitution and the responsibility to combat it wherever it arises. Kafka is an author who assumed this vigilance and this responsibility with the utmost seriousness. This is the reason that he is an author whose works reverberate with laughter.

Postscript

A Triple or a Single Will?

> Man has free will, and of three sorts:
>
> First, he was free when he wanted this life; now admittedly he cannot take back his decision, because he is no longer the one who wanted it then, he must do his own will then by living.
>
> Second, he is free inasmuch as he can choose the pace and the course of his life.
>
> Third, he is free in that as the person he will one day be, he has the will to go through life under any condition and so come to himself, on some path of his own choosing, albeit sufficiently labyrinthine that it leaves no little spot of life untouched.
>
> This is the triple nature of the free will, but being simultaneous, it is also single, and is in fact so utterly single that it has no room for a will at all, whether free or unfree.
>
> —Kafka, *Zürau Aphorisms*, 104

I would like to pick a thread that has run throughout this book. This is the idea that the freedom from the free will is more primary than the free will itself.[1] Mediated freedom is in excess of voluntarism and the subjective expression of the will. Differently put, mediated freedom is not a reaction against the free will, which will only make it subservient to it—a move whose difficulties I described in the context of Brod's theological interpretation in chapter 1 and of Agamben's antinomianism in chapter 4. Rather, it is the free will that is a reaction or an effect of mediated freedom. We have seen several examples in Kafka's works of the way in which laughter is the means to present that excess of mediated freedom, and thereby suggests that the free will presupposes a different sense of freedom. I would like now to make a few observations about this move that we have repeatedly encountered in Kafka's texts.

First, I want to point to the different spheres within which we have described this move. We discovered it in the ontological, the exegetical, the ethical, the legal, and the political spheres—in chapters 1, 2, 3, 4, and 5 respectively. From this perspective, the idea of a freedom which is free from the free will forges connections between different ways in which we can understand our being in the world in relation to others. Differently put, the freedom from the free will can function as a heuristic category that animates thinking about being in relation to others—or about being with.

Second, the concept of freedom has a specific historicity. This historicity within the Western tradition is imbued in the conception of the free will. And the free will has two registers, one theological and the other political. It is theological because, as I explain in chapter 1, Augustine's conception of the free will was in response to a specific problem faced by Christian metaphysics, namely, about how to account for the existence of evil within an all-encompassing God. Augustine's solution was to posit the separation between two realms, the paradise of the Garden of Eden where there is absolute freedom (the spiritual realm), and the Fallen world in which the humans are confined in an unending unfreedom (the material and corporeal realm). But this separation was an effect of the first decision—the first exercise of the free will—by Adam and Eve, namely, the decision to eat from the tree of knowledge. Thus the genesis of the free will ties it to the separation between an ideal freedom and an absolute confinement. This theological provenance reverberates every time, within a political context, freedom is touted as an ideal. In fact, given the prominence of freedom within the thinking of the political, we could say, paraphrasing Carl Schmitt, that all significant political concepts are an effect of the separation between an ideal freedom and an absolute imprisonment—or of the free will. I do not want to—nor can I—defend this claim here, but I merely want to point out, once again, the political and theological nexus of the free will.

From the perspective of the theological and political nexus of the free will—that is, from the perspective of the historicity of the free will—the most important avenue of approaching the free will is that of power, in particular through the conceptualization of power that I delineated in chapter 5. Let us look at aphorism 104 from the *Zürau Aphorisms*, cited as the motto of the "Postscript," to see how Kafka himself, without having recourse to the specific theory of power that I put forward, is nevertheless expressing its salient points. We can read the tripartite articulation of freedom presented in aphorism 104 as the structure of the free will in the three forms of power I explained in chapter 5.

Kafka opens aphorism 104 by indicating that we can conceive of three kinds of free will. The first consists of wanting "this life," and one cannot "take back his decision." This is the life that the decision of the protoplasts had bequeathed to humanity—life in the Fallen world. This corresponds to the ancient conception of sovereign power, according to which there is an ideal or end that dictates action—and that is expressed here as that which is now separated from the free will. The second kind of free will described by aphorism 104 corresponds to modern power. Here the subject is conceived as an individual who is free to act so long as it does not confront the will of the sovereign. Individuals can choose the "pace and course" of their lives freely so long as they do not become outlaws. Third, there is the subject that is ab initio confined in the biopolitical cage without walls. For such an individual, the only option to enjoy free will is to look for it "one day" in the future, or, in the language of *The Trial*, to defer it indefinitely.

The problem with this triple free will is that the three conceptions of power that underlie its articulation are in fact cosupponible. They each entail the other. But, as discussed earlier, this single logic of power also entails that the different modalities of power as well as their corresponding articulations of the free will contradict each other. The upshot is that there is "no room for a will, whether free or unfree." Within the context of Western metaphysics—that is, the metaphysics that created the free will and relied on it as a political concept—the freedom from the free will is achieved by recognizing that the economy of power is self-contradictory and self-dissolving.

Third, how are we to explain that it is through literary texts—Kafka's works—that we approached the question of the free will? A response to this question cannot revert to an understanding of literature, or of art more broadly, as giving us some privileged access to concepts or ideas. A separation between two discourses—one of high literature that supposedly enjoys a privileged access to ideas that are fundamental to our lives, and another one that is supposedly inferior—simply idealizes these discourses and reproduces the dichotomy that we have examined between an ideal freedom and an absolute imprisonment.

There is a more straightforward answer to the question "why literature?" or "why Kafka?"—an answer related to the previous two points. If asking about the free will plays a heuristic function that animates different spheres of discourse, then literature has the capacity to mobilize this concept to broaden its scope, and to broaden it specifically by taking a stand on the ontologico-political resister that characterizes the historicity of the free will. To put this the other way round, so long as literature has the capacity to ask political questions and to animate thinking about the political, we can discover in its practice ideas that pertain to and respond to the construction of freedom in the Western philosophical tradition.

But there is another aspect here—and this returns us to the point about the primacy of mediated freedom over the free will. If that's the case, even the most banal and otiose expressions of the free will can unravel and disclose the freedom from the free will. All that is needed is the means or the technique. Kafka is not unique in addressing the free will or in making astute observations about it or in raising political questions in his literature. In the course of doing so, however, he perfected a laughter that he used as a means to show how the free will is untenable and as a matter of fact presupposes a different, an ethical or mediated freedom. Kafka's laughter is his unique contribution in presenting us with a way to free ourselves from the free will.

Notes

Preamble

1. Dimitris Vardoulakis, "Kafka's Other Freedom," essay for the program of the play *The Trial*, based on Franz Kafka's novel, adapted by Louise Fox, directed by Matthew Lutton. The Malthouse Theatre, Melbourne, August 13 to September 4, 2010. The Sydney Theatre Company, Sydney, September 9 to September 30, 2010.

2. Max Brod, *Franz Kafka: A Biography*, trans. G. Humphreys Roberts and Richard Winston (New York: Schocken, 1960), 178. This is not an isolated testimony about the laughter that Kafka's readings provoked. Another well-known example comes from a letter to Felice dated March 1, 1913. The letter, written at two in the morning, narrates how he had read a story—probably the *Metamorphosis*—to a group of friends at Brod's house earlier in the evening. In Kafka's own words, he "read himself into a frenzy" and "we let ourselves go, and laughed a lot." Kafka, *Letters to Felice*, eds. Erich Hellen and Jürgen Born, trans. James Stern and Elizabeth Duckworth (New York: Schocken, 1973).

3. Felix Weltsch, *Religion und Humor im Leben und Werk Franz Kafkas* (Berlin: Herbig, 1957), 78, 79.

4. Milan Kundera, *The Art of the Novel*, trans. Linda Asher (New York: Grove, 1986), 104–5, emphasis in the original.

5. Simon Critchley, *On Humour* (London: Routledge, 2002), 43.

6. I should note that in this context I am using the words "homor" and "laughter" interchangeably, and in a narrow sense as responses to the illusion of the free will, as I explain shortly.

7. Michel Foucault, "The Subject and Power," in *Michel Foucault: Beyond Structuralism and Hermeneutics*, 2nd ed., eds. Hubert L. Dreyfus and Paul Rabinow (Chicago: University of Chicago Press, 1983), 221.

8. When I refer throughout the book to a "Western" conception of freedom, I mean a conception of freedom that relies on this separation, as I will also

explain in chapter 1. The key in such a metaphysics of freedom is the free will. I argue that Kafka's laughter is directed against this metaphysics, and its product, the free will, as a way to confine my inquiry to the Western conception of freedom, but I do not thereby suggest that there are no other ways of conceiving of freedom that Kafka may or may not have been aware of.

9. Mladen Dolar,"Kafka's Immanence, Kafka's Transcendence," in *Transcendence: Philosophy, Literature, and Theology Approach the Beyond*, ed. Regina Schwarz (New York: London, 2004), 192–93.

10. In taking Kafka's work as a provocation to think philosophically, I follow in the footsteps of several significant philosophers. For some, this is explicit, because they have devoted books or essays to Kafka; I will be referring to the most important of these throughout the present book. In other cases, the connection may be more obscure, as with Judith Butler, who reveals in the Preface to the 1999 edition of *Gender Trouble* that the inspiration for the notion of performativity was Kafka's parable "Before the Law," as well as Derrida's reading of the same parable. Judith Butler, *Gender Trouble: Feminism and the Subversion of Identity* (New York: Routledge, 1999), xiv. It is neither possible nor the aim of the present book to survey all the philosophical approaches to Kafka, but after even a cursory perusal of the material it is still possible to say that Kafka is one of the philosophers' writers par excellence.

11. Bill Dodd, "The Case for a Political Reading," in *The Cambridge Companion to Kafka*, ed. Julian Preece (Cambridge, UK: Cambridge University Press, 2002), 131–49.

12. Ibid., 133.

13. Peter Fenves, "'Workforce without Possessions': Kafka, 'Social Justice,' and the Word *Religion*," in *Freedom and Confinement in Modernity: Kafka's Cages*, eds. Kiarina Kordela and Dimitris Vardoulakis (New York: Palgrave, 2011), 107–26.

14. Judith Butler, "Who Owns Kafka," *London Review of Books* 33.5 (March 3, 2011), 3–8.

15. These decisions make more sense if viewed from my own personal trajectory. The present book is, in one sense, a rewriting and expansion of the last chapter of my book *The Doppelgänger*. At the same time, these ideas percolated while I was writing my two subsequent books, *Sovereignty and Its Other* and *Stasis: On Agonistic Democracy*. My reflections on Kafka are embedded in the thinking recorded in these books. But this also means that I am forced either to briefly summarize arguments from these books or, more often, to state the conclusion and direct the reader to where the argument is developed. This is an inevitable effect of the contingent process through which the present book was conceived and developed.

16. See Quentin Meillassoux, *After Finitude: An Essay on the Necessity of Contingency*, trans. Ray Brassier (London: Continuum, 2009).

17. See, for instance, chapter 1 of *Sovereignty and Its Other*. See also Dimitris Vardoulakis, "A Matter of Immediacy: The Artwork and the Political in Walter Benjamin and Martin Heidegger," in *Sparks Will Fly: Benjamin and Heidegger*, eds. Andrew Benjamin and Dimitris Vardoulakis (New York: SUNY Press, 2015), 237–57.

18. Genevieve Lloyd and Moira Gatens, *Collective Imaginings: Spinoza, Past and Present* (London: Routledge, 1999), 51.

19. Peter Szendy, *Kant in the Land of the Extraterrestrials: Cosmopolitical Philosofictions*, trans. Will Bishop (New York: Fordham University Press, 2013), 46.

20. Gilles Deleuze, "Power and Classical Natural Right," seminar conducted on December 9, 1980, transcribed by Simon Duffy, available at www.webdeleuze.com.

21. The other philosopher of laughter is, of course, Nietzsche. Stanley Corngold and Benno Wagner draw attention to the connection between Nietzsche and Kafka in their *Ghost in the Machine*. As they put it, "we have spoken of Kafka as Nietzsche's stringent interlocutor . . . [and] we have taken . . . the position that scarcely a line in Nietzsche's published works went unread or uncommented by Kafka." Corngold and Wagner, *Franz Kafka: The Ghost in the Machine* (Evanston, IL: Northwestern University Press, 2011), 151.

1. Kafka's Cages: Laughter and the Free Will

1. I am referring to narratives that have at least the rudiments of a plot, even though Kafka does not follow plots faithfully because he often takes writing to extremes. Thus, the letters and diaries, for instance, will not be the focus of my attention—which of course does not mean that I will not have recourse to them in seeking material related to the argument at hand.

2. Max Brod, *Franz Kafka: A Biography*, trans. G. Humphreys Roberts and Richard Winston (New York: Schocken, 1960), 178.

3. The examples here can easily proliferate, but I will mention only one more: Henry Sussman observes in "The Burrow" the "blunt literality" characteristic of cartoons. See his *Franz Kafka: Geometrician of Metaphor* (Madison, WI: Coda, 1979), 154.

4. I therefore disagree with Bill Dodd, who asserts that "once we accept that irony and travesty are part of Kafka's treatment of religious themes, it becomes possible to conceive of the social and political dimensions of his critique of metaphysics." Dodd, "The Case for a Political Reading," in *The Cambridge Companion to Kafka*, ed. Julian Preece, 146. The problem with irony and travesty is the assertion of a position of superiority, which ends up reaffirming the very politics of metaphysics that it is supposed to overcome. If we substitute "irony and

travesty" with the term "laughter" as developed in the present book, a different picture emerges.

5. I am using here a series of terms—such as *submission*, *oppression*, *unfreedom*, *confinement*, and *imprisonment*—as synonymous for the purpose of designating their opposite, namely, an ideal freedom.

6. In other words, I am concerned here to read Kafka's plots of confinement as giving us the means to think of freedom philosophically. The figure of the cage in Kafka offers itself to a variety of different possible approaches, as demonstrated by the contributions to the book I coedited with Kiarina Kordela, *Freedom and Confinement in Modernity: Kafka's Cages*. I could, for example, mention the following: Stanley Corngold's contribution, "Special Views on Kafka's Cages," points to Max Weber's idea of the "iron cage" as a metaphor of modern capitalism. I was particularly intrigued by this idea, and I was fascinated to see it further elaborated in Stanley Corngold and Benno Wagner, *Frank Kafka: The Ghost in the Machine*. Chris Fleming and John O'Carroll showed me, in "Delusions of Agency: Kafka, Imprisonment, and Modern Victimhood," how it is also possible to do an anthropological study of Kafka's cages. John Mowitt "Kafka's Cage" made Kafka's plot of confinement reverberate with the music of John Cage and thereby confirmed in my mind that the cages Kafka constructs are illusions awaiting their self-implosion. And so on. I will have occasion in the course of this book to refer to all the essays collected in *Freedom and Confinement in Modernity: Kafka's Cages*. I would like to register here my gratitude for the intellectual stimulation generated by each chapter in the volume, which formed the indispensable basis for writing the present book.

7. Erica Weitzman, "Almost Necessary: Kafka's Kantian Situation Comedy," *Modern Language Notes* 126 (2011), 590–613. For a more recent book, see Peter Rehberg, *Lachen Lesen: Zur Komik der Moderne bei Kafka* (Bielefeld, Germany: Transcript, 2007). See also the earlier book, Pavel Petr, *Kafkas Spiele: Selbststilisierung und literarische Komik* (Heidelberg: Carl Winter Universitätsverlag, 1992); and the article by Joseph Vogl, "Kafkas Komik," in *Kontinent Kafka: Mosse-Lectures an der Humboldt-Universität zu Berlin*, eds. Klaus R. Scherpe and Elisabeth Wagner (Berlin: Vorwerk 8, 2006), 72–87. Neither of these pays any attention to the connection between laughter and freedom. (I read Erica Weitzman's *Irony's Antics: Walser, Kafka, and the German Comic Tradition* (Evanston, ILL: Northwestern University Press, 2015) too late to engage with it here, but I highly recommend it as a perceptive and original work—and in particular her discussion of Kafka's comedy there significantly exceeds the scope of Weitzman's article mentioned above.)

8. Hannah Arendt insists most forcefully on the distinction between a conception of freedom as praxis within the political community, which characterizes the Greek polis, and the conception of the free will within the Christian tradition, which comes to dominate the Western idea of freedom. The most succinct presentation of this argument can be found in "What Is Freedom?,"

in *Between Past and Future: Six Exercises in Political Thought* (New York: Viking, 1961), 143–71. But this idea informs Arendt's thought from the early writings, such as *The Human Condition* (Chicago: University of Chicago Press, 1998) to the late, unfinished manuscript *The Life of the Mind* (New York: Harcourt, 1978).

9. For a fascinating account of the development of the idea of providence, see Genevieve Lloyd, *Providence Lost* (Cambridge, MA: Harvard University Press, 2008).

10. Antonio Negri has produced significant work that shows the mutual support between a hierarchical ontology and the stratification of constituted power. See, for instance, his *The Political Descartes: Reason, Ideology, and the Bourgeois Project*, trans. Matteo Mandarini and Alberto Toscano (London: Verso, 2006).

11. I am summarizing here Augustine's account as it can be found in Books XXII and XXIII of *The City of God Against the Pagans*, ed. and trans. R. W. Dyson (New York: Cambridge University Press, 1998). See also Augustine's *On the Free Choice of the Will, on Grace and Free Choice, and Other Writings*, ed. Peter King (Cambridge, UK: Cambridge University Press, 2010).

12. The classic account of the Augustinian theodicy is John Hick, *Evil and the God of Love* (New York: Palgrave Macmillan, 2010 [1st ed. 1966]).

13. Quoted in Walter Benjamin, "Franz Kafka," *Selected Writings*, Vol. 4, eds. Michael W. Jennings, Gary Smith, and Howard Eiland (Cambridge, MA: Belknap, 2003), 798.

14. Gustav Janouch, *Conversations with Kafka* (London: Derek Verschoyle, 1953). See also the final section of chapter 3.

15. I should note here that I do not intend to explore every facet of laughter in Kafka or to present a comprehensive theory of laughter in general. Instead, I am concerned with how laughter comes to deconstruct the separation of an ideal world from a fallen world, and thus to derail the operation of the free will. For this reason, I have intentionally refrained from extensive digressions into various theories of laughter—such as, for instance, Freud's or Bergson's. And I have not indexed all references to laughter in Kafka's manuscripts, unless they are directly related to the free will. For instance, there is a famous letter to Felice, dated January 8–9, 1913, in which Kafka describes how he had an uncontrollable bout of laughter during an audience with the president of the insurance company he worked for—an occasion "tantamount to meeting the Emperor," as he writes. The president is described as an imperial figure with unassailable authority (*auctoritas*). And, as is well-known, the most effective way to undermine authority is to laugh at it. Hence, Kafka's laughter in front of the president is qualitatively different from laughter at the illusion of the free will, which explains my decision not to discuss instances such as the one in the January 1913 letter.

16. Isaiah Berlin concedes that the conception of freedom that relies on the free will of the individual is "absent in the ancient world" and cannot be

found in other civilizations, such as the Chinese. Isaiah Berlin, "Two Concepts of Liberty," in *Liberty*, ed. Henry Hardy (Oxford, UK: Oxford University Press, 2002), 176.

17. Ibid., 168.

18. Ibid., 168.

19. Kant repeatedly returns to this issue. The entire *Metaphysics of Morals* can be read as an attempt to bring the moral realm into communication with the political realm. Another significant attempt is made in the larger part of "Perpetual Peace"—the part that follows the articles.

20. Berlin, "Two Concepts of Liberty," 174.

21. Michael Foucault defines biopolitics for the first time in the final lecture of his course *Society Must Be Defended: Lectures at the Collège de France 1975–1976*, trans. David Macey (New York: Picador, 2003).

22. Theodor Adorno, "Notes on Kafka," in *Prisms*, eds. Samuel and Shierry Weber (London: Neville Spearman, 1967), 256–57. For an overview of Adorno's engagement with Kafka, see Brian O'Connor, "On the Mimesis of Reification: Adorno's Critical Theoretical Interpretation of Kafka," in *Philosophy and Kafka*, eds. Brendan Moran and Carlo Salzani (Lanham, MD: Lexington, 2013), 229–42.

23. For a detailed discussion of the separation of ancient and modern sovereignty from biopolitics in Foucault, see Vardoulakis, *Sovereignty and Its Other: Toward the Dejustification of Violence* (New York: Fordham University Press, 2013), chapter 5.

24. Howard Caygill shows that Derrida's failure to mention the publication of the parable in journals during Kafka's lifetime is actually damaging for Derrida's argument. See Caygill's "Kafka and Derrida *Before the Laws*," in Kordela and Vardoulakis, *Freedom and Confinement in Modernity: Kafka's Cages*, 49–59.

25. Jacques Derrida, "Before the Law," in *Acts of Literature*, ed. Derek Attridge, trans. Avital Ronell and Christine Roulston (New York: Routledge, 1992), 181–220.

26. Ibid., 185–88.

27. Ibid., 203.

28. Ibid., 204.

29. Gilles Deleuze and Félix Guattari, *Kafka: Towards a Minor Literature*, trans. Dana Polan (Minneapolis: University of Minnesota Press, 1986), 6. I will refrain here from entering into a discussion of what the key, and much-discussed, term "minor literature" means. For an astute analysis, see Gregg Lambert, "The Bachelor-Machine: Kafka and the Question of a Minor Literature," in *Franz Kafka: Minority Report*, eds. Petr. Kouba and Tomáš Pivoda (Prague: Literraria Pragnesia, 2011), 7–31.

30. Deleuze and Guattari, *Kafka*, 41.

31. Walter Benjamin, [Notes on Kafka], *Gesamelte Schriften*, eds. Rolf Tiedemann and Hermann Schweppenhäuser (Frankfurt am Main: Suhrkamp, 1991), 2.3:1262.

32. Kafka, *Amerika*, trans. Willa and Edwin Muir (New York: Schocken, 1962), 297–98. For a more extensive discussion of this scene, see the section titled "Ethical Laughter: The Nature Theater of Oklahoma" in chapter 3.

33. I cannot here do a detailed reading of Benjamin's essay on Kafka. See, however, chapter 5 of Dimitris Vardoulakis, *The Doppelgänger: Literature's Philosophy* (New York: Fordham University Press, 2010) for a lengthy analysis as well as references to the secondary literature.

34. Benjamin, "Franz Kafka," 795.

35. Ibid., 818, trans. modified/"Franz Kafka: Zur sehnten Wiederkehr seines Todestages," *Gesammelte Schriften*, eds. Rolf Tiedemann and Hermann Schweppenhäuser (Frankfurt am Main: Suhrkamp, 1991), 2.2, 437.

36. Kafka, cited in Benjamin, "Franz Kafka," 815–16/437, trans. modified.

37. For another reading of the story, see Winfried Kudszus, "Kafka's Cage and Circus," in Alan Udoff, ed., *Kafka and the Contemporary Critical Performance* (Bloomington: Indiana University Press, 1987), 158–64.

38. Benjamin, "Franz Kafka," 816/437.

39. Franz Kafka, *Letters to Felice*, eds. Erich Hellen and Jürgen Born, trans. James Stern and Elizabeth Duckworth (New York: Schocken, 1973), dated January 14 to 15, 1913.

40. If we take this prison within which writing flourishes as the space of ideal freedom, and the subsequent dissolution of ideal freedom in the moment of madness, then the structure of this letter is remarkably similar to the structure of "A Hunger Artist." See my reading of this story in chapter 3.

41. I suggested in the beginning that Kafka's cages are related to Kafka's plots of confinement. I am trying to read here this letter to Felice as part of a "plot" that Kafka constructs in his correspondence—a plot to marry Felice on his own terms, for which he has recourse to his characteristic laughter.

42. For an insightful review of the volume, written shortly after its publication, see Siegfried Kracauer, "Franz Kafka: On His Posthumous Works," in *The Mass Ornament: The Weimar Essays*, trans. Thomas Y. Levin (Cambridge, MA: Harvard University Press, 1995), 267–78.

43. Brod is referring here explicitly to the Zürau aphorisms, which contain references to the Indestructible. Blanchot notes that the Indestructible is a concept that Brod himself develops. Thus Brod's interpretation overplays a concept that Kafka had borrowed from Brod's writings. See also chapter 2.

44. Brod, *Kafka*, p. 49. See also Max Brod, *Verzweiflung und Erlösung im Werk Franz Kafkas* (Frankfurt am Main: Fischer, 1959).

45. Franz Kafka, *The Zürau Aphorisms*, trans. Michael Hofmann (London: Harvill Secker, 2006). Hereafter referred to in text by aphorism number.

46. See Roberto Calasso, "Veiled Splendor," trans. Geoffrey Brock, in Kafka, *The Zürau Aphorisms*, 109–34.

47. The idea about the relation between mediated freedom and the free will that I present here parallels the idea of the relation between democracy and

sovereignty that I articulate in *The Ruse of Sovereignty: Stasis and Democracy* (New York: Fordham University Press, forthcoming 2017).

2. The Abrahamic Laughter: The Topography of Freedom in "The Judgment" and *The Metamorphosis*

1. Maurice Blanchot, "Kafka and the Work's Demand," *The Space of Literature*, trans. Ann Smock (Lincoln: University of Nebraska Press, 1982), 67.

2. Blanchot's fascination with Kafka's *Diaries* has to do with the fact that Kafka actually uses the same notebooks to write most of his short stories and often sketches for his longer writings too. It is literally in the same pages, then, that Blanchot discovers an Abrahamic figure who is called to sacrifice a nonexistent son, and the series of figures who suffer confinement. See Blanchot, "Kafka and the Work's Demand," 57.

3. Ibid. 61–2.

4. On Abraham and modern philosophy and literature in general, as well as for detailed reflections on Kafka in particular, see the exceptional book by Chris Danta, *Literature Suspends Death: Sacrifice and Storytelling in Kierkegaard, Kafka and Blanchot* (London: Continuum, 2011).

5. I have developed the distinction between the theologico-political and political theology in Dimitris Vardoulakis, "Spinoza's Empty Law: The Possibility of Political Theology," in *Spinoza Beyond Philosophy*, ed. Beth Lord (Edinburgh: Edinburgh University Press, 2012), 135–48. See also chapter 4.

6. See Blanchot's comparison between *The Trial* and *The Castle* in "Kafka and the Work's Demand," 77–80. Cf. also Maurice Blanchot, "Kafka and Brod," in *Friendship*, trans. Elizabeth Rottenberg (Stanford, CA: Stanford University Press, 1997), 246–47.

7. Jane Bennett, "Kafka, Genealogy, and the Spiritualization of Politics," *Journal of Politics* 56.3 (1994), 665.

8. On resistance and counter-resistance, see Howard Caygill, *Resistance: A Philosophy of Defiance* (London: Bloomsbury, 213); and Dimitris Vardoulakis, *Sovereignty and Its Other: Toward the Dejustification of Violence* (New York: Fordham University Press, 2013), chapter 5.

9. See also chapter 5 for an extended discussion of the figure of substitution.

10. James Martel, *Textual Conspiracies: Walter Benjamin, Idolatry and Political Theory* (Ann Arbor: University of Michigan Press, 2011), 63.

11. Cited in Blanchot, "Kafka and the Work's Demand," 68.

12. Cf. Henry Sussman, *Afterimages of Modernity: Structure and Indifference in Twentieth-Century Literature* (Baltimore, MD: Johns Hopkins University Press, 1990), 95–122.

13. Blanchot, "Kafka and the Work's Demand," 70.

14. Franz Kafka, *The Diaries*, ed. Max Brod, trans. Joseph Kresh and Martin Greenberg (London: Vintage, 1999), 213.

15. Ibid., 214.

16. Claude-Edmonde Magny, "The Objective Depiction of Absurdity," *Quarterly Review of Literature*, 2.3 (1945), 211–27.

17. Kafka, *The Diaries*, 213–14/*Tagebücher*, eds. Hans-Gerd Koch, Michael Müller, and Malcolm Pasley (Frankfurt am Main: Fischer, 2002), 462–63.

18. Max Brod, *Franz Kafka: A Biography*, trans. G. Humphreys Roberts and Richard Winston (New York: Schocken, 1960), 141.

19. Ibid., 49.

20. Maurice Blanchot, "The Last Word," *Friendship*, trans. Elizabeth Rottenberg (Stanford, CA: Stanford University Press, 1997), 255.

21. In a brilliant analysis of the function of the legal concept of property in Kafka, Peter Fenves suggests an entirely different notion of the religious in Kafka's work, one that characterizes a community without possessions that are regulated by church or state. See Peter Fenves, " 'Workforce without Possessions': Kafka, 'Social Justice,' and the Word *Religion*," in *Freedom and Confinement in Modernity: Kafka's Cages*, eds. Kiarina Kordela and Dimitris Vardoulakis (New York: Palgrave, 2011), 107–26.

22. Walter Sokel, *The Myth of Power and the Self: Essays on Franz Kafka* (Detroit: Wayne State University Press, 2002), 297, 300.

23. Stanley Corngold both affirms this gnostic element and shows that it need not be just an assertion of the gnostic perspective, or of any religious perspective for that matter. Corngold instead describes what he calls a "gnosticism with a small-cap" because "Gnostic elements permeate Kafka's writing; but because they do not supersaturate it, his writing is *tout dit* a lower-case gnosticism, importantly including mythic elements of his own devising." Stanley Corngold, *Lambent Traces: Franz Kafka* (Princeton, NJ: Princeton University Press, 2004), 11. My own analysis here is indebted to Corngold's distinction. See also the further refinement of this argument in chapter 8 of Stanley Corngold and Benno Wagner, *Frank Kafka: The Ghost in the Machine*. See, finally, Stanley Corngold, "Kafka's Later Stories and Aphorisms," in *The Cambridge Companion to Kafka*, ed. Julian Preece, 93–110.

24. Theodor Adorno, "Notes on Kafka," in *Prisms*, eds. Samuel and Shierry Weber, 245–71.

25. Franz Kafka, "The Judgment," trans. Willa and Edwin Muir, in *The Complete Stories* (New York: Schocken, 1995)/"Die Urteil," in *Drucke zu Lebzeiten*, eds. Wolf Kitler, Hans-Gerd Koch and Gerhard Neuman (Frankfurt am Main: Fischer, 2002). All references to "The Judgment" are made in-text parenthetically.

26. Stanley Corngold points out that the same process of undermined subjective identity pertains not only to his characters but to Kafka himself: "His self is defined not by particular interests but by its narrating attentiveness to the

products of a dream play in which he is the dreamer. The self is precisely its lucid tolerance of whatever arises in the place where control, for the sake of mastery and reward, has been relinquished." *Franz Kafka: The Necessity of Form* (Ithaca, NY: Cornell University Press, 1988), 160–61.

27. On letter writing as practiced by Kafka himself and as depicted in "The Judgment," see Bernhard Siegert, *Relays: Literature as an Epoch of the Postal System* (Stanford, CA: Stanford University Press, 1999), 207–18.

28. The second time that Georg repeats twice that he is happy occurs when he recounts to his father what he had written on this letter: "If he's a good friend of mine, I said to myself, my being happily engaged should make him happy too" (82).

29. The Muirs' translation refers to the friend from Petersburg as "a returned prodigal" (77). This reference to the prodigal is never made explicit in Kafka's own text, although, as I suggest, it is implied in it. Jill Robbins discusses the theme of the prodigal son in Kafka's works, but she does not mention "The Judgment." See her *Prodigal Son/Elder Brother: Interpretation and Alterity in Augustine, Petrarch, Kafka, Levinas* (Chicago: University of Chicago Press, 1991), 81–99.

30. Brod, *Franz Kafka*, 129. The word "Verkehr" in German means both "traffic" and "intercourse." It can also denote the communication that takes place over a telephone line. Henry Sussman notes the use of "Verkehr in this way in *The Castle*, where it denotes the exchanges between the castle and the villagers." See Sussman, *Afterimages of Modernity*, 101. See also Corngold and Wagner, *The Ghost in the Machine*, 134.

31. All of Blanchot's essays are collected in his *De Kafka à Kafka* (Paris: Gallimard, 1981).

32. For the notion of the outside in Blanchot, see Leslie Hill, *Blanchot: Extreme Contemporary* (London: Routledge, 1997), 121–27. For the related concept of the neuter, which I cannot deal with in any detail here, see Christophe Bident, "The Movements of the Neuter," in *After Blanchot: Literature, Criticism, Philosophy*, eds. Leslie Hill, Brian Nelson, and Dimitris Vardoulakis (Newark: University of Delaware Press, 2005), 13–34.

33. Blanchot, "Kafka and the Work's Demand," 70.

34. Ibid., 71.

35. Ibid., 73.

36. See Kevin Hart, *Losing the Power to Say "I"* (Melbourne, 1996).

37. Michael Foucault, "Maurice Blanchot: The Thought from Outside," in *Foucault/Blanchot*, trans. Brian Massumi (New York: Zone Books, 1987), 22.

38. Ibid., 38–39.

39. Maurice Blanchot, "Reading Kafka," *The Work of Fire*, trans. Charlotte Mandell (Stanford, CA: Stanford University Press, 1995), 7.

40. Blanchot, "Kafka and the Work's Demand," 77.

41. Ibid., 79.

42. Franz Kafka, *Metamorphosis*, trans. Willa and Edwin Muir, in *The Complete Stories* (New York: Schocken, 1995), 89–139, in this section cited parenthetically in text without further qualification.

43. Blanchot, "Reading Kafka," 9.

44. Ibid., 10.

45. Brod, *Franz Kafka*, 134.

46. Franz Kafka, *Letters to Friends, Family, and Editors*, trans. Richard and Clara Winston (New York: Schocken, 1987).

47. Eric Santner, *My Own Private Germany: Daniel Paul Schreber's Secret History of Modernity* (Princeton, NJ: Princeton University Press, 1986), 135–37. Santner observes: "Gregor's peculiar attachment to this piece of pornographic kitsch is obviously central to the text. Indeed, the entire story seems to crystallize around it as an elaborate punishment scenario called forth by guilt-ridden sexual obsessions. The indications of putrescence that proliferate in the course of the story suggest fantasies of the consequences of a young man's autoerotic activities. In this perspective, many hitherto unintelligible details take on importance" (Ibid., 136).

48. Gilles Deleuze, *Masochism: Coldness and Cruelty*, in Gilles Deleuze, *Masochism: Coldness and Cruelty*; and Leopold von Sacher-Masoch, *Venus in Furs*, trans. Jean McNeil and Aude Willm (New York: Zone, 1991).

49. Danta also points to the essential similarity of the transformation of the sister: "The problem is that Grete's apparently natural transformation might not eclipse the monstrosity of Gregor's because it might not in fact be of a different order to Gregor's." Danta, *Literature Suspends Death*, 75.

3. The Return of the Body: The Ethics of Laughter

1. Emmanuel Levinas, *Totality and Infinity: An Essay on Exteriority*, trans. Alphonso Lingis (Pittsburgh: Duquesne University Press, 1969). All references to this book in this section are given in text without further clarification.

2. I am indebted to Howard Caygill's *Levinas and the Political* (London: Routledge, 2002) for helping me realize that Levinas's trajectory is just as much political as it is ethical. Caygill also provides important thoughts on Levinas's development of the idea of freedom.

3. See Dimitris Vardoulakis, *The Ruse of Sovereignty: Stasis and Democracy* (New York: Fordham University Press, forthcoming 2017); and *Stasis: On Agonistic Democracy* (New York: Fordham University Press, forthcoming 2017).

4. Caygill, *Levinas and the Political*, 121.

5. The fear that the privileging of alterity would make freedom disappear is recorded in the philosophical tradition as the accusation of determinism against

Spinoza. See, for instance, Levinas, *Totality and Infinity*, 105. Despite Levinas's seeming dismissal of Spinoza, they have a lot in common, as Hent de Vries has shown in "Levinas, Spinoza, and the Theologico-Political Meaning of Scripture," in *Political Theologies: Public Religions in a Post-Secular World*, eds. Hent de Vries and Lawrence E. Sullivan (New York: Fordham University Press, 2006), 232–48. See also the last section of the present chapter for parallels between Kafka and Spinoza. I take up the connection between Kafka and Spinoza in much more detail in chapter 4.

6. For a different attempt to bring Kafka in conversation with Levinas, see Laura Stahman, "Franz Kafka's 'The Burrow' as Model of Ipseity in Levinasian Theory," *Mosaic* 37.3 (2004), 19–32.

7. For an account for the two most famous but very different versions of the Gyges story, see Gabriel Danzig, "Rhetoric and the Ring: Herodotus and Plato on the Story of Gyges as a Politically Expedient Tale," *Greece & Rome* 55.2 (2008), 169–92.

8. Cf. Plato, *Republic*, trans. Paul Shorey (Cambridge, MA: Harvard University Press, 2003), 359d–360a.

9. Caygill, *Levinas and the Political*, 78.

10. Kafka, *Amerika*, trans. Willa and Edwin Muir (New York: Schocken, 1962)/*Der Verschollene*, ed. Von Jost Schillemeit (Frankfurt am Main: Fischer, 2002). All references to these editions will be provided parenthetically within the text.

11. Walter Benjamin, [Notes on Kafka], *Gesammelte Schriften*, eds. Rolf Tiedemann and Hermann Schweppenhäuser (Frankfurt am Main: Suhrkamp, 1991), 2.3:1262.

12. For a discussion of Benjamin's essay on Kafka, see my *The Doppelgänger: Literature's Philosophy* (New York: Fordham University Press, 2010), chapter 5.

13. In an exhilarating reading of *Amerika*, Henry Sussman describes this as Kafka's most political work precisely because it depicts conditions of oppression. See Sussman, *Idylls of the Wanderer: Outside in Literature and Theory* (New York: Fordham University Press, 2007), 178–98.

14. Caygill's article is published in the journal *College Literature*, 38.1 (2011), 1–14. I will present here the general point he raises about the publication history of *Amerika* and its effect on the reception of the novel and its last chapter in particular, and I will eschew the discussion of Arendt, as Caygill himself uses it as indicative and in the context of the discussion here it will take away from the point that I am making.

15. The further inference is made that the Nature Theater of Oklahoma is the *only* space in Kafka's works where such a religious experience of freedom takes place. In an important article, Peter Fenves analyzes the concept of property in various texts by Kafka, showing that he develops a notion of the religious that relies on a sense of community without property. It would be very

interesting to apply Fenves's findings to the Nature Theater of Oklahoma—which Fenves does not do—to not only challenge the idea that it is the only space where redemption really takes places in Kafka's works, but to challenged perceived ideas about what constitutes the religious in that space. See Fenves, "'Workforce without Possessions': Kafka, 'Social Justice,' and the Word *Religion*," in *Freedom and Confinement in Modernity: Kafka's Cages*, eds. Kiarina Kordela and Dimitris Vardoulakis, 107–26.

16. Caygill, "The Fate of the Pariah," 2.

17. Ibid., 9, 14. We know from Brod that Kafka owned a copy and very much liked Arthur Holitscher's travel account *Amerika heute und morgen*, which was serialized in 1911 and 1912. For further discussion of the connection between Holitscher's travel account and Kafka's novel, see Anne Fuchs, "A Psychoanalytic Reading of *The Man Who Disappeared*," in *The Cambridge Companion to Kafka*, ed. Julian Preece, 27; Mark M. Anderson, *Kafka's Clothes: Ornament and Aestheticism in the Habsburg Fin de Siècle* (Oxford, UK: Clarendon, 1992), 104–5; and Hans-Peter Rüsing, "Quellenforschung als Interpretation: Holitscher und Soukups Reiseberichte über Amerika und Kafkas Roman *Der Verschollene*," *Modern Austrian Literature* 20 (1987), 1–38.

18. Caygill, "The Fate of the Pariah," 9. Caygill supports this conclusion by noting that the last chapter of *Amerika* is written in 1914, that is, the year in which Kafka writes works such as "In the Penal Colony."

19. Stanley Corngold and Benno Wagner arrive at a similar conclusion through a very different kind of analysis, namely, by comparing the Nature Theater of Oklahoma to Weber's concept of the "iron cage." See *Franz Kafka: The Ghost in the Machine*, 36–37.

20. Heinz Politzer suggests that at the end of *Amerika* Karl Rossmann "has lost his name and will never more be heard of." Politzer then goes on to link this idea to the original title of the novel, *Der Veschollene*: "From now on the nameless one will be what he always was in Kafka's mind, *Der Verschollene*." Politzer, *Franz Kafka: Parable and Paradox* (Ithaca, NY: Cornell University Press, 1966), 162.

21. One could possibly ask the following question here: How far does the similarity between Kafka and Levinas actually go, given that Levinas would understand the Other only as human? The question essentially asks whether Levinas's notion of the ethical actually remains trapped in humanism. It can be argued, however, that it is a profound misunderstanding of Levinas to ask whether the Other is human or nonhuman. Instead, the Other is the "Jewish" challenge to the "Greek" question of existence. Therefore, one should not try to define the Other as such and thereby ontologize or totalize it—one cannot ask whether the Other is human or nonhuman—but one should rather seek to explore the formal relations that arise when the "Jew" and the "Greek" come face to face. Cf. Jacques Derrida, "Violence and Metaphysics: An Essay on the Thought of Emmanuel Levinas," in *Writing and Difference*, trans. Allan Bass (London: Routledge, 2002), 97–192.

Although I cannot examine these issues in any detail here, the implicit argument is that such a notion of relationality is really what binds Kafka and Levinas.

22. This is what Theodor Adorno calls the "deadly aesthetic error": "Kafka's works protected themselves against the deadly aesthetic error of equating the philosophy that an author pumps into a work with its metaphysical substance. Were this so, the work of art would be stillborn: it would exhaust itself in what it says and would not unfold itself in time. To guard against this short-circuit, which jumps directly to the significance intended by the work, the first rule is: take everything literally; cover up nothing with concepts invoked from above. Kafka's authority is textual." "Notes on Kafka," in *Prisms*, eds. Samuel and Shierry Weber, 247.

23. Franz Kafka, "A Report to an Academy," trans. Willa and Edwin Muir, in *The Complete Stories* (New York: Schocken, 1995)/"Ein Bericht für eine Akademie," in *Drucke zu Lebzeiten*, eds. Wolf Kitler, Hans-Gerd Koch, and Gerhard Neuman (Frankfurt am Main: Fischer, 2002). Hereafter cited parenthetically in the text.

24. In other words, the notion of play-acting effects the separation between the animal and the human, since it is only humans who are meant to have hypocritical abilities.

25. Cf. Christophe Bident, "How Is the Trapeze Possible?," in *Freedom and Confinement in Modernity: Kafka's Cages*, eds. Kiarina Kordela and Dimitris Vardoulakis, 204–6.

26. For a different analysis of the sense of freedom put forward by Rotpeter, see Fenves, " 'Workforce without Possessions,' " 115–17.

27. Gilles Deleuze and Félix Guattari, *Kafka: Towards a Minor Literature*, trans. Dana Polan (Minneapolis: University of Minnesota Press, 1986), 41.

28. Ibid., 35.

29. Marthe Robert provides illuminating insights on Kafka's humor by departing from a comparison with *Don Quixote* in *The Old and the New: From Don Quixote to Kafka*, trans. Carol Cosman (Berkeley: University of California Press, 1977). Robert argues that "quixotism" is the drive to relate literature to the real, the correlation of work and life that characterizes modernity. She further identifies the connection between humor and imitation as one of the ways that this quixotism is carried out: "Like those insects who protect themselves against their nearest and strongest enemies by a mimetic ruse, quixotism apes the manner, tone, and gestures of its anonymous adversary, whose indifferent, self-interested or simply lazy conformity it perceives on all sides." Robert compares Cervantes's creation to Kafka's land surveyor in *The Castle*, but this description of imitation is even more apt to Rotpeter. The ape's imitation is related to life so long as freedom is an issue that has to do with "our" world. Robert continues: "Here, however, the tactic of simulation is not only a defensive consideration, it is a formidable weapon" (27). Imitation exposes that which is imitated and ultimately dismantles or deconstruct it. Rotpeter imitates the human desire for

freedom to show its absurdity. But this absurdity can only be demonstrated if the ape imitates the humans, if the ape appears to have humanized itself.

30. Franz Kafka, "A Hunger Artist"/"Ein Hungerkünstler," in *Drucke zu Lebzeiten*. Hereafter cited parenthetically in the text.

31. According to Walter Vandereycken and Ron van Deth, in 1926 there were six simultaneous performances by hunger artists in Berlin. *From Fasting Saints to Anorexic Girls: The History of Self-Starvation* (New York: New York University Press, 1994), 88. See also Peter Payer, *Hungerkünstler in Wien: Eine verschwundene Attraktion (1896–1926)* (Vienna: Sonderzahl, 2002).

32. See Astrid Lange-Kirchheim, "Nachrichten vom italienischen Hungerkünstler Giovanni Succi: Neue Materialien zu Kafkas *Hungerkünstler*," *Freiburger literaturpsychologische Gespräche: Jahrbuch für Literatur und Psychoanalyse* 18 (1999), 315–40; and Breon Mitchell, "Kafka and the Hunger Artists," in *Kafka and the Contemporary Critical Performance*, ed. Alan Udoff (Bloomington: Indiana University Press, 1987), 236–55.

33. See Vandereycken and Deth, *From Fasting Saints to Anorexic Girls*, 14–32; for the Jewish tradition specifically, see Eliezier Diamond, *Holy Men and Hunger Artists: Fasting and Asceticism in Rabbinic Culture* (Oxford, UK: Oxford University Press, 2004).

34. For Gregory Palamas, the major defender of Hesychasm, see John Meyendorff's classic *A Study of Gregory Palamas*, 2nd ed. (Bedfordshire, UK: Faith Press, 1974). For a description of the techniques of the movement, see Kallistos of Diokleia, "Praying with the Body: The Hesychast Method and non-Christian Parallels," *Sobornost* 14.2 (1993), 6–35.

35. Aldous Huxley, for instance, provides an explanation of why extreme fasting came to be associated with mystical experiences:

> By reducing the amount of available sugar, fasting lowers the brain's biological efficiency and so makes possible the entry into consciousness of material possessing no survival value. Moreover, by causing a vitamin deficiency, it removes from the blood that known inhibitor of visions, nicotinic acid. Another inhibitor of visionary experience is ordinary, everyday, perceptual experience. Experimental psychologists have found that, if you confine a man to a "restricted environment," where there is no light, no sound, nothing to smell and, if you put him in a tepid bath, only one, almost imperceptible thing to touch, the victim will very soon start "seeing things," "hearing things" and having strange bodily sensations. Milarepa, in his Himalayan cavern, and the anchorites of the Thebaid followed essentially the same procedure and got essentially the same results. A thousand pictures of the Temptations of St. Anthony bear witness to

the effectiveness of restricted diet and restricted environment. Aldous Huxley, *The Doors of Perception* (London: Penguin, 1959), 74, and cf. 118–19.

36. It has often been observed that Kafka was doing the proofs of "The Hunger Artist" as he was dying, no longer able to eat due to his disease. See, for example, Ernst Pawel, *The Nightmare of Reason: A Life of Franz Kafka* (New York: Vintage, 1985), 445. The lack of nutrition may be a common feature, but the differences seem to me more important: Kafka was forced to refrain from nutrition because of his illness and, even more importantly, he did not construct this fasting into a spiritual quest.

37. Contrary to the Muirs' translation, Kafka never talks of a "professional" hunger artist. Indeed, his disdain for the commercial aspect of his trade may be evidence to argue that Kafka had primarily in mind the religious, rather than the "professional," *Hungerkünstler*. From this perspective, the correct translation of the title may be "A Fasting Artist."

38. For Felix Weltsch, in *Religion und Humor in Leben und Werk Kafkas* (Berlin: Herbig, 1957), the humor in "A Hunger Artist" consists in the chaotic string of reasons proffered for the fasting—as entertainment, as business, as a means of attracting admiration—which are resolved in the final explanation that the artist was disgusted by food. According to Weltsch, this explanation reorders the crazy chaos of different reasons (83). Such an interpretation sees the work as a self-subsisting entity, whose only connection to the "outside" is the notion of unity, that is, the religious impulse. Conversely, the interpretation of humor proposed here locates laughter and the connection to the "outside" in the way that unity—such as the unity of the ideal of freedom—is shattered. Whereas for Weltsch, Kafka's humor entails the reconstitution of a totality, for the present interpretation laughter is the effect of totality's impossibility.

39. This is not to say, of course, that every instance when the starting point is imprisonment would necessarily lead to this joyous reversal. A case in point is Josef K. in *The Trial*. Josef K. has his chance to let the joyous laughter reverberate at the end of the dialogue with the priest in the Cathedral. However, he fails to grasp the comical implications of concluding the conversation by saying "*Die Lüge wird zur Weltordnung gemacht.*" For a closer analysis, see chapter 4. But the point is that a typology of laughter in Kafka is not exhausted in the distinction between a joyous and what I will call in a moment "lugubrious" laughter. See also the following note.

40. As I indicated in the note above, the typology of laughter in Kafka is not exhausted in the distinction between a joyous and a lugubrious laughter. There is a third major category that I cannot discuss here in detail but I would like, nevertheless, to outline briefly. It is characterized by a hysterical or surface laughter that is reminiscent of farce. One of the best examples of this laughter is

the histrionics of the soldier and the condemned man in "In the Penal Colony." In general (although this point needs a careful reading of Kafka's texts), this kind of laughter is only associated with secondary characters. That's why Walter Benjamin is correct in his essay on Kafka to indicate that the secondary characters are outside the nexus of the world of law and the Nature Theater. See chapter 5 for further analysis.

41. Janouch, Gustav, *Conversations with Kafka* (London: Derek Verschoyle, 1953), 55. I am quoting from Janouch's volume despite the doubts about their provenance. It is fascinating that in the conversations, Kafka functions in a certain sense as Janouch's other. From that point of view, the issue of whether the conversations are accurate transcripts is of secondary importance. I also note that the citations are to the first edition, but they can all be found in the second edition as well.

42. Cf. A. Kiarina Kordela, *$urplus: Spinoza, Lacan* (New York: SUNY Press, 2007).

43. Janouch, *Conversations*, 65.

44. *Ibid.*, 74.

4. The Law of Freedom: Reading *The Tria*l through Spinoza

1. Hannah Arendt, "Franz Kafka, Appreciated Anew," in *Reflections on Literature and Culture* (Stanford, CA: Stanford University Press, 2007), 106–7.

2. We read the following entry in Kafka's diary, dated December 31, 1914: "Have been working since August, in general not little and not badly." He then provides a list of what he has written in that period. And he concludes: "I don't know why I am drawing up this summary, it's not at all like me!" Franz Kafka, *The Diaries*, ed. Max Brod, trans. Joseph Kresh and Martin Greenberg (London: Vintage, 1999).

3. The English translation of the *Trial* referenced in this chapter is Franz Kafka, *The Trial*, trans. Willa and Edwin Muir, rev. trans. E. M. Butler (New York: Schocken, 1995)/*Der Prozeß*, eds. Malcolm Paysley (Frankfurt am Main: Fischer, 2002). All references to *The Trial* are provided parenthetically in the text.

4. Kiarina Kordela describes this encagement in terms of the Kafkaesque: "The Kafkaesque is the paradoxical cage one can be confined in only by being outside, and vice versa." Kordela, "Kafkaesque: (Secular) Kabbalah and Allegory," in *Freedom and Confinement in Modernity: Kafka's Cages*, eds. Kordela and Vardoulakis, 141.

5. Max Brod, *Franz Kafka: A Biography*, trans. G. Humphreys Roberts and Richard Winston (New York: Schocken, 1960), 178.

6. This is consistent with the insight that "Kafka's works have a striking ability to anticipate their own reception, to inscribe into themselves the logics

of readings to come," as Stanley Corngold and Benno Wagner put it in *Frank Kafka: The Ghost in the Machine*, 75. There is also a different way to approach the connection between Kafka and biopolitics, which I will not be discussing here. This consists in paying attention to his legal work, recently published as Franz Kafka, *The Office Writings*, eds. Stanley Corngold, Jack Greenberg, and Benno Wagner, trans. Eric Patton with Ruth Hein (Princeton, NJ: Princeton University Press, 2008). See also Corngold and Wagner, *The Ghost in the Machine*, chapter 10.

7. Michael Foucault, *The Birth of Biopolitics: Lectures at the Collège de France, 1978–79*, trans. Graham Burchell (New York: Palgrave, 2008), 41–42.

8. Cf. Nikolas Rose, *Powers of Freedom: Reframing Political Thought* (Cambridge, UK: Cambridge University Press, 2004). Rose, writing prior to the publication of Foucault's lectures on *The Birth of Biopolitics*, but still influenced by Foucault's other writings, also diagnoses the subordination of freedom to government—with the important difference, however, that for Rose this contains a redemptive potential. In other words, Rose, even before the term "affirmative biopolitics" becomes common currency in the vocabulary of political philosophy, describes a positive "spin" of the subordination of freedom to government. The term *affirmative biopolitics* has come to the fore through the work of Roberto Esposito. For a succinct presentation of his position, see his essay "Totalitarianism or Biopolitics: Toward a Philosophical Interpretation of the Twentieth Century," in Esposito, *The Terms of the Political: Community, Immunity, Biopolitics*, trans. Rhiannon Noel Welch (New York: Fordham University Press, 2013), 100–11. In her introductory essay to the same volume, Vanessa Lemm notes that this chapter "offers the hermeneutical key to understanding what is at stake in Esposito's rethinking of community," and that "the exclusive *either/or* [of this essay] stands at the center of a new and affirmative strategy for immunity." Lemm, "Introduction: Biopolitics and Community in Roberto Esposito," in *The Terms of the Political*, 3, 8.

9. Foucault, *Birth of Biopolitics*, 63–64.

10. One notable exception is Miguel Vatter's *The Republic of the Living: Biopolitics and the Critique of Civil Society* (New York: Fordham University Press, 2014). Vatter provides a brilliant analysis of biopolitics from the perspective of republicanism, which is incommensurate with antinomianism.

11. I use this theological vocabulary partly inspired by a description of biopolitics in Michael Hardt and Antonio Negri's *Empire* (Cambridge, MA: Harvard University Press, 2000), xiv–xv, and partly to allude to the possibility of the theological nesting within biopolitics—to which I return in the final section of the present chapter.

12. Henry Sussman, in *Around the Book: Systems and Literacy* (New York: Fordham University Press, 2011), 49–84, draws an incisive comparison between the graphic novel and what he calls "Kafka's visual imagination." This book of law that is in fact an erotic graphic novel forms part of the same visual universe Sussman describes.

13. If the law does indeed elide proscription in *The Trial*, then a relevant point can be raised (that I cannot, however, take up in any detail here) about the concluding remark of the novel, when Josef K. is executed "like a dog." If the law is an expression of desire, then being a "dog" is not an offensive appellative. Rather, it is a reiteration of the way that the elusive law of *The Trial* conceives of agency.

14. Patrick J. Glen, "The Deconstruction and Reification of Law in Kafka's 'Before the Law' and *The Trial*," *Southern California Interdisciplinary Law Journal* 17 (2007), 26 and passim.

15. The English translation of the *Tractatus* referenced in this chapter is Spinoza, *Theologico-Political Treatise*, in *Complete Works*, trans. Samuel Shirley, ed. Michael L. Morgan (Indianapolis, IN: Hackett, 2002). All references to the *Tractatus* in this section are provided parenthetically in the text.

16. For instance, we find the following comment in the transcript of "Power and Classical Natural Right," a lecture by Deleuze delivered on December 9, 1980: "[T]here are some very comical pages in Spinoza's *Ethics*. . . . It is a very particular kind of laughter and Spinoza is one of the most cheerful authors in the world. . . . It is Ethical laughter!" Available at http://www.webdeleuze.com/php/texte.php?cle=20&groupe=Spinoza&langue=2; Date of access: October 2006. And of Kafka, Deleuze and Guattari write: "He is an author who laughs with a profound joy, a *joie de vivre*, in spite of, or because of, his clownish declarations that he offers like a trap or a circus." Gilles Deleuze and Félix Guattari, *Kafka: Towards a Minor Literature*, 41. I will discuss further both of these assertions by Deleuze in due course.

17. The most explicit articulation of what I call here philonomianism—that is, the impossibility of disengaging being and the law, or the impossibility of positing a space outside the law—in chapter 4 of the *Tractatus Theologico-Politicus*. See Dimitris Vardoulakis, "Philonomianism: Spinoza and Arendt on Authority, Legality and History," *Theory & Event* (forthcoming).

18. That Spinoza's *Treatise* is about freedom is made clear from the subtitle, which says that the treatise is about the freedom to philosophize and to judge as necessary for the peace of the state. The subtitle says exactly: "Containing Various Disquisitions, By means of which it is shown not only that Freedom of Philosophising can be allowed in Preserving Piety and the Peace of the Republic: but also that it is not possible for such Freedom to be upheld except when accompanied by the Peace of the Republic and Piety Themselves."

19. My reading of Spinoza's *Tractatus Theologico-Politicus* here is based on, combines, and augments two earlier attempts: Dimitris Vardoulakis, "Spinoza's Empty Law: The Possibility of Political Theology," in *Spinoza Beyond Philosophy*, ed. Beth Lord (Edinburgh: Edinburgh University Press, 2012), 135–48; and Dimitris Vardoulakis, *Sovereignty and Its Other*, chapter 4.

20. For a discussion of this point, see Arthur Jacobson, "Prophesy without Prophets: Spinoza and Maimonides on Law and the Democracy of Knowledge,"

in *Spinoza Now*, ed. Dimitris Vardoulakis, (Minneapolis: University of Minnesota Press, 2011), 135–59.

21. Spinoza in the *Tractatus* describes this perception of necessity as superstition.

22. Alain Badiou, *Saint Paul: The Foundation of Universalism*, trans. Ray Braissier (Stanford, CA: Stanford University Press, 2003).

23. Étienne Balibar, *Spinoza and Politics*, trans. Peter Snowdon (London: Verso, 1998), 68.

24. I will return to this point in the last section to show how it differs fundamentally from the antinomianism and messianism of Agamben.

25. The opposition to teleology can be traced throughout Spinoza's work. It can already be found, for instance, in Part I of the *Ethics* where teleology is associated with the anthropomorphic understanding of God. See, for example, the "Appendix" to *Ethics*, Part I.

26. For the distinction between constituent power or *potentia* and constituted power or *potestas* in Spinoza, see Antonio Negri, *The Savage Anomaly: The Power of Spinoza's Metaphysics and Politics*, trans. Michael Hardt (Minneapolis: University of Minnesota Press, 2002).

27. Despite the great merit of clearly drawing the distinction between constituted and constituent power, Negri's interpretation of constituent power still fails to grasp that this distinction in Spinoza never leads to a separation of the two. I take this issue up in the chapter on Negri in *Stasis: On Agonistic Democracy* (New York: Fordham University Press, forthcoming).

28. This is why, I argue in *Sovereignty and Its Other*, in *The Ruse of Sovereignty*, and in *Stasis*, there must be something more primary than sovereignty. I name that other of sovereignty "agonistic democracy."

29. Cf. Vardoulakis, "Spinoza's Empty Law."

30. Deleuze, "Power and Classical Natural Right."

31. It is well known that "Before the Law" was also published independently as a short prose piece in Kafka's collection *A Country Doctor* (1919). What is less known is that it was previously published in journals three times. The first publication was in the Zionist journal *Selbstwehr: Unabhängige judische Wochenschrift*, in September 1915. This was followed by a publication in *Vom jüngsten Tag: Ein Almanach neuer Dichtung* in 1916, and in a second, amended edition of the same volume in 1917. See Franz Kafka, *Drucke zu Lebzeiten: Apparatband*, ed. Wolf Kittler, Hans-Gerd Koch and Gerhard Neumann (Frankfurt am Main: Fischer, 2002), 328.

32. Jacques Derrida starts from a different distinction, namely, the universality and the singularity of the law. See Derrida, "Before the Law," in *Acts of Literature*, ed. Derek Attridge, trans. Avital Ronell and Christine Roulston (New York: Routledge, 1992), 181–220. For a powerful discussion of freedom in Derrida and Spinoza, see Alexander Garcia Düttmann, "A Matter of Life and Death: Spinoza and Derrida," in *Spinoza Now*, ed. Dimitris Vardoulakis (Minneapolis:

University of Minnesota Press, 2011), 351–62. See also the analysis of Derrida's text above, in chapter 1.

33. See a recent discussion in Slavoj Zizek, *Iraq: The Borrowed Kettle* (London: Vero, 2004), 160–61.

34. As already noted, much of the impetus for the religious interpretations in general comes from Max Brod himself. In relation to *The Trial*, in particular, we need to note also the possible influences from the Jewish mystical tradition, which are thoroughly explored in Karl Erich Grözinger, *Kafka and Kabbalah*, trans. Susan Hecker Ray (New York: Continuum, 1994).

35. Augustine, *Confessions*, trans. Henry Chadwick (Oxford, UK: Oxford University Press, 1991). See also Jean-François Lyotard's discussion of this non-response in *The Confession of Augustine*, trans. Richard Beardsworth (Stanford, CA: Stanford University Press, 2000).

36. See Theodor Adorno's critique of the negative theological interpretation of Kafka in "Notes on Kafka," *Prisms*, eds. Samuel and Shierry Weber, 245–71.

37. I am not suggesting here that the theological and the biopolitical dimensions are separated. On the contrary, the suggestion is that they are intimately connected. See also chapter 5.

38. Or, more accurately, *almost* everyone becomes such a guardian, because there are certain ambiguous characters, the foremost being Leni, the attorney's assistant, who seem to escape the law's snare.

39. Michel Foucault, *Society Must Be Defended: Lectures at the Collège de France 1975–1976*, 259.

40. Michael Hardt and Antonio Negri show in *Empire* (Cambridge, MA: Harvard University Press, 2000) that biopolitics does rely on moralizing. I do not mean to suggest here that the theological, the biopolitical, and the moral interpretations are separate—I only want to argue that they are distinct. I take this issue up extensively in my *Sovereignty and Its Other*.

41. Immanuel Kant, *Groundwork of the Metaphysics of Morals*, trans. Mary Gregor (Cambridge, UK: Cambridge University Press, 2002).

42. The distance that separates Kant from Spinoza can be gleaned by comparing Kant's proscription against lying to the argument in chapter 16 of the *Tractatus* that a promise depends on its utility (see 529). See also Dimitris Vardoulakis, "The Freedom to Lie," *Philosophy Today*, 58.2 (2014), 141–62.

43. J. Hillis Miller, *The Ethics of Reading: Kant, de Man, Eliot, Trollope, James, and Benjamin* (New York: Columbia University Press, 1987), 36.

44. Miller, *Ethics of Reading*, 38. Cf. Jacques Derrida, "Justices," trans. Peggy Kamuf, in *Critical Inquiry* 31 (2005), 715.

45. It may be objected that I contradict myself here: If I argued in the first section of the present chapter that the pervasive imprisonment is an effect of biopolitics, then how can it also be the effect of the three modalities of sovereign power? To respond to such an objection thoroughly requires a detour via the

argument I develop in detail in *Sovereignty and Its Other*. Given that such a lengthy detour is not possible, I will say in brief that I describe the combination and mutual support of the three modalities as the chief characteristic of the logic of sovereignty. I refer to this as the cosupponibility of the three modalities of sovereignty. Further, I show that biopolitics is the culmination of this sovereign logic. (Some of these issues are further elaborated on in chapter 5.)

46. Deleuze and Guattari, *Kafka*, 43.

47. Ibid., 44–45.

48. For the figures of suffering, priesthood, consolation, and nihilism, see Friedrich Nietzsche's third essay of *The Genealogy of Morals*.

49. For a more detailed discussion of judgment as well as arbitrary judgment (or "justification," as it is called there), see my *Sovereignty and Its Other*, chapter 1.

50. Deleuze and Guattari, *Kafka*, 35.

51. For a discussion of the nasal hair, see Jacques Derrida, "Before the Law."

52. I do not have the space here to review the extensive—and expanding—secondary literature on the animal in Kafka's works. The only point I am making here is that the expression "like a dog" can be seen, among other things, as part of the structure of the humor directed toward Josef K. in *The Trial* in the sense that it undermines his superiority to the "country buffoon." For an interesting article on Kafka and animals, see Chris Danta, "Animal Bachelors and Animal Brides: Fabulous Metamorphosis in Kafka and Garnett," in *Philosophy and Kafka*, eds. Brendan Moran and Carlo Salzani (Lanham, MD: Lexington, 2013), 123–39.

53. Cf. Mikhail Bakhtin, *Rabelais and His World*, trans. Hélène Iswolky (Bloomington: Indiana University Press, 1984).

54. The other side of this is Simon Critchley's observation—mentioned earlier in the "Preamble"—that "What makes us laugh . . . is the return of the physical into the metaphysical." Critchley, *On Humour* (London: Routledge, 2002), 43.

55. Deleuze and Guattari, *Kafka*, 43.

56. Ibid., 45.

57. Ibid., 45.

58. Paul Alberts notes the origins of the idea of the empty law in Kant and legal positivism in "Knowing Life Before the Law: Kafka, Kelsen, Derrida," in *Philosophy and Kafka*, eds. Moran and Salzani, 179–97.

59. Carlo Salzani, "In a Messianic Gesture: Agamben's Kafka," in *Philosophy and Kafka*, 265.

60. Giorgio Agamben, *Homo Sacer: Sovereign Power and Bare Life*, trans. Daniel Heller-Roazen (Stanford, CA: Stanford University Press, 1998), hereafter cited parenthetically in the text. For a discussion of Kafka inspired by the concepts in *Homo Sacer*, see Henry Sussman, "With Impunity," in Kordela and Vardoulakis, *Freedom and Confinement in Modernity: Kafka's Cages*, 213–37.

61. Jessica Whyte, *Catastrophe and Redemption: The Political Thoughts of Giorgio Agamben* (Albany, NY: SUNY, 2014), 6, 9.

62. For a slightly different interpretation of "Before the Law," see Giorgio Agamben, *Nudities*, trans. David Kishik and Stefan Pedatella (Stanford, CA: Stanford University Press, 2011), 30–31.

63. I take this this to be the most likely interpretation, given that the figure of the *Homo Sacer* (the one who can be killed but cannot be sacrificed) is the inversion of the image of Christ (the one who can be sacrificed but who cannot be killed). See Gil Anidjar "The Meaning of Life," *Critical Inquiry* 37.4 (2011), 723.

5. Executing Violence: The Drama of Power in "In the Penal Colony"

1. Elias Canetti, *Kafka's Other Trial: The Letter to Felice*, trans. Christopher Middleton (Harmondsworth, UK: Penguin, 1974), 62.

2. This culminated in the thoughts contained in Elias Canetti, *Crowds and Power*, trans. Carol Stewart (New York: Continuum, 1973). *Masse und Macht* was originally published in 1960, and the book on Kafka nine years later.

3. Michel Foucault, *Discipline and Punish: The Birth of the Prison*, trans. Alan Sheridan (Harmondsworth, UK: Penguin, 1979), 4–5.

4. Franz Kafka, "In the Penal Colony," trans. Willa and Edwin Muir, in *The Complete Stories* (New York: Schocken, 1995)/"In der Strafkolonie," in *Drucke zu Lebzeiten*, eds. Wolf Kitler, Hans-Gerd Koch, and Gerhard Neuman (Frankfurt am Main: Fischer, 2002). All references in text parenthetically.

5. For instance, see Walter Müller-Seidel, *Die Deportation des Menschen: Kafkas Erzählung "In der Strafkolonie" im europäischen Kontext* (Frankfurt am Main: Fischer, 1989); and John Frow, "In the Penal Colony," *Journal of Australian Studies* 64 (2000), 1–13.

6. Michel Foucault, *Security, Territory, Population: Lectures at the Collège de France, 1977–1978*, ed. Michel Senellart, trans. Graham Burchell (New York: Palgrave Macmillan, 2007), 89–94.

7. See Ernst H. Kantorowicz, *The King's Two Bodies: A Study in Mediaeval Political Theology* (Princeton, NJ: Princeton University Press, 1970 [1957]).

8. Vardoulakis, *Sovereignty and Its Other.*

9. There are, nevertheless, attempts to read "In the Penal Colony" in a nonpolitical manner. For instance, Mark Anderson criticizes such political readings because they ignore the fin de siècle aestheticism that he identifies in the elaborate drawing of the torture machine. See Mark M. Anderson, *Kafka's Clothes: Ornament and Aestheticism in the Habsburg Fin de Siècle* (Oxford, UK: Clarendon, 1992).

10. As a piece of biographical information, it may be worth noting here that Kafka's uncle, Alfred Loewy, was indirectly involved in the Dreyfus affair. See Anthony Northey, *Kafka's Relatives: Their Lives and His Writings* (New Haven, CT: Yale University Press, 1991), 12–13.

11. See Franz Kafka, *In der Strafkolonie: Eine Geschichte aus dem Jahr 1914*, ed. Klaus Wagenbach (Berlin: Verlag Klaus Wagenbach, 2010), 72–76. Stanley Corngold and Benno Wagner also draw attention to the parallels between Kafka's description of the island of the penal colony and Theodor Herzl's description of "Freiland" in *The Jewish State*, thereby linking this text to Zionist discourses. See Corngold and Wagner, *Frank Kafka: The Ghost in the Machine*, 79–80.

12. In his commentary on the short story, Wagenbach mentions explicitly Joseph Mason Cox's "rotary machine" (77).

13. Stanley Corngold, *Lambent Traces* (Princeton, NJ: Princeton University Press, 2004), chapter 4.

14. I assume here—as is the most commonly held interpretation in Foucault scholarship—that Foucault understands biopolitics as an extension and intensification of disciplinary power. Mark Kelly even argues that it is *necessary* for disciplinary power to precede biopower: "disciplinary institutions are indispensable to the monitoring, and even more so to the interventions, of biopolitics. For this reason, it indeed seems necessary that the introduction of anatomo-politics preceded that of biopolitics." Mark Kelly, *Foucault's History of Sexuality*, Vol. I (Edinburgh: Edinburgh University Press, 2013), 99–100.

15. Foucault, *Discipline and Punish*, 7.

16. Michel Foucault, *Society Must Be Defended*, 241.

17. Carl Schmidt, *The Concept of the Political*, trans. George D. Schwab (Chicago: University of Chicago Press, 1996).

18. Michael Hardt and Antonio Negri, *Empire* (Cambridge, MA: Harvard University Press, 2000).

19. Arnold Weinstein, in *The Fiction of Relationship* (Princeton, NJ: Princeton University Press, 1998), asserts that "in becoming the prisoner, the officer undergoes the fundamental Kafkaesque transformation. . . . The officer 'becomes' a prisoner no less than Gregor Samsa becomes an insect" (170). I am not convinced by this analysis. As I argued in chapter 2, the theme of metamorphosis leads to a destabilization of subjective identity. Here, we have a substitution that does not destabilize the identity of the officer, but rather, as I show, collapses the sharp distinction between different regimes of power. This is not an insignificant shift. I am much more convinced by Samolsky's reading, according to which the officer's substitution can be read according to the Derridean logic of autoimmunity, that is, the logic that characterizes sovereign power. See Russell Samolsky, *Apocalyptic Futures: Marked Bodies and the Violence of the Text in Kafka, Conrad, and Coetzee* (New York: Fordham University Press, 2011), 59.

20. Kafka uses both *der Reisende* and *der Forschungsreisende* to describe the traveler or explorer.

21. Margot Norris argues that this structure of the "then and now" is common to "In the Penal Colony" and "The Hunger Artist." See her "Sadism and Masochism in 'In the Penal Colony' and 'A Hunger Artist,'" in *Reading Kafka: Prague, Politics and the Fin de Siècle*, ed. Mark Anderson (New York: Schocken, 1988), 170–86.

22. Peter Fenves describes the register of the divine in the short story by reading "In the Penal Colony" as a continuation of Leibniz's theodicy. See "Continuing the Fiction: From Leibniz' 'petite fable' to Kafka's *In der Strafkolonie*," *MLN* 116 (2001), 502–20.

23. For a thorough discussion of the connections between *The Trial* and "In the Penal Colony," see Corngold, *Franz Kafka: The Necessity of Form*, 228–49.

24. See, for example, Matthew 19:14, Luke 18:16, and Mark 10:14.

25. I should note that Foucault himself complicates this clear separation in various places. For a discussion and references, see *Sovereignty and Its Other*, chapter 5.

26. George Bataille has developed the idea of sovereignty as an economy that does not rely on substitution but is rather an exchange beyond measure. See his *The Accursed Share: An Essay on General Economy*, Vols. 1–3, trans. Robert Hurley (New York: Zone Books, 1988–1991). For an excellent exegesis of the economy of sovereignty as understood by Bataille, see Nick Mansfield, *The God Who Deconstructs Himself: Sovereignty and Subjectivity Between Freud, Bataille, and Derrida* (New York: Fordham University Press, 2010).

27. Jacques Derrida, "Autoimmunity: Real and Symbolic Suicides," in *Philosophy in a Time of Terror: Dialogues with Jürgen Habermas and Jacques Derrida*, ed. Giovanna Borradori (Chicago: University of Chicago Press, 2003), 85–136.

28. Gilles Deleuze, "Postscript on Control Societies," in *Negotiations: 1972–1990*, trans. Martin Joughin (New York: Columbia University Press, 1995), 179, emphasis added.

29. Roland Bogue arrives at a similar idea about the way that Deleuze understands the function of power in Kafka, and yet he does so without referring to the "Postscript." See Roland Bogue, "'In the Penal Colony' in the Philosophy of Gilles Deleuze," in *Philosophy and Kafka*, eds. Brendan Moran and Carlo Salzani, 241–60

30. See, for instance, Wayne Burns, "'In the Penal Colony': Variations on a Theme by Gustave Mirbeau," *Accent* 17.1 (1957), 45–51.

31. Anderson, *Kafka's Clothes*, 176.

32. For a paper that looks at the significance of the figure of Robinson Crusoe in the contemporary understanding of the human, see Jessica Whyte, "The

Fortunes of Natural Man: Robinson Crusoe, Political Economy and the Universal Declaration of Human Rights," *Humanity* 5 (2014), 301–21.

33. Michèle Le Doeuff draws some interesting parallels between the literary and the philosophical use of the island metaphor in *The Philosophical Imaginary*, trans. Colin Gordon (London: Athlone, 1989), 9–20.

34. Octave Mirbeau, *The Torture Garden*, trans. Alvah Bessie (London: Bookkake, 2008).

35. Ibid., 83.

36. Ibid., 1.

37. Ibid., 9.

38. Ibid., 9.

39. See Schmitt, *The Concept of the Political*; Georges Sorel, *Reflections on Violence*, ed. Jeremy Jennings (Cambridge, UK: Cambridge University Press, 1999); and Walter Benjamin, "Critique of Violence," trans. Edmund Jephcott, in *Selected Writings*, Vol. 1, ed. Marcus Bullock and Michael W. Jennings (Cambridge, MA: Belknap, 2002), 236–52.

40. See especially *Sovereignty and Its Other*, chapter 1.

41. We can recall here that Yiddish theater, which is one of the influences shaping Kafka's humor, started as performances on makeshift stages, often outside the synagogue. For Kafka's fascination with Yiddish theater, see Evelyn Torton Beck, *Kafka and Yiddish Theater: Its Impact on His Work* (Madison: University of Wisconsin Press, 1971).

42. It would be interesting to compare these Kafkaesque gestures to the descriptions of the Trauerspiel as the expression of the sovereign. From this perspective, Benjamin's essay on Kafka may be the philosophical and political counterweight to his mediations on the Baroque. But of course this is a whole other story, which needs its own separate analysis.

43. Cited in Reiner Stach, *Kafka: The Years of Insight*, trans. Shelley Frisch (Princeton, NJ: Princeton University Press, 2013), 135–36. I thank Stanley Corngold for this reference.

44. Stach introduces the citation of the eyewitness account thus: "The only eyewitness account appears to be a cock-and-bull story" (ibid.).

45. For his fascination with the cinema, see Hanns Zischler, *Kafka Goes to the Movies*, trans. Susan H. Gillespie (Chicago: University of Chicago Press, 2003). For an analysis of gestures from a theatrical perspective, see Joseph Vogl, *Der Ort der Gewalt: Kafkas literalische Ethik* (Munich: Fink, 1990).

46. We do know, however, from Kafka's letter to Felice that they met when he traveled to Munich for the reading of "In the Penal Colony." The meeting was in fact a disaster, as they seemed to have argued in a café. We do not find any entries in Kafka's diary for that period, but again from the letters to Felice we know that he was dissatisfied with the reading.

47. Mikhail Bakhtin, *Rabelais and His World*, trans. Hélène Iswolky (Bloomington: Indiana University Press, 1984).

48. Perhaps this is the reason that Foucault insisted that any direct resistance to sovereignty leads to nothing but an amplification of sovereignty. See also Howard Caygill, *On Resistance: A Philosophy of Defiance* (London: Bloomsbury, 2013).

49. Needless to say, I am not concerned with either a normative or a constitutional description of democratic regimes. I am rather concerned with the political articulation of a conception of being, assuming that ontology and politics are related.

50. See Simon During, *Against Democracy: Literary Experience in the Era of Emancipations* (New York: Fordham University Press, 2012).

Postscript: A Triple or a Single Will?

1. For this reason, it could be said that the conception of freedom that I develop here is a monist conception of freedom. But the concept of monism is understood here in the way it is defined in my *The Ruse of Sovereignty* and in *Stasis*. To avoid an extensive digression on this point, I will not develop this concept here, pointing the interested reader instead to the aforementioned works.

Bibliography

Adorno, Theodor. "Notes on Kafka." In *Prisms*, translated by Samuel and Shierry Weber, 243–71. London: Neville Spearman, 1967.

Agamben, Giorgio. *Homo Sacer: Sovereign Power and Bare Life*. Translated by Daniel Heller-Roazen. Stanford, CA: Stanford University Press, 1998.

———. *Nudities*. Translated by David Kishik and Stefan Pedatella. Stanford, CA: Stanford University Press, 2011.

Alberts, Paul. "Knowing Life Before the Law: Kafka, Kelsen, Derrida." In *Philosophy and Kafka*, edited by Brendan Moran and Carlo Salzani, 179–97. Lanham, MD: Lexington, 2013.

Anderson, Mark M. *Kafka's Clothes: Ornament and Aestheticism in the Habsburg Fin de Siècle*. Oxford, UK: Clarendon, 1992.

Anidjar, Gil. "The Meaning of Life," *Critical Inquiry* 37, no. 4 (2011): 97–723.

Arendt, Hannah. "Franz Kafka, Appreciated Anew." In *Reflections on Literature and Culture*, edited by Susannah Young-ah Gottlieb, 94–109. Stanford, CA: Stanford University Press, 2007.

———. *The Human Condition*. Chicago: University of Chicago Press, 1998.

———. *The Life of the Mind*. New York: Harcourt, 1978.

———. "What Is Freedom?" In *Between Past and Future: Six Exercises in Political Thought*, 143–71. New York: Viking, 1961.

Augustine. *Confessions*. Translated by Henry Chadwick. Oxford, UK: Oxford University Press, 1991.

———. *On the Free Choice of the Will, On Grace and Free Choice, and Other Writings*. Translated and edited by Peter King. Cambridge, UK: Cambridge University Press, 2010.

———. *The City of God Against the Pagans*. Translated and edited by R. W. Dyson. New York: Cambridge University Press, 1998.

Badiou, Alain. *Saint Paul: The Foundation of Universalism*. Translated by Ray Brassier. Stanford, CA: Stanford University Press, 2003.

Bakhtin, Mikhail. *Rabelais and His World*. Translated by Hélène Iswolky. Bloomington: Indiana University Press, 1984.

Balibar, Étienne. *Spinoza and Politics*. Translated by Peter Snowdon. London: Verso, 1998.

Bataille, George. *The Accursed Share: An Essay on General Economy*. Vols. 1–3. Translated by Robert Hurley. New York: Zone Books, 1988–1991.

Beck, Evelyn Torton. *Kafka and Yiddish Theater: Its Impact on His Work*. Madison: University of Wisconsin Press, 1971.

Benjamin, Walter. *Selected Writings*. Edited by Marcus Bullock and Michael W. Jennings. Cambridge, MA: Belknap, 2001.

———. *Gesamelte Schriften*. Edited by Rold Tiedemann and Hermann Schweppenhauser. Frankfurt am Main: Suhrkamp, 1991.

Bennett, Jane. "Kafka, Genealogy, and the Spiritualization of Politics." *Journal of Politics* 56, no. 3 (1994): 650–70.

Berlin, Isiah. *Liberty*. Edited by Henry Hardy. Oxford, UK: Oxford University Press, 2002.

Bident, Christophe. "How Is the Trapeze Possible?" In *Freedom and Confinement in Modernity: Kafka's Cages*, edited by A. Kiarina Kordela and Dimitris Vardoulakis, 201–12. New York: Palgrave, 2011.

———. "The Movements of the Neuter." In *After Blanchot: Literature, Criticism, Philosophy*, edited by Leslie Hill, Brian Nelson and Dimitris Vardoulakis, 13–34. Newark: University of Delaware Press, 2005.

Blanchot, Maurice. *De Kafka à Kafka*. Paris: Gallimard, 1981.

———. *Friendship*. Translated by Elizabeth Rottenberg. Stanford, CA: Stanford University Press, 1997.

———. *The Space of Literature*. Translated by Ann Smock. Lincoln: University of Nebraska Press, 1982.

———. In *The Work of Fire*. Translated by Charlotte Mandell. Stanford, CA: Stanford University Press, 1995.

Bogue, Roland. "'In the Penal Colony' in the Philosophy of Gilles Deleuze." In *Philosophy and Kafka*, edited by Brendan Moran and Carlo Salzani, 243–60. Lanham, MD: Lexington, 2013.

Brod, Max. *Franz Kafka: A Biography*. Translated by G. Humphreys Roberts and Richard Winston. New York: Schocken, 1960.

———. *Verzweiflung und Erlösung im Werk Frank Kafkas*. Frankfurt am Main: Fischer, 1959.

Burns, Wayne. "'In the Penal Colony': Variations on a Theme by Gustave Mirbeau." *Accent* 17, no. 1 (1957): 45–51.

Butler, Judith. *Gender Trouble: Feminism and the Subversion of Identity*. New York: Routledge, 1999.

———. "Who Owns Kafka?" *London Review of Books* 33, no. 5 (March 3, 2011): 3–8.

Calasso, Roberto. "Veiled Splendour." In Franz Kafka, *The Zürau Aphorisms*. Translated by Geoffrey Brock, 109–34. London: Harvill Secker, 2006.

Canetti, Elias. *Crowds and Power*. Translated by Carol Stewart. New York: Continuum, 1973.

Caygill, Howard. "The Fate of the Pariah: Arendt and Kafka's 'Nature Theatre of Oklahama.'" *College Literature* 38, no. 1 (2011): 1–14.

———. "Kafka and Derrida 'Before the Laws.'" In *Freedom and Confinement in Modernity: Kafka's Cages*, edited by A. Kiarina Kordela and Dimitris Vardoulakis, 49–62. New York: Palgrave, 2011.

———. *Levinas and the Political*. London: Routledge, 2002.

———. *On Resistance: A Philosophy of Defiance*. London: Bloomsbury, 2013.

Corngold, Stanley. *Franz Kafka: The Necessity of Form*. Ithaca, NY: Cornell University Press, 1988.

———. "Kafka's Later Stories and Aphorism." In *The Cambridge Companion to Kafka*, edited by Julian Preece, 93–110. Cambridge, UK: Cambridge University Press, 2002.

———. *Lambent Traces: Franz Kafka*. Princeton: Princeton University Press, 2004.

———. "Special Views on Kafka's Cages." In *Freedom and Confinement in Modernity: Kafka's Cages*, edited by A. Kiarina Kordela and Dimitris Vardoulakis, 9–28. New York: Palgrave, 2011.

Corngold, Stanley, and Benno Wagner. *Franz Kafka: The Ghost in the Machine*. Evanston, IL: Northwestern University Press, 2011.

Critchley, Simon. *On Humour*. London: Routledge, 2002.

Danta, Chris. "Animal Bachelors and Animal Brides: Fabulous Metamorphosis in Kafka and Garnett." In *Philosophy and Kafka*, edited by Brendan Moran and Carlo Salzani, 123–39. Lanham, MD: Lexington, 2013.

———. *Literature Suspends Death: Sacrificing and Storytelling in Kierkegaard, Kafka and Blanchot*. London: Continuum, 2011.

Danzig, Gabriel. "Rhetoric and the Ring: Herodotus and Plato on the Story of Gyges as a Politically Expedient Tale." *Greece & Rome* 55, no. 2 (2008): 169–92.

Deleuze, Gilles. *Masochism: Coldness and Cruelty*. In *Masochism: Coldness and Cruelty and Venus in Furs*, edited by Gilles Deleuze and Leopold von Sacher-Masoch. Translated by Jean McNeil and Aude Willm, 15–142. New York: Zone, 1991.

———. "Postscript on Control Societies." In *Negotiations: 1972–1990*. Translated by Martin Joughin, 177–82. New York: Columbia University Press, 1995.

———. "Power and Classical Natural Right," 9 December, 1980, transcribed by Simon Duffy, available at www.webdeleuze.com. Accessed October 2006.

Deleuze, Gilles, and Félix Guattari. *Kafka: Towards a Minor Literature*. Translated by Dana Polan. Minneapolis: University of Minnesota Press, 1986.

Derrida, Jacques. "Autoimmunity: Real and Symbolic Suicides." In *Philosophy in a Time of Terror: Dialogues with Jürgen Habermas and Jacques Derrida*.

Giovanna Borradori, 85–136. Chicago: University of Chicago Press, 2003.

———. "Before the Law." In *Acts of Literature*, edited by Derek Attridge, 181–220. Translated by Avital Ronell and Christine Roulston. New York: Routledge, 1992.

———. "Justices." Translated by Peggy Kamuf. In *Critical Inquiry* 31 (2005): 689–721.

———. "Violence and Metaphysics: An Essay on the Thought of Emmanuel Levinas." In *Writing and Difference*. Translated by Alan Bass, 97–192. London: Routledge, 2002.

de Vries, Hent. "Levinas, Spinoza, and the Theologico-Political Meaning of Scripture." In *Political Theologies: Public Religions in a Post-Secular World*, edited by Hent de Vries and Lawrence E. Sullivan, 232–48. New York: Fordham University Press, 2006.

Diamond, Eliezier. *Holy Men and Hunger Artists: Fasting and Asceticism in Rabbinic Culture*. Oxford, UK: Oxford University Press, 2004.

Dodd, Bill. "The Case for a Political Reading." In *The Cambridge Companion to Kafka*, edited by Julian Preece, 131–49. Cambridge, UK: Cambridge University Press, 2002.

During, Simon. *Against Democracy: Literary Experience in the Era of Emancipations*. New York: Fordham University Press, 2012.

Düttmann, Alexander Garcia. "A Matter of Life and Death: Spinoza and Derrida." In *Spinoza Now*, edited by Dimitris Vardoulakis, 351–62. Minneapolis: University of Minnesota Press, 2011.

Esposito, Roberto. "Totalitarianism or Biopolitics: Toward a Philosophical Interpretation of the Twentieth Century." In *The Terms of the Political: Community, Immunity, Biopolitics*. Translated by Rhiannon Noel Welch, 100–11. New York: Fordham University Press, 2013.

Fenves, Peter. "Continuing the Fiction: From Leibniz's 'petite fable' to Kafka's *In der Strafkolonie*." *MLN* 116 (2001): 502–20.

———. "'Workforce without Possessions': Kafka, 'Social Justice,' and the Word *Religion*." In *Freedom and Confinement in Modernity: Kafka's Cages*, edited by A. Kiarina Kordela and Dimitris Vardoulakis, 107–26. New York: Palgrave, 2011.

Fleming, Chris, and John O'Carroll. "Delusions of Agency: Kafka, Imprisonment, and Modern Victimhood." In *Freedom and Confinement in Modernity: Kafka's Cages*, edited by A. Kiarina Kordela and Dimitris Vardoulakis, 29–48. New York: Palgrave, 2011.

Foucault, Michel. *The Birth of Biopolitics: Lectures at the Collège de France, 1978–79*. Translated by Graham Burchell. New York: Palgrave, 2008.

———. *Discipline and Punish: The Birth of the Prison*. Translated by Alan Sheridan. Harmondsworth: Penguin, 1979.

———. "Maurice Blanchot: The Thought from Outside." In *Foucault/Blanchot*. Translated by Brian Massumi, 7–60. New York: Zone Books, 1987.

———. *Security, Territory, Population: Lectures at the Collège de France, 1977–1978*. Edited by Michel Senellart. Translated by Graham Burchell. New York: Palgrave Macmillan, 2007.

———. *Society Must Be Defended: Lectures at the Collège de France, 1975–1976*. Translated by David Macey. New York: Picador, 2003.

———. "The Subject and Power." In *Michel Foucault: Beyond Structuralism and Hermeneutics*, 2nd ed., edited by Hubert L. Dreyfus and Paul Rabinow, 208–26. Chicago: University of Chicago Press, 1983.

Frow, John. "In the Penal Colony." *Journal of Australian Studies* 64 (2000): 1–13.

Fuchs, Anne. "A Psychoanalytic Reading of *The Man Who Disappeared*." In *The Cambridge Companion to Kafka*, edited by Julian Preece, 25–41.Cambridge, UK: Cambridge University Press, 2002.

Glen, Patrick J. "The Deconstruction and Reification of Law in Kafka's 'Before the Law' and *The Trial*." *Southern Californian Interdisciplinary Law Journal* 17 (2007): 23–66.

Grözinger, Karl Erich. *Kafka and Kabbalah*. Translated by Susan Hecker Ray. New York: Continuum, 1994.

Hardt, Michael, and Antonio Negri. *Empire*. Cambridge, MA: Harvard University Press, 2000.

Hart, Kevin. *Losing the Power to Say "I."* Melbourne, 1996.

Hick, John. *Evil and the God of Love*. New York: Palgrave Macmillan, 2010 [1st ed. 1966].

Huxley, Aldous. *The Doors of Perception*. London: Penguin, 1959.

Jacobson, Arthur J. "Prophesy without Prophets: Spinoza and Maimonides on Law and the Democracy of Knowledge." In *Spinoza Now*, edited by Dimitris Vardoulakis, 135–59. Minneapolis: University of Minnesota Press, 2011.

Janouch, Gustav. *Conversations with Kafka*. London: Derek Verschoyle, 1953.

Kafka, Franz. *Amerika*. Translated by Willa and Edwin Muir. New York: Schocken, 1962.

———. *The Complete Stories*. Translated by Willa and Edwin Muir. New York: Schocken, 1995.

———. *The Diaries*. Edited by Max Brod. Translated by Joseph Kresh and Martin Greenberg. London: Vintage, 1999.

———. *Drucke zu Lebzeiten: Apparatband*, edited by Wolf Kittler, Hans-Gerd Koch, and Gerhard Neumann. Frankfurt am Main: Fischer, 2002.

———. *In der Strafkolonie: Eine Geschichte aus dem Jahr 1914*. Edited by Klaus Wagenbach. Berlin: Verlag Klaus Wagenbach, 2010.

———. *Letters to Felice*. Edited by Erich Hellen and Jürgen Born. Translated by James Stern and Elizabeth Duckworth. New York: Schocken, 1973.

———. *Letters to Friends, Family, and Editors*. Translated by Richard and Clara Winston. New York: Schocken, 1987.

———. *The Office Writings*. Translated by Eric Patton and Ruth Hein. Edited by Stanley Corngold, Jack Greenberg, and Benno Wagner. Princeton, NJ: Princeton University Press, 2008.

———. *The Trial.* Translated by Willa and Edwin Muir. Revised translation by E. M. Butler. New York: Schocken, 1995.

———. *The Zürau Aphorisms*. Translated by Michael Hofmann. London: Harvill Secker, 2006.

Kallistos of Diokleia. "Praying With the Body: The Hesychast Method and non-Christian Parallels." *Sobornost* 14, no. 2 (1993): 6–35.

Kant, Immanuel. *Groundwork of the Metaphysics of Morals.* Translated by Mary Gregor. Cambridge, UK: Cambridge University Press, 2002.

Kantorowicz, Ernst H. *The King's Two Bodies: A Study in Medieval Political Theology*. Princeton, NJ: Princeton University Press, 1970 [1957].

Kelly, Mark. *Foucault's History of Sexuality*. Vol. 1. Edinburgh: Edinburgh University Press, 2013.

Kordela, A. Kiarina. "Kafkaesque: (Secular) Kabbalah and Allegory." In *Freedom and Confinement in Modernity: Kafka's Cages*, edited by A. Kiarina Kordela and Dimitris Vardoulakis, 127–58. New York: Palgrave, 2011.

———. *Surplus: Spinoza, Lacan*. New York: SUNY Press, 2007.

Kordela, A. Kiarina, and Dimitris Vardoulakis, eds. *Freedom and Confinement in Modernity: Kafka's Cages*. New York: Palgrave, 2011.

Kracauer, Siegfried. "Franz Kafka: On His Posthumous Works." In *The Mass Ornament: The Weimar Essays*. Translated by Thomas Y. Levin, 267–78. Cambridge, MA: Harvard University Press, 1995.

Kudszus, Winfried. "Kafka's Cage and Circus." In *Kafka and the Contemporary Critical Performance*, edited by Alan Udoff, 158–64. Bloomington: Indiana University Press, 1987.

Kundera, Milan. *The Art of the Novel.* Translated by Linda Asher. New York: Grove, 1986.

Lambert, Gregg. "The Bachelor-Machine: Kafka and the Question of a Minor Literature." In *Franz Kafka: Minority Report*, edited by Petr. Kouba and Tomáš Pivoda, 7–31. Prague: Literraria Pragnesia, 2011.

Lange-Kirchheim, Astrid. "Nachrichten vom italienischen Hungerkünstler Giovanni Succi: Neue Materialien zu Kafkas *Hungerkünstler*." *Freiburger literaturpsychologische Gespräche: Jahrbuch für Literatur und Pscyhoanalyse* 18 (1999): 315–40.

Le Doeuff, Michèle. *The Philosophical Imaginary*. Translated by Colin Gordon. London: Athlone, 1989.

Lemm, Vanessa. "Introduction: Biopolitics and Community in Roberto Esposito." In *The Terms of the Political: Community, Immunity, Biopolitics*. Translated by Rhiannon Noel Welch, 1–13. New York: Fordham University Press, 2013.

Levinas, Emmanuel. *Totality and Infinity: An Essay on Exteriority*. Translated by Alphonso Lingis. Pittsburgh: Duquesne University Press, 1969.

Lloyd, Genevieve. *Providence Lost*. Cambridge, MA: Harvard University Press, 2008.

Lloyd, Genevieve, and Moira Gatens. *Collective Imaginings: Spinoza, Past and Present*. London: Routledge, 1999.

Lyotard, Jean-François. *The Confessions of Augustine*. Translated by Richard Beardsworth. Stanford, CA: Stanford University Press, 2000.

Magny, Claude-Edmonde. "The Objective Depiction of Absurdity." *Quarterly Review of Literature* 2, no. 3 (1945): 211–27.

Mansfield, Nick. *The God Who Deconstructs Himself: Sovereignty and Subjectivity Between Freud, Bataille, and Derrida*. New York: Fordham University Press, 2010.

Martel, James. *Textual Conspiracies: Walter Benjamin, Idolatry and Political Theory*. Ann Arbor: University of Michigan Press, 2011.

Meillassoux, Quentin. *After Finitude: An Essay on the Necessity of Contingency*. Translated by Ray Brassier. London: Continuum, 2009.

Meyendorff, John. *A Study of Gregory Palamas*. 2nd ed. Bedfordshire, UK: Faith Press, 1974.

Miller, J. Hillis. *The Ethics of Reading: Kant, de Man, Eliot, Trollope, James, and Benjamin*. New York: Columbia University Press, 1987.

Mirbeau, Octave. *The Torture Garden*. Translated by Alvah Bessie. London: Bookkake, 2008.

Mitchell, Breon. "Kafka and the Hunger Artists." In *Kafka and the Contemporary Critical Performance*, edited by Alan Udoff, 236–55. Bloomington: Indiana University Press, 1987.

Mowitt, John. "Kafka's Cage." In *Freedom and Confinement in Modernity: Kafka's Cages*, edited by A. Kiarina Kordela and Dimitris Vardoulakis, 63–86. New York: Palgrave, 2011.

Müller-Seidel, Walter. *Die Deportation des Menschen: Kafkas Erzählung "In der Strafkolonie" im europäischen Kontext*. Frankfurt am Main: Fischer, 1989.

Negri, Antonio. *The Political Descartes: Reason, Ideology, and the Bourgeois Project*. Translated by Matteo Mandarini and Alberto Toscano. London: Verso, 2006.

———. *The Savage Anomaly: The Power of Spinoza's Metaphysics and Politics*. Translated by Michael Hardt. Minneapolis: Minnesota University Press, 2002.

Norris, Margaret. "Sadism and Masochism in 'In the Penal Colony' and 'A Hunger Artist.'" In *Reading Kafka: Prague, Politics and the Fin de Siècle*, edited by Mark Anderson, 170–86. New York: Schocken, 1988.

O'Connor, Brian. "On the Mimesis of Reification: Adorno's Critical Theoretical Interpretation of Kafka." In *Philosophy and Kafka*, edited by Brendan Moran and Carlo Salzani, 229–42. Lanham, MD: Lexington, 2013.

Pawel, Ernst. *The Nightmare of Reason: A Life of Franz Kafka*. New York: Vintage, 1985.

Payer, Peter. *Hungerkünstler in Wein: Eine verschwundene Attraktion (1986–1926)*. Vienna: Sonderzahl, 2002.

Petr, Pavel. *Kafkas Spiele: Selbststilisierung und literarische Komik*. Heidelberg: Carl Winter Universitätsverlag, 1992.

Plato. *Republic*. Translated by Paul Shorey. Cambridge, MA: Harvard University Press, 2003.

Politzer, Heinz. *Franz Kafka: Parable and Paradox*. Ithaca, NY: Cornell University Press, 1966.

Rehberg, Peter. *Lachen Lesen: Zur Komik der Moderne bei Kafka*. Bielefeld, Germany: Transcript, 2007.

Robbins, Jill. *Prodigal Son/Elder Brother: Interpretation and Alterity in Augustine, Petrarch, Kafka, Levinas*. Chicago: University of Chicago Press, 1991.

Robert, Marthe. *The Old and the New: From Don Quixote to Kafka*. Translated by Carol Cosman. Berkeley: University of California Press, 1977.

Rose, Nikolas. *Powers of Freedom: Reframing Political Thought*. Cambridge, UK: Cambridge University Press, 2004.

Salzani, Carlo. "In a Messianic Gesture: Agamben's Kafka." In *Philosophy and Kafka*, edited by Brendan Moran and Carlo Salzani, 261–81. Lanham, MD: Lexington, 2013.

Samolsky, Russell. *Apocalyptic Futures: Marked Bodies and the Violence of the Text in Kafka, Conrad, and Coetzee*. New York: Fordham University Press, 2011.

Santner, Eric. *My Own Private Germany: Daniel Paul Schreber's Secret History of Modernity*. Princeton, NJ: Princeton University Press, 1986.

Schmidt, Carl. *The Concept of the Political*. Translated by George D. Schwab. Chicago: University of Chicago Press, 1996.

Siegert, Bernhard. *Relays: Literature as an Epoch of the Postal System*. Stanford, CA: Stanford University Press, 1999.

Sokel, Walter. *The Myth of Power and the Self: Essays on Franz Kafka*. Detroit: Wayne State University Press, 2002.

Sorel, Georges. *Reflections on Violence*. Edited by Jeremy Jennings. Cambridge, UK: Cambridge University Press, 1999.

Spinoza, Baruch. *Complete Works*. Edited by Michael L. Morgan. Translated by Samuel Shirley. Indianapolis: Hackett, 2002.

Stach, Reiner. *Kafka: The Years of Insight*. Translated by Shelley Frisch. Princeton, NJ: Princeton University Press, 2013.

Stahman, Laura. "Franz Kafka's 'The Burrow' as Model of Ipseity in Levinasian Theory." *Mosaic* 37, no. 3 (2004): 19–32.

Sussman, Henry. *Afterimages of Modernity: Structure and Indifference in Twentieth-Century Literature*. Baltimore, MD: John Hopkins University Press, 1990.

———. *Around the Book: Systems and Literacy*. New York: Fordham University Press, 2011.

———. *Franz Kafka: Geometrician of Metaphor*. Madison, WI: Coda, 1979.

———. *Idylls of the Wanderer: Outside in Literature and Theory*. New York: Fordham University Press, 2007.

———. "With Impunity." In *Freedom and Confinement in Modernity: Kafka's Cages*, edited by A. Kiarina Kordela and Dimitris Vardoulakis, 213–37. New York: Palgrave, 2011.

Szendy, Peter. *Kant in the Land of the Extraterrestrials: Cosmopolitical Philosofictions*. Translated by Will Bishop. New York: Fordham University Press, 2013.

Vandereycken, Walter, and Ron van Deth. *From Fasting Saints to Anorexic Girls: The History of Self-Starvation*. New York: New York University Press, 1994.

Vardoulakis, Dimitris. "A Matter of Immediacy: The Artwork and the Political in Walter Benjamin and Martin Heidegger." In *"Sparks Will Fly": Benjamin and Heidegger*, edited by Andrew Benjamin and Dimitris Vardoulakis, 237–57. New York: SUNY Press, 2015.

———. *The Doppelgänger: Literature's Philosophy*. New York: Fordham University Press, 2010.

———. "The Freedom to Lie." *Philosophy Today* 58, no. 2 (2014): 141–62.

———. "Kafka's Other Freedom." In the program for the play *The Trial*, based on Kafka's novel. Adapted by Louise Fox. Directed by Matthew Lutton. The Malthouse Theatre, Melbourne: August 13–September 4, 2010; the Sydney Theatre Company, Sydney: September 9–September 30, 2010.

———. "Philonomianism: Spinoza and Arendt on Authority, Legality and History." In *Theory & Event* (forthcoming).

———. *Sovereignty and Its Other: Towards the Dejustification of Violence*. New York: Fordham University Press, 2013.

———. *The Ruse of Sovereignty: Stasis and Democracy*. New York: Fordham University Press, 2017.

———. "Spinoza's Empty Law: The Possibility of Political Theology." In *Spinoza Beyond Philosophy*, edited by Beth Lord, 135–48. Edinburgh: Edinburgh University Press, 2012.

———. *Stasis: On Agonistic Democracy*. New York: Fordham University Press, forthcoming.

Vatter, Miguel. *The Republic of the Living: Biopolitics and the Critique of Civil Society*. New York: Fordham University Press, 2014.

Vogl, Joseph. *Der Ort der Gewalt: Kafkas literalische Ethik*. Munich: Fink, 1990.

———. "Kafkas Komik." In *Kontinent Kafka: Mosse-Lectures an der Humboldt-Universität zu Berlin*, edited by Klaus R. Scherpe and Elisabeth Wagner, 72–87. Berlin: Virwek 8, 2006.

Weinstein, Arnold. *The Fiction of the Relationship*. Princeton, NJ: Princeton University Press, 1998.

Weitzman, Erica. "Almost Necessary: Kafka's Kantian Situation Comedy." *Modern Language Notes* 126 (2011): 590–613.

———. *Irony's Antics: Walser, Kafka, and the German Comic Tradition*. Evanston, IL: Northwestern University Press, 2015.

Weltsch, Felix. *Religion und Humor im Leben und Werk Franz Kafkas*. Berlin: Herbig, 1957.

Whyte, Jessica. *Catastrophe and Redemption: The Political Thoughts of Giorgio Agamben*. Albany, NY: SUNY Press, 2014.

———. "The Fortunes of Natural Man: Robinson Crusoe, Political Economy and the Universal Declaration of Human Rights." *Humanity* 5, no. 3 (2014): 301–21.

Zischler, Hanns. *Kafka Goes to the Movies*. Translated by Susan H. Gillespie. Chicago: University of Chicago Press, 2003.

Zizek, Slavoj. *Iraq: The Borrowed Kettle*. London: Vero, 2004.

Index